Visual Basic 6 Core Language Little Black Book Quick Reference

This handy tip sheet presents the nuts and bolts of Visual Basic programming. Use it to quickly look up items such as code syntax, operator precedence, and how-to reminders.

Naming Conventions In Visual Basic

The names of the procedures, variables, and constants that you declare in your Visual Basic code should follow these rules:

- They must begin with a letter.
- They can't contain embedded periods or characters that specify a data type.
- They can't be longer than 255 characters.
- They can't be the same as restricted keywords.
- The names of controls, forms, classes, and modules can't exceed 40 characters.
- The body of constant and variable names should be mixed case with capitals starting each word.
- Ideally, constant and variable names should be prefixed to indicate their data type and scope.

The Const Statement

```
[Public | Private] Const constname _
[As type] = expression
```

The Dim Statement

```
Dim [WithEvents] varname[([subscripts])] _
[As [New] type] [, [WithEvents] _
varname[([subscripts])] [As [New] type]]
```

Redimensioning Arrays

```
ReDim [Preserve] varname(subscripts) _
[As type] [, varname(subscripts) [As type]]
```

Creating A User-Defined Type

```
[Private | Public] Type varname
elementname [([subscripts])] As type
[elementname [([subscripts])] As type]
```

The If Statement

```
If condition Then
[statements]
[ElseIf condition-n Then
[elseifstatements] ...
[Else
[elsestatements]]]
End If
```

The Choose Function

```
Choose(index, choice-1[, choice-2, _
... [, choice-n]])
```

The Switch Function

```
Switch(expr-1, value-1[, expr-2, _
value-2 ... [, expr-n, value-n]])
```

The Select Case Structure

```
Select Case testexpression
[Case expressionlist-n
[statements-n]] ...
[Case Else
[elsestatements]]
End Select
```

The While Loop

```
While condition
[statements]
Wend
```

The For Loop

```
For index = start To end [Step step]
[statements]
[Exit For]
[statements]
Next [index]
```

The Do Loop

The **Do** loop has two versions. You can evaluate a condition at the beginning, like this:

```
Do [{While | Until} condition]
[statements]
[Exit Do]
[statements]
Loop
```

Or, you can evaluate a condition at the end, like this:

```
Do
[statements]
[Exit Do]
[statements]
Loop [{While | Until} condition]
```

The For Each Statement

```
For Each element In group
[statements]
[Exit For]
[statements]
Next [element]
```

The With Statement

```
With object
[statements]
End With
```

The Exit Statements

```
Exit Do
Exit For
Exit Function
Exit Sub
```

The End Statements

```
End
End Function
End If
End Select
End Sub
End Type
End With
```

Declaring Subroutines

```
[Private | Public | Friend] [Static] _
Sub name [(arglist)]
    .
    .
[statements]
    .
    .
[Exit Sub]
    .
    .
[statements]
    .
    .
End Sub
```

Declaring Functions

```
[Private | Public | Friend] [Static] _
Function name [(arglist)] [As type]
    .
    .
[statements]
    .
    .
[name = expression]
    .
    .
[Exit Function]
    .
    .
[statements]
    .
    .
End Function
```

The GoSub Statement

```
GoSub line
    .
    .
    .
line
    .
    .
    .
Return
```

Showing And Hiding Forms

To show a form on the screen, you use the **Show** method; to hide it, you use the **Hide** method.

Creating And Opening Files

```
Open pathname For mode [Access access] _
[lock] As [#]filenumber [Len=reclength]
```

Sequential Access File-Handling Statements

```
Open
Line Input #
Print #
Write #
Input$
Input #
Close
```

Random Access File-Handling Statements

```
Type...End Type (to create and format
    records)
Open
Put #
Len
Seek
Loc
Get #
Close
```

Binary File-Handling Statements

```
Open
Get
Put
Seek
Close
```

Creating A Class

You use a class module to create a new class. To add a class module to a project, select the Add Class Module item in the Project menu.

Visual Basic 6
Core Language

Little Black Book

Steven Holzner

Publisher
Keith
Weiskamp

Acquisitions Editor
Stephanie Wall

Marketing Specialist
Gary Hull

Project Editor
Meredith
Brittain

Technical Reviewer
Harry
Henderson

Production Coordinator
Wendy Littley

Layout Design
April Nielsen

Cover Design
Anthony Stock

Visual Basic 6 Core Language Little Black Book

The Coriolis Group, LLC
14455 N. Hayden Road, Suite 220
Scottsdale, Arizona 85260

480/483-0192
FAX 480/483-0193
http://www.coriolis.com

Library of Congress Cataloging-in-Publication Data
Holzner, Steven.
    Visual Basic 6 core language little black book / by Steven Holzner.
        p.   cm.
    Includes index.
    ISBN 1-57610-390-0
    1. Microsoft Visual BASIC.   2. BASIC (Computer program language)   3. Coding
theory.   I. Title.
QA76.73.B3H76   1999
005.2'768–dc21   98-31314
                                                         CIP

Printed in the United States of America
10   9   8   7   6   5   4   3

CORIOLIS

14455 North Hayden, Suite 220 • Scottsdale, Arizona 85260

Dear Reader:

Coriolis Technology Press was founded to create a very elite group of books: the ones you keep closest to your machine. Sure, everyone would like to have the Library of Congress at arm's reach, but in the real world, you have to choose the books you rely on every day *very* carefully.

To win a place for our books on that coveted shelf beside your PC, we guarantee several important qualities in every book we publish. These qualities are:

- *Technical accuracy:* It's no good if it doesn't work. Every Coriolis Technology Press book is reviewed by technical experts in the topic field and sent through several editing and proofreading passes in order to create the piece of work you now hold in your hands.

- *Innovative editorial design:* We've put years of research and refinement into the ways we present information in our books. Our books' editorial approach is uniquely designed to reflect the way people learn new technologies and search for solutions to technology problems.

- *Practical focus:* We put only pertinent information into our books and avoid any fluff. Every fact included between these two covers must serve the mission of the book as a whole.

- *Accessibility:* The information in a book is worthless unless you can find it quickly when you need it. We put a lot of effort into our indexes, and we heavily cross-reference our chapters, to make it easy for you to move right to the information you need.

Here at The Coriolis Group we have been publishing and packaging books, technical journals, and training materials since 1989. We're programmers and authors ourselves, and we take an ongoing active role in defining what we publish and how we publish it. We have put a lot of thought into our books; please write to us at **ctp@coriolis.com** and let us know what you think. We hope that you're happy with the book in your hands, and that in the future, when you reach for software development and networking information, you'll turn to one of our books first.

Keith Weiskamp
President and Publisher

Jeff Duntemann
VP and Editorial Director

To my sweetie, Nancy: forever and ever!

❧

About The Author

Steven Holzner wrote the book on Visual Basic…a couple of times. He co-authored with Peter Norton the bestseller *Peter Norton's Visual Basic for Windows* and *Peter Norton's Guide to Visual Basic 4 for Windows 95*. He wrote *Advanced Visual Basic 4.0 Programming*, a 650-pager that came out in three editions, and *Internet Programming With Visual Basic 5*. His most recent project was *Visual Basic 6 Black Book*, a 1,100-page book with more than 800 examples. All in all, this former contributing editor for *PC Magazine* has authored 44 books ranging in subjects from assembly language to Visual C++, but Visual Basic is his favorite topic. Steven's books have sold over a million copies and have been translated into 15 languages.

Steven was on the faculty of Cornell University for 10 years, where he earned his Ph.D. He's also been on the faculty of his undergraduate school, Massachusetts Institute of Technology. Because he loves to travel, Steven has been to more than 30 countries, from Afghanistan to India, from Borneo to Iran, from Sweden to Thailand, with more to come. He and Nancy live in a small, picturesque town on the New England coast and spend summers in their house in the Austrian Alps.

Acknowledgments

The book you are holding is the result of many people's dedication. I would especially like to thank Stephanie Wall, acquisitions editor, for her hard work; Meredith Brittain, the project editor who did such a great job of bringing this project together and shepherding it along; Wendy Littley, the production coordinator who kept things on track; Tiffany Taylor, the copyeditor who waded through everything and got it into such good shape; April Nielsen, who did the interior design; and Tony Stock, who did the cover design. Special thanks to Harry Henderson for the terrific tech edit. Thanks to all: great job!

Contents At A Glance

Table Of Contents

Part II   The Visual Basic Tools

Chapter 10
The Integrated Development Environment 175

Part III   Common Tasks

Chapter 16
Coding ActiveX 297

Chapter 19
Programming With Database Objects 361

Introduction

Welcome to *Visual Basic 6 Core Language Little Black Book*. This book is designed to give you the core programming information you need to code effectively in Visual Basic, from the essentials to more advanced material. In this handy reference, you'll be able to quickly find the solution you want and put it to work without extraneous details to bog you down.

Get in, fix it, and get out—that's the philosophy. Here, you're going to find the solutions you need, not a lot of extra chat.

How This Book Works

Because programming is a task-based business, the task-based format of this book is one most programmers will appreciate. Rather than reading about subjects in the order the author thinks best, you can go directly to your topic of interest and find the bite-sized nugget of information you need—such as constructing a particular kind of **While** loop, adding a method to an ActiveX control, creating an error handler, opening a database, and numerous other topics.

Because this book is written for programmers, each chapter is broken up into dozens of practical programming tasks. After selecting the chapter you want, turn to the first page in that chapter to look up the page number where the task you're interested in can be found. This book covers hundreds of tasks that were chosen because they're the ones that programmers will find useful.

Besides programming tasks and examples, this book also contains brief topic overviews in each chapter. These In Brief sections give you background on the subject of the chapter, and the Immediate Solutions sections that follow dig into the specifics.

What's In This Book

To best cover the Visual Basic core programming practices, this book is divided into three parts:

- *Part I: Core Programming*—Chapters 1 through 9 cover the essentials and syntax of Visual Basic programming.
- *Part II: The Visual Basic Tools*—Chapters 10 through 12 discuss the tools that come with Visual Basic, such as the Integrated Development Environment (IDE) and the debugger.
- *Part III: Common Tasks*—Chapters 13 through 20 explain common programming tasks, including working with databases, ActiveX, and the core Visual Basic controls.

This book covers a lot of ground. Some of the topics you'll find in these pages include:

- Visual Basic syntax
- Good programming practices
- ActiveX controls
- DAO database applications
- Code clients that call methods in programs like Microsoft Excel
- Code components (OLE automation servers)
- Applications that use the Windows common dialogs
- Customized toolbars with embedded controls like combo boxes
- Database editing applications
- Direct connections to the Windows API
- Error handlers
- File handlers for text and binary data
- Dialog boxes
- Status bars and toolbars
- Windows Help files
- Compiled HTML Help files
- MDI applications
- Pop-up menus activated with right mouse clicks
- Application deployment
- Applications that create controls at runtime
- Mouse capture
- Setup programs

That's just a sampling of what's coming up. Visual Basic is a very large subject, and the topics we'll cover number in the hundreds.

What You'll Need

To use this book, you should have some experience with Visual Basic—not necessarily very much, but enough to create rudimentary programs. You should have some familiarity with the essentials of Visual Basic (although those essentials are not very hard to pick up).

As far as software goes, just about all you need to use this book is already in Microsoft Visual Basic; we'll use version 6 in this book. Visual Basic comes with an enormous set of tools and resources, and we'll have our hands full putting them to work.

Where can you go for additional Visual Basic support? You can find Visual Basic user groups all over, and more are appearing every day. You can also find Visual Basic information (and advertising) at the Microsoft Visual Basic home page, **www.microsoft.com/vbasic/**; free Visual Basic downloads at **http://www.microsoft.com/vbasic/download/**; and technical documents (white papers) at **http://www.microsoft.com/vbasic/techmat/**.

Many Usenet groups are dedicated to Visual Basic as well, but remember that what you read there is not guaranteed to be accurate. About two dozen of these groups are hosted by Microsoft, including:

- **microsoft.public.vb.bugs**
- **microsoft.public.vb.addins**
- **microsoft.public.vb.controls**
- **microsoft.public.vb.database**
- **microsoft.public.vb.installation**
- **microsoft.public.vb.ole**
- **microsoft.public.vb.ole.automation**
- **microsoft.public.vb.syntax**

Groups that are not hosted by Microsoft include these popular Usenet forums:

- **comp.lang.basic.visual**
- **comp.lang.basic.visual.3rdparty**
- **comp.lang.basic.visual.announce**
- **comp.lang.basic.visual.database**
- **comp.lang.basic.visual.misc**

That's all the introduction we need. It's time to start delving into Visual Basic now.

Part I

Core Programming

Chapter 1

Visual Basic Programming Essentials

In Brief

This chapter begins your guided tour of coding in Visual Basic. Here you'll see everything that you need to know from the time you start up Visual Basic to the point at which you start entering code.

In preparation for writing your own code in later chapters, let's look at a sample of Visual Basic code now:

```
Sub OnButton_Click(Index As Integer)
    If (Index = 1) Then
        AlarmOn = True
    Else
        AlarmOn = False
    End If
End Sub
```

This is Visual Basic code, all right, but it's out of context—you must cover a lot of ground before you can put lines like these into an application and expect it to run. This chapter is all about getting ready to enter such code into your applications.

In brief, the process of writing the code for a new Visual Basic application is as follows:

1. Use Visual Basic to start a new *project*.
2. Open or create the code *modules* in which you want to place your code.
3. Use the Visual Basic *code editor* to start writing your code.

In this chapter, we'll begin taking a look at this process by seeing how Visual Basic projects work and how they help organize the files needed to create an application. We'll also examine Visual Basic programming in overview, discuss some good programming practices, and cover a few general points about writing Visual Basic code (such as how to comment your code and break a line of code over multiple lines). This discussion will give you the start you need—in the following chapters, you'll write the actual code.

Let's start by taking a look at Visual Basic projects.

Visual Basic Projects

A *project* is a collection of files you use to build an application. Since every Visual Basic application starts with a Visual Basic project, projects are the natural starting point for this chapter: You must create a project before you can begin writing code. (Because we expect that you've already done some Visual Basic programming, this section will be along the lines of a review.)

Here are the types of projects you can create in Visual Basic:

- Standard EXE
- ActiveX EXE
- ActiveX DLL
- ActiveX Control
- VB Application Wizard
- VB Wizard Manager
- Data Project
- IIS Application
- Visual Basic Add-in
- ActiveX Document DLL
- ActiveX Document EXE
- Dynamic HTML Application
- Visual Basic Enterprise Edition Controls

From a coding point of view, a project is the backbone of a Visual Basic application, because the project holds all the code files needed for the application. For example, if your application displays several separate windows, each of those windows (or *forms*, in Visual Basic terminology) has its own code file in the application's project. Each form may, in turn, contain *controls* like buttons, list boxes, and so on; the code to handle those controls is typically placed in the form's code file.

In fact, a project may contain three types of code files: *form modules*, each of which holds the code for exactly one form in your application; *standard modules* (often simply called *code modules* by programmers), which hold Visual Basic code not associated with any particular form; and *class modules*, which you use to create Visual Basic objects that other applications can use.

An application's project contains the information Visual Basic needs to create the application, including what files make up the project. Visual Basic keeps track of that information in a project file.

Visual Basic Project Files

A *project file*, which has the extension .vbp, keeps track of a particular project's code files. The project file also performs a great deal of internal bookkeeping, such as tracking version numbers, what ActiveX controls you've added to a project, and which workspace file the project uses. (A *workspace file*, which has the extension .vbw, stores information that the Visual Basic environment uses—which code files are open, where you're currently working in each code file, and more.)

Everything Visual Basic needs to know about a project is in its project file. When you first start Visual Basic, it uses a series of dialog boxes to determine if you want to create a new project or open an existing one—which really means whether you want to create a new project file or open an existing one.

For the sake of reference, a typical project file appears in Listing 1.1. You can pick out such items as the name of the startup form, the name of the project, the fact that the project uses the ActiveX control msinet.ocx, and more.

Listing 1.1 *A typical Visual Basic project file.*

```
Type=Exe
Form=http.frm
Reference=*\G{00020430-0000-0000-C000- _
000000000046}#2.0#0#..\..\WINDOWS\SYSTEM\STDOLE2.TLB#OLE _
   Automation
Object={48E59290-9880-11CF-9754-00AA00C00908}#1.0#0; MSINET.OCX
IconForm="Form1"
Startup="Form1"
Command32=""
Name="Project1"
HelpContextID="0"
CompatibleMode="0"
MajorVer=1
MinorVer=0
RevisionVer=0
AutoIncrementVer=0
ServerSupportFiles=0
CompilationType=0
OptimizationType=0
FavorPentiumPro(tm)=0
```

```
CodeViewDebugInfo=0
NoAliasing=0
BoundsCheck=0
OverflowCheck=0
FlPointCheck=0
FDIVCheck=0
UnroundedFP=0
StartMode=0
Unattended=0
Retained=0
ThreadPerObject=0
MaxNumberOfThreads=1
```

You can *group* multiple projects together. This is useful if the projects are related in some way—for example, you might want to develop a code component (such as OLE automation server) for use by other applications. By creating a project group, you can simultaneously develop the code component and an application to test that code component. Visual Basic keeps track of groups of projects with a group file that has the extension .vbg. You'll learn how to create project groups later in this chapter.

Now, let's take a look at the types of code modules you can include in a project: form modules, standard modules, and class modules.

Form Modules

Forms are familiar to all Visual Basic programmers—they're the templates you base windows on. Besides standard forms, Visual Basic also supports Multiple Document Interface (MDI) forms, as well as many predefined forms.

Each form module contains *event procedures*—sections of code in which you place the instructions that will execute in response to specific events. Forms can contain controls; for each control on a form, the form module holds a corresponding set of event procedures. In addition to event procedures, form modules can contain general procedures that are executed in response to a call from any event procedure.

By default, each new Visual Basic project contains one form module (and no modules of any other type).

A typical form file appears in Listing 1.2. You can see in the listing how the names and positions of the controls are specified in the form, as well as how the code connected to those controls is stored.

Listing 1.2 *A typical Visual Basic form file.*

```
VERSION 6.00
Object = "{48E59290-9880-11CF-9754-00AA00C00908}#1.0#0"; _
  "MSINET.OCX"
Begin VB.Form Form1
    Caption         =   "Form1"
    ClientHeight    =   3195
    ClientLeft      =   60
    ClientTop       =   345
    ClientWidth     =   4680
    LinkTopic       =   "Form1"
    ScaleHeight     =   3195
    ScaleWidth      =   4680
    StartUpPosition =   3  'Windows Default
    Begin InetCtlsObjects.Inet Inet1
        Left        =   2040
        Top         =   2520
        _ExtentX    =   1005
        _ExtentY    =   1005
        _Version    =   393216
    End
    Begin VB.CommandButton Command2
        Caption     =   "Read binary"
        Height      =   495
        Left        =   3120
        TabIndex    =   2
        Top         =   2520
        Width       =   1215
    End
    Begin VB.TextBox Text1
        Height      =   2175
        Left        =   480
        MultiLine   =   -1  'True
        ScrollBars  =   3  'Both
        TabIndex    =   1
        Top         =   120
        Width       =   3855
    End
    Begin VB.CommandButton Command1
        Caption     =   "Read HTML"
        Height      =   495
        Left        =   480
        TabIndex    =   0
        Top         =   2520
        Width       =   1215
    End
```

```
End
Attribute VB_Name = "Form1"
Attribute VB_GlobalNameSpace = False
Attribute VB_Creatable = False
Attribute VB_PredeclaredId = True
Attribute VB_Exposed = False
Private Sub Command1_Click()
    Text1.Text = _
Inet1.OpenURL("http://www.server.com/default.htm")
End Sub

Private Sub Command2_Click()
    Dim bytData() As Byte

    bytData() = Inet1.OpenURL_
("http://www.server.com/library/sample.gif", icByteArray)

    Open "c:\sample.gif" For Binary Access Write As #1
    Put #1, , bytData()
    Close #1

    MsgBox "sample.gif downloaded"
End Sub
```

Standard Modules

You place code that isn't necessarily connected to a particular form in a standard module (often simply called a *code module* or just a *module* by programmers). This code can include general-purpose routines, as well as items that Visual Basic requires you to place in standard modules (such as the definition of a data type). These modules are saved in files with the extension .bas. You'll see how useful these modules are throughout the book, when it comes to setting up code that can span several forms.

A typical Visual Basic standard module file appears in Listing 1.3; in that module, we set up a new data type named **Record** that holds two strings of fixed length.

Listing 1.3 A typical Visual Basic standard module file.

```
Attribute VB_Name = "Module1"
Type Record
    Name As String * 50
    Number As String * 50
End Type
```

Class Modules

Besides standard modules, Visual Basic also supports *class modules*. Programming with class modules brings you close to true object-oriented programming (OOP), because you use the classes you create with these modules to form *objects*. You'll get a great deal of insight into what Visual Basic considers to be an object later in this book; briefly, whereas a standard module contains only code, a class module can contain both code and data, wrapping them into a single package. Class modules form the foundation of ActiveX and Component Object Model (COM) programming in Visual Basic, as you'll see.

Besides projects and project files, you should become acquainted with several other subjects before you start writing code, such as various project options, coding conventions (how to comment your code, for instance), and coding recommendations put together by experienced programmers and by Microsoft. It's best to see all this material at work, however, and not in dry overview form, so we'll do that now, as we turn to the Immediate Solutions part of this chapter.

Immediate Solutions

Creating Or Opening Projects

When you start Visual Basic, it uses the New Project dialog box to ask if you want to create a new project or open an existing one, as shown in Figure 1.1.

To create a new project, just select the project type on the New tab of the New Project dialog box and click on Open. Visual Basic will automatically create the type of project you request.

To open an existing project, click on the Existing tab in the New Project dialog box, find the project you want to open, and click on Open. Visual Basic also maintains a list of projects you've opened recently; to select a project from that list, click on the Recent tab in the New Project dialog box and choose one of the projects listed there.

After you've started Visual Basic, you can also create a new project by choosing File|New Project; this menu item displays a New Project dialog box (but one that doesn't allow you to open existing projects). To open an existing project after you've started Visual Basic, choose File|Open Project; this menu item displays the Open Project dialog

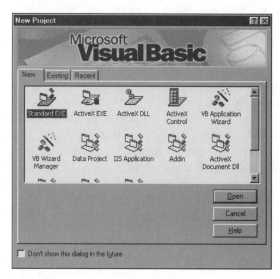

Figure 1.1   *Creating or opening a new project.*

box, in which you can open an existing project or select a project to open from the Visual Basic recent-project list.

Saving Projects

To save a project you're working on, choose File|Save Project As or File|Save Project. These menu items update or create the VBP project files for the currently open project.

The Save Project As menu item lets you name the project you're saving, so use that item the first time you save a new project. Note also that if the project contains modules that haven't yet been saved—such as code for FRM files—Visual Basic will prompt you for names for those files before saving the entire project.

Entering Code Into A Code Module

By default, each new project has one code module: a form module. You can add other code modules as required, of course (see the next topic).

In this book, we're assuming that you've used Visual Basic enough to know the rudiments of entering code; however, we'll cover the process briefly now. If you need more than a review, Chapter 10 discusses in detail the complete mechanics of handling code in code modules (including entering and editing code).

To enter code into a code module, you must first open that code module. To do so, double-click on the module's name in the Visual Basic project window (which appears at upper right in Figure 1.2). Visual Basic will open the code module in the code editor (which appears as the large central window in Figure 1.2), and you can enter code directly using standard editing techniques, described next.

To add code to a specific component (such as a control), find that component in the code editor's left list box; also, locate the event you want to add code for in the right list box. When you've selected the component and the event, Visual Basic will create or open the associated procedure in the code editor. You then enter the code by simply typing it in.

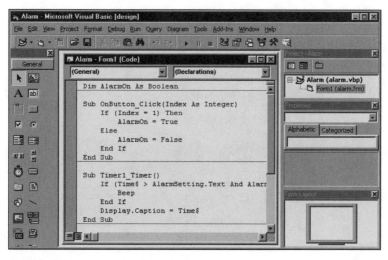

Figure 1.2   *Entering code in a code module.*

To go beyond the bare overview of the coding process presented here, see the cross-references to other parts of this book listed below.

Related solution:	Found in:
Entering Code	Chapter 10

Adding Or Removing Form, Standard, And Class Modules

To add a new code module to a Visual Basic project, choose one of the following items from the Project menu:

- Add Form
- Add MDI Form
- Add Module
- Add Class Module

These menu items open dialog boxes that let you select the type of form or module you want to add. For example, when you choose Project|Add Form, the Add Form dialog box appears, as shown in Figure 1.3, which lists the available forms you can add. Select the Form option and click on Open to add a standard form to the project.

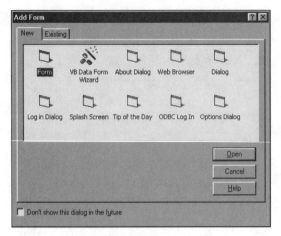

Figure 1.3   *Adding a new form to a project.*

TIP: *Don't forget to save the new module you've added to a project. (If you do forget, Visual Basic will ask you to do so when you close the project.)*

To remove a module from a project, just select the module in the project window and select Project|Remove. Alternatively, you can right-click on the module in the project window and select Remove from the pop-up menu that appears.

Adding Or Removing Project Files

You add files to your project by selecting Project|Add File. Selecting this menu item opens the Add File dialog box, in which you can select the file you want to add. Click on Open to add the selected file to the project or click on Cancel to dismiss the dialog box without adding any files.

Adding files to a project is particularly useful if you've already developed a set of FRM or BAS files and you want to use them in all your applications.

To remove a file from a project, select its module in the project window and select Project|Remove. Alternatively, you can right-click on the module in the project window and select Remove from the pop-up menu that appears.

Project Options: The Project Name And Description

After you've created a project, you may want to change its name from the default name Visual Basic assigns. For example, the default name for a standard EXE file is simply Project1; when you compile the EXE file, it will be named project1.exe. To change the name of the EXE file, you change the name of the project file when you save it from project1.vbp to, say, calculator.vbp. When you create the EXE file, Visual Basic will call it calculator.exe.

However, the name you give the project file isn't the same as the project name. Even if you rename project1.vbp to calculator.vbp, the program will still register itself as Project1 with Windows when you run it. To change the Registry name of an application (especially important when you're creating ActiveX controls), follow these steps:

1. Select Project|*Projectname* Properties. The Project Properties dialog box will open, as shown in Figure 1.4.

2. Click on the General tab.

3. Select the project's name, as shown in Figure 1.4.

4. Enter the new name you want to give the project.

5. Click on OK to dismiss the Project Properties dialog box.

You can also set the Project Description on the General tab of the Project Properties dialog box. This description is the text a programmer will

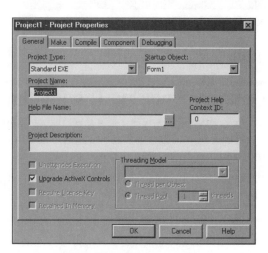

Figure 1.4   *The Project Properties dialog box.*

see when adding a reference to a component you've created or when selecting your component in the Components dialog box. To give your project a description, enter the description text in the Project Description box in the Project Properties dialog box and click on OK.

Project Options: The Startup Object

You can start a Visual Basic program in two primary ways: with a startup form (which appears on screen as soon as you start an application) or with a subroutine named **Main**.

By default, an application will start by displaying the application form named **Form1**. But, you might also want to do some behind-the-scenes preparation before placing any windows on screen; in that case, you can set up a **Main** subroutine in a standard module and use it as the startup object. You can also make any other form the startup object—not just **Form1**. Here's how to set the startup object:

1. Select Project|*Projectname* Properties. The Project Properties dialog box will open (refer back to Figure 1.4).
2. Click on the General tab.
3. Select the startup object you want in the Startup Object list box.
4. Click on OK to close the Project Properties dialog box.

Related solution:	*Found in:*
Setting A Project's Startup Procedure	Chapter 10

Project Options: Favoring The Pentium Pro

If you know the code you're writing is targeted at the Pentium Pro processor, you can direct Visual Basic to optimize the code it writes for that processor. To do so, follow these steps:

1. Select Project|*Projectname* Properties. The Project Properties dialog box will open (refer back to Figure 1.4).
2. Click on the Compile tab.
3. Click on the Favor Pentium Pro checkbox.
4. Click on OK to close the Project Properties dialog box.

TIP: *Visual Basic code automatically checks for floating-point division (FDIV) errors in Pentium processors. If you want to disable this feature for some reason, follow Steps 1 and 2, click on Advanced Optimizations, and then click on the Remove Safe Pentium FDIV Checks box. Click on OK to close the Advanced Optimizations dialog box.*

Project Options: Optimizing For Small Or Fast Code

You can direct Visual Basic to optimize the code you write in two ways: to make the code faster or to make the created EXE or DLL file smaller. Here's how you can do that:

1. Select Project*Projectname* Properties. The Project Properties dialog box will open (refer back to Figure 1.4).

2. Click on the Compile tab.

3. Click on the desired option button: Optimize For Fast Code or Optimize For Small Code.

4. Click on OK to close the Project Properties dialog box.

Project Options: Setting The Application Version Number

While developing software, you may want to give version numbers—such as 1.00 or 3.02—to the various editions of your software. The user can also determine the version number of your software using the Windows Explorer. Follow these steps to set an application's version number:

1. Select Project*Projectname* Properties. The Project Properties dialog box will open (refer back to Figure 1.4).

2. Click on the Make tab, as shown in Figure 1.5.

3. Enter the project's new version number in the Version Number boxes.

4. Click on OK to dismiss the Project Properties dialog box.

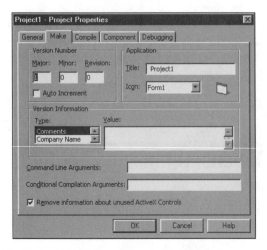

Figure 1.5   *The Project Properties dialog box's Make tab.*

Creating A Project Group

When you want to associate a number of projects, you can create a project *group*. Creating a project group is a good idea if, for example, you have an application you're developing and an application you're using to test the application under development. (Project groups are especially useful when you're developing code components, which rely on OLE automation to work between applications.)

To create a project group, simply add a new project to an existing project. To add a new project to an open project, select File|Add Project; this menu item opens the Add Project dialog box. Select the New, Existing, or Recent tab, as appropriate, and select the project you want to add; then, click on Open to add the new project and dismiss the Add Project dialog box.

Visual Basic will automatically create a project group and let you save that group in a Visual Basic group file. The first project in the group serves as the startup object for the group, but you can change that in the Visual Basic project window. Just select a project, right-click, and select Set As Start Up from the pop-up menu that appears.

Breaking Lines Of Code

Visual Basic is capable of handling very long lines of code, and sometimes you'll get tired scrolling to the end of them. To break a single line of Visual Basic code across several lines, you can use the underscore *continuation character*. Using this character, you can break lines of code at any whitespace character, but you shouldn't break a quotation. For example, consider the single line of Visual Basic code highlighted here:

```
Private Sub Command1_Click()
    Text1.Text = "Hi there!"
End Sub
```

To comply with Visual Basic's line-breaking conventions, this line of code should be broken as follows:

```
Private Sub Command1_Click()
    Text1.Text = _
    "Hi there!"
End Sub
```

Combining Statements On One Line

You'll usually write one Visual Basic statement per line. However, you can place two or more statements on a line if you use a colon to separate them, like this (note that doing so doesn't improve the readability of your code):

```
Text1.Text = "Hello" : Text2.Text = "there"!"
```

Adding Comments To Your Code

Comments are non-code text items you add to your program to indicate what's going on and to make the code more readable to yourself and other programmers. To add a comment, insert an apostrophe; Visual Basic will ignore everything after the apostrophe. Here's an example:

```
Private Sub Command1_Click()
    Text1.Text = "Hi there!"      'Display greeting message
End Sub
```

In general, you should add a comment when you declare a new and important variable or wish to make clear some implementation method. Ideally, procedures should have only one purpose and be named clearly enough that excessive comments aren't required.

In addition, each procedure should begin with a comment describing what it does; you should break that comment into various sections. The Microsoft recommendations for these comment block sections appear in Table 1.1 (note that not all sections are required for all procedures).

Here's an example, which shows how to set up a comment preceding a function named **dblSquareRoot( )**:

```
'*******************************************************
' dblSquareRoot()
' Purpose: Returns a square root
' Inputs: dblSquare, the value you want the square root of
' Returns: The input value's square root
'*******************************************************
Function dblSquareRoot(dblSquare As Double) As Double
    dblSquareRoot = Sqr(dblSquare)      'Find square root
End Function
```

Table 1.1   Procedure starting comment block sections.

Section Heading	Comment Description
Purpose	What the procedure does.
Assumptions	List of each external variable, control, open file, or other element that isn't obvious.
Effects	List of each affected external variable, control, or file and the effect it has (only if this isn't obvious).
Inputs	Each argument that may not be obvious. Arguments appear on separate lines, with inline comments.
Returns	Explanation of the values returned by functions.

Following Good Programming Practices

All of the good coding practices in this topic come from professional programmers or Microsoft. Of course, whether you implement them is up to you. Here they are:

- *Avoid magic numbers when you can*—A *magic number* is a number (excluding 0 or 1) that's hardwired into your code, like this:

```
Function blnCheckSize(dblParameter As Double) As Boolean

    If dblParameter > 1024 Then
        blnCheckSize = True

    Else
        blnCheckSize = False

    End If
End Function
```

Here, 1024 is a magic number. It's better to declare such numbers as constants, especially if you have several of them. Then, when the time comes to change your code, you must change the constant declaration in only one place—not try to find all the magic numbers scattered through your code.

- *Be modular*—Putting code and data together in modules hides the code from the rest of the program, makes it easier to debug, makes it easier to work with conceptually, and even quickens load time of procedures in the same module. Being modular— also known as incorporating *information-hiding* (and *encapsulation*, in true OOP)—is the backbone of working with larger programs. Divide and conquer is the idea here.

- *Program defensively*—For example, check data passed to you in a procedure before you use it. Doing so can prevent a bug from propagating throughout your program and help pinpoint its source. Make no assumptions.

- *Write procedures that have only one purpose*—This rule is also an aid in larger programs, when the code starts to get complex. If a procedure has two distinct tasks, you should certainly consider breaking it up.

- *Avoid deep nesting of conditionals or loops*—This tip is important because debugging them visually is very, very inefficient. If you need to, place some of the inner loops or conditionals in new

procedures and call them. Three levels of nesting should be about
the maximum.

- *Use access procedures to protect sensitive data*—This guideline
  is part of programming defensively. Access procedures—also
  called **Get/Set** procedures—are called by the rest of the program
  when you want to work with sensitive data. If the rest of the
  program must call a **Set( )** procedure to set that data, you can
  test to be sure that the new value is acceptable, thereby providing
  a screen between that data and the rest of the program.

- *Define variables with the smallest scope possible*—Global
  variables can create enormously complex conditions. (In fact,
  Microsoft recommends using global variables only when there's
  no other convenient way to share data between forms.)

- *Don't pass global variables to procedures*—If you do, the procedure to which you pass that variable might give it one name (as a
  passed parameter) and also reference it as a global variable,
  which can lead to some serious bugs, because then the procedure
  would have two different names for the variable.

- *Use specific operators for specific tasks*—Use the **&** operator
  when linking strings and the **+** operator when working with
  numerical values, per Microsoft's recommendations.

- *Break long strings*—Use the underscore continuation character
  to create multiple lines of code from a long string, breaking the
  long string into shorter ones with the **&** operator so that you can
  read or debug the string easily. For example:

```
Dim Msg As String
Msg = "Well, there is a problem " _
& "with your program. I am not sure " _
& "what the problem is, but there is " _
& "definitely something wrong."
```

- *Avoid using **Variants** if you can*—Although convenient, they
  waste not only memory, but—perhaps surprisingly—time. Visual
  Basic has to convert the data in a **Variant** to the proper type
  when it learns what's required, and that conversion takes a great
  deal of time.

- *Indent your code with four spaces*—This is Microsoft's recom-
  mendation. (Believe it or not, serious studies have been undertaken, and those studies found two to four spaces to be best for
  maximum code readability.) Be consistent.

- *Watch out for misspelled variables*—This is a big Visual Basic pitfall. Because you don't have to declare a variable in Visual Basic to use it, you might be surprised when Visual Basic creates a new variable after you've misspelled a variable's name. For example, here's some perfectly legal code modified from a tic-tac-toe project; the code compiles and runs, but because of a misspelling—**xNoww** instead of **xNow**—it doesn't work:

```
Private Sub Command_Click(Index As Integer)
    If xNow Then
        Command(Index).Caption = "x"
    Else
        Command(Index).Caption = "o"
    End If

    xNoww = Not xNow

End Sub
```

Because Visual Basic treats **xNoww** as a legal variable, this kind of bug is very hard to find when debugging.

- *If you work in teams, use version control*—Several well-known utilities help programmers work in teams, such as Microsoft's Visual SourceSafe. This utility—which is designed to work with programming environments like Visual Basic—restricts access to code so that two programmers can't modify independent copies of the same file.

Data Types And Data Declaration

In Brief

In this chapter, we're going to start taking a look at how to set up data in Visual Basic programs. Storing the data a program works on is fundamental to programming—after all, computer programs wouldn't be much use if they couldn't work on data—and we'll examine that process here.

You'll see how to set aside storage space for your data in variables and how to name and work with those variables. Visual Basic has specific data types already set up for you to use—such as the **Integer**, **Double**, and so on—and you'll learn how to create variables using those types. We'll also examine how to name those variables, and what range of data they can store. Finally, we'll take a look at related topics, such as declaring constants and how to convert one data type to another.

Declaring Variables

You can store numeric or string data in Visual Basic variables in a number of ways; perhaps the easiest is simply to start using a variable by name in your program. In this technique—called *implicit declaration*—you declare a variable implicitly by using it. For example, the following code creates a new variable named **NumberFiles** by using the = operator to assign that variable a value of 12:

```
Private Sub Form_Load()
    NumberFiles = 12
End Sub
```

If this is the first time Visual Basic has encountered the **NumberFiles** variable, it creates that variable as a *Variant*. A **Variant** (the default type for Visual Basic variables) is a special data type that can hold any kind of data.

It isn't recommended practice to declare variables implicitly, however, because in longer programs you can lose track of those variables. It's far better to declare your variables *explicitly*.

TIP: *If you include the line **Option Explicit** in the (General) part of a module, Visual Basic requires that you declare all variables before using them.*

As you'll see in this chapter, you use Visual Basic keywords like **Dim** to declare variables explicitly. This code declares a variable named **NumberFiles**:

```
Dim NumberFiles
```

As with implicit variables, if you don't specify the type of variable when declaring it, Visual Basic makes the variable a **Variant**. **Variant**s can simplify writing short programs, but they use up a lot of space and can slow program performance because of all the testing and conversions that must occur. You should usually declare the type of variable you're creating, as in this code, which declares a **NumberFiles** variable of type **Integer**:

```
Dim NumberFiles As Integer
```

Now you're free to use **NumberFiles** in your code:

```
Dim NumberFiles As Integer

Private Sub Form_Load()
    NumberFiles = 12
End Sub
```

In this chapter, then, we'll cover the process of setting up elementary variables using keywords like **Dim**, and we'll examine the kinds of data you can store in those variables. Besides variables, you can declare constants in Visual Basic. They work much like variables, with one exception, of course: You can't change a constant's value when the application is running. You'll also see how to declare constants in this chapter.

Where you declare a variable in a program is also important, because its placement can have a significant bearing on where you can use it. For example, declaring a variable in one procedure may mean that you can't use it in another. The parts of an application in which you can use a variable are collectively called the variable's *scope*; you'll get an overview of variable scope in this chapter. (We examine variable scope in this chapter with the assumption that you're familiar with the idea of Visual Basic procedures—if you want more information, see Chapter 5.)

Now that you have an idea of what's coming up, let's turn to the Immediate Solutions part of this chapter.

Immediate Solutions

Understanding The Visual Basic Numbering System

Most programmers use decimal numbers when programming, but Visual Basic provides other possibilities. You can represent numbers in octal and hexadecimal, as well; use the "&O" and "&H" prefixes, respectively, as shown in Table 2.1.

Table 2.1   Decimal, octal, and hexidecimal number representation.

Decimal	Octal	Hexadecimal
1	&O1	&H1
15	&O17	&HF
16	&O20	&H10
255	&O377	&HFF

Naming Conventions In Visual Basic

When writing Visual Basic code, you declare and name many elements, such as procedures, variables, and constants. The names of the procedures, variables, and constants that you declare in your Visual Basic code should follow these rules, according to Microsoft:

- They must begin with a letter.
- They can't contain embedded periods or characters that specify a data type.
- They can be no longer than 255 characters.
- The names of controls, forms, classes, and modules shouldn't exceed 40 characters.
- They can't be the same as restricted keywords. (A restricted keyword is a word that Visual Basic uses as part of its language.)
- The body of a constant or variable name should be mixed case, with a capital letter starting each word.
- Ideally, you should add prefixes to constant and variable names to indicate their data type and scope.

Variable Data Types

You've decided you want to set up a few variables—but what types are available in Visual Basic? You'll find those types listed in Table 2.2.

Note that each variable type has a suggested prefix, such as "int" for **Integer**s and "lng" for **Long** variables. Giving your variables prefixes that indicate their type can be very helpful when you're working on long applications.

Table 2.2   Data types and prefixes.

Data Type	Prefix	Example
Boolean	bln	blnOpen
Byte	byt	bytData
Collection object	col	colRecords
Currency	cur	curDebt
Date (Time)	dtm	dtmHoliday
Double	dbl	dblValue
Error	err	errDiskSpace
Integer	int	intNumber
Long	lng	lngValue
Object	obj	objScreen
Single	sng	sngTotal
String	str	strName
User-defined type	udt	udtOwner
Variant	vnt	vntBigValue

Variable Ranges

You're considering setting up an integer variable—but will Visual Basic set aside enough memory to store the values you want? You'll find the answer to that question in Table 2.3, which lists the ranges of the standard Visual Basic variable types.

When you're declaring variables, be generous with memory space—it's a rare program these days that can't afford a few more bytes of space to ensure the accuracy of your data. You'll make an exception,

Table 2.3   Variable types.

Variable Type	Bytes Of Storage	Range
Boolean	2	True, False
Byte	1	0 to 255
Currency	8	-922,337,203,685,477.5808 to 922,337,203,685,477.5807
Date	8	1 January 100 to 31 December 9999 and times from 0:00:00 to 23:59:59
Decimal	12	-79,228,162,514,264,337,593,543,950,335 to 79,228,162,514,264,337,593,543,950,335
Double	8	-1.79769313486232E308 to -4.94065645841247E-324 (negative values) and 4.94065645841247E-324 to 1.79769313486232E308 (positive values)
Integer	2	-32,768 to 32,767
Long	4	-2,147,483,648 to 2,147,483,647
Object	4	N/A
Single	4	-3.402823E38 to -1.401298E-45 (negative values) and 1.401298E-45 to 3.402823E38 (positive values)
String	N/A	Variable-length strings can hold about 2 billion characters; fixed-length strings can hold 1 to about 64K characters
User-defined type	N/A	N/A
Variant	N/A	N/A

of course, when you have huge arrays of variables! In that case, check your math and be sure the numbers you're storing in various variables will fit in them.

Declaring Variables

You can declare variables several ways. Most often, you use the **Dim** keyword to declare a variable. If you don't specify the variable type when you use **Dim**, Visual Basic creates a **Variant**, which can operate as any variable type.

You can specify the variable type by using the **As** keyword, like this:

```
Dim IntegerValue As Integer
```

TIP: The **Option Explicit** statement requires that you declare all the variables in your Visual
Basic program.

The **Dim** Statement

Here's how you use the **Dim** statement:

```
Dim [WithEvents] varname[([subscripts])] [As [New] type] _
  [, [WithEvents] varname[([subscripts])] [As [New] type]] . . .
```

The **WithEvents** keyword is valid only in class modules. This keyword specifies that *varname* is an object variable used to respond to
events triggered by an ActiveX object.

The ***varname*** identifier is the name of the variable you're declaring.

You use ***subscripts*** if you're declaring an array. Set up the ***subscripts***
argument this way:

```
[lower To] upper [, [lower To] upper]
```

TIP: In Visual Basic, you may declare up to 60 dimensions for an array.

The **New** keyword enables creation of an object. If you use **New** when
declaring an object variable, Visual Basic creates a new instance of
the object on first reference to it—you don't have to use the **Set** statement to assign the object reference. Here's an example:

```
Dim DataSheet As New Worksheet
```

The ***type*** argument specifies the data type of the variable, which may
be **Boolean**, **Byte**, **Currency**, **Date**, **Decimal** (not currently supported),
Double, **Integer**, **Long**, **Object**, **Single**, **String** (for variable-length
strings), **String * length** (for fixed-length strings), a user-defined type,
Variant, or an object type. If you don't specify a type, the default is
Variant, which means the variable can act as any type.

TIP: *By default in Visual Basic, numeric variables are initialized to zero, variable-length strings are initialized to a zero-length string (""), and fixed-length strings are filled with zeros.* **Variant** *variables are initialized to* **Empty**.

Besides **Dim**, you can also use **ReDim** to redimension space for dynamic arrays (see the next chapter), **Private** to restrict a variable to a module or form, **Public** to make a variable global—that is, accessible to all modules or forms—or **Static** to make sure its value doesn't change between procedure calls. Table 2.4 summarizes these ways of declaring variables.

Table 2.4   Visual Basic declaring statements.

Keyword	Does This
Dim	Using Dim alone creates Variants. Use the As keyword to specify a variable type.
Private	Makes the variable available only in the current form/module.
Public	Makes the variable global—available to the rest of your program.
ReDim	Reallocates storage space for dynamic-array variables.
Static	Preserves the variable's value between procedure calls.
Type	Declares a user-defined type.

Related solution:	Found in:
Redimensioning Arrays	Chapter 3

Setting Variable Scope

The scope of a variable indicates where in your program you can refer to that variable and have Visual Basic find it. For example, if you declare a variable named **NumberFiles** in a subroutine that is itself in a form module, the declaration might look like this:

```
Private Sub Form_Load()
    Dim NumberFiles As Integer

    .
    .
    .
End Sub
```

Now you can use the variable in that procedure:

```
Private Sub Form_Load()
    Dim NumberFiles As Integer
    NumberFiles = 12
End Sub
```

However, you can't use the same variable in another subroutine in the same module, like this:

```
Private Sub Form_Load()
    Dim NumberFiles As Integer
    NumberFiles = 12
End Sub

Private Sub Form_Click()
    NumberFiles = 100          'Not the same variable as above!
End Sub
```

In fact, the variable **NumberFiles** in the second procedure is completely separate from the variable of the same name in the first procedure. This fact points out a weakness of implicit declaration in Visual Basic—a programmer ignorant of variable scope could well believe the second variable is the same as the first, and Visual Basic won't indicate otherwise.

To let both subroutines use the same variable named **NumberFiles**, you can declare that variable in the form module's (General) section:

```
Dim NumberFiles As Integer
```

Now both procedures will use the same variable:

```
Dim NumberFiles As Integer

Private Sub Form_Load()
    NumberFiles = 12
End Sub

Private Sub Form_Click()
    NumberFiles = 100
End Sub
```

Levels Of Scope In Visual Basic

Visual Basic uses three levels of variable scope: at the procedure level, at the form or module level, and at the global level. Schematically, Figure 2.1 shows how variable scope works.

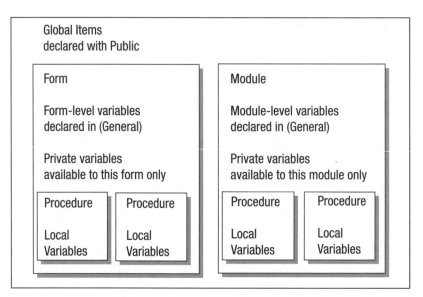

Figure 2.1 *Schematic of Visual Basic project scope.*

When you're designing a program, Microsoft suggests you limit your variables to the minimum possible scope, in order to make things simpler and to avoid conflicts.

Related solution:	Found in:
Giving An ActiveX Control A Method	Chapter 16

Using Variable Prefixes

Ideally, you should add prefixes to variable names to indicate their data type. These prefixes let you determine a variable's type at a glance, and they can be extraordinarily helpful if someone else will be reading your code.

TIP: *It's also a good idea to prefix function names, using the same prefixes to indicate the return type of the function.*

In this topic, we'll take a look at the standard Microsoft prefixes for the various variable types.

Simple Variable Prefixes

Let's start with simple variable prefixes; you can find the prefixes Microsoft suggests for simple variables in Table 2.5.

Here are some examples of simple prefixed variable names:

```
blnTrueFalse      'Boolean
intCounter        'Integer
sngDividend       'Single
```

Control Variable Prefixes

Microsoft's suggested control prefixes appear in Table 2.6—as you can see, there's a suggested prefix for every standard type of control.

Table 2.5   Variable prefixes.

Data Type	Prefix
Boolean	bln
Byte	byt
Collection object	col
Currency	cur
Date (Time)	dtm
Double	dbl
Error	err
Integer	int
Long	lng
Object	obj
Single	sng
String	str
User-defined type	udt
Variant	vnt

Table 2.6   Control prefixes.

Control Type	Prefix
3D panel	pnl
ADO data	ado
Animated button	ani
Checkbox	chk

(continued)

Table 2.6   Control prefixes (continued).

Control Type	Prefix
Combo box, drop-down list box	cbo
Command button	cmd
Common dialog	dlg
Communications	com
Control (used within procedures when the specific type is unknown)	ctr
Data	dat
Data-bound combo box	dbcbo
Data-bound grid	dbgrd
Data-bound list box	dblst
Data combo	dbc
Data grid	dgd
Data-bound list	dbl
Data repeater	drp
Date picker	dtp
Directory list box	dir
Drive list box	drv
File list box	fil
Flat scroll bar	fsb
Form	frm
Frame	fra
Gauge	gau
Graph	gra
Grid	grd
Header	hdr
Hierarchical flexgrid	flex
Horizontal scroll bar	hsb
Image	img
Image combo	imgcbo
Image list	ils
Label	lbl
Lightweight checkbox	lwchk
Lightweight combo box	lwcbo
Lightweight command button	lwcmd
Lightweight frame	lwfra

(continued)

Table 2.6   Control prefixes (continued).

Control Type	Prefix
Lightweight horizontal scroll bar	lwhsb
Lightweight list box	lwlst
Lightweight option button	lwopt
Lightweight text box	lwtxt
Lightweight vertical scroll bar	lwvsb
Line	lin
List box	lst
List view	lvw
MAPI message	mpm
MAPI session	mps
MCI	mci
Menu	mnu
Month view	mvw
MS chart	ch
MS flexgrid	msg
MS tab	mst
OLE container	ole
Option button	opt
Picture box	pic
Picture clip	clp
Progress bar	prg
Remote data	rd
Rich text box	rtf
Shape	shp
Slider	sld
Spin	spn
Status bar	sta
Sys info	sys
Tab strip	tab
Text box	txt
Timer	tmr
Toolbar	tlb
Tree view	tre
Up down	upd
Vertical scroll bar	vsb

Data Variable Prefixes

If you work with databases, take a look at Table 2.7; it holds the prefixes for data-access objects.

Besides these prefixes, Microsoft recommends prefixes for menus and constants; we'll take a look at them now, to round off our discussion on this topic.

Menu And Constant Prefixes

Microsoft recommends that you name menu controls starting with the prefix **mnu** followed by the menu name and the menu item name. For example, the File menu's Open item would be named **mnuFileOpen**, and the Edit menu's Cut item would be named **mnuEditCut**.

Microsoft also recommends that you name constants (declared with the **Const** statement) using mixed case with a capital letter starting each word. For example:

```
Const DiskDriveNumber = 1        'Constant
Const MaximumFileCount = 1024    'Constant
```

Table 2.7   Data-access object prefixes.

Data Access Object	Prefix
Container	con
Database	db
DBEngine	dbe
Document	doc
Field	fld
Group	grp
Index	ix
Parameter	prm
QueryDef	qry
Recordset	rec
Relation	rel
TableDef	tbd
User	usr
Workspace	wsp

TIP: *Although standard Visual Basic constants don't include data type and scope information, prefixes such as "i", "s", "g", and "m" can be useful in understanding the value or scope of a constant.*

That completes the prefix and naming conventions. As you can see, prefixes exist for just about every type of programming construct available. You aren't required to use them, but they can be extremely helpful.

Variable Scope Prefixes

As a project's size grows, it becomes more important to recognize a variable's scope quickly. A one-letter scope prefix preceding the type prefix provides this information without significantly increasing the size of variable names. Microsoft's recommended variable-scope prefixes appear in Table 2.8.

Table 2.8   Variable-scope prefixes.

Scope	Prefix	Example
Global	g	gstrUserName
Module-level	m	mblnCalcInProgress
Local to procedure	None	dblVelocity

Declaring Constants

You use constants to store unchanging values in a Visual Basic program. So, what's the use of doing that? Constants improve your program's readability and help you avoid "magic numbers" (see the topic "Following Good Programming Practices" in Chapter 1's Immediate Solutions section). For example, here's a little code that's understandable, but not very enlightening:

```
Dim NumberFiles As Integer

Private Sub Form_Load()
    NumberFiles = 33
End Sub
```

The code's meaning is much clearer when you use a named constant instead:

```
Dim NumberFiles As Integer
Const MaxPossibleFiles As Integer = 33

Private Sub Form_Load()
    NumberFiles = MaxPossibleFiles
End Sub
```

You use the **Const** statement to declare a constant:

```
[Public | Private] Const constname [As type] = expression
```

The **Const** statement has these parts:

- *Public*—Keyword used at module level to declare constants that are available to all procedures in all modules. Not allowed in procedures.

- *Private*—Keyword used at module level to declare constants that are available only in the module where the declaration is made. Not allowed in procedures.

- *constname*—Name of the constant (follows standard variable-naming conventions).

- *type*—Data type of the constant; may be **Byte**, **Boolean**, **Currency**, **Date**, **Decimal** (not currently supported), **Double**, **Integer**, **Long**, **Single**, **String**, or **Variant**.

- *expression*—Literal, other constant, or any combination that includes all arithmetic or logical operators except **Is**.

Here's an example showing how to declare and use constants:

```
Dim NumberFiles As Integer
Const LowValue As Integer = 12
Const HighValue As Integer = 100

Private Sub Form_Load()
    NumberFiles = LowValue
End Sub

Private Sub Form_Click()
    NumberFiles = HighValue
End Sub
```

Naming Constants

According to Microsoft, the body of a constant name should be mixed case with a capital letter starting each word. Although standard Visual Basic constants don't include data type and scope information, prefixes like "i", "s", "g", and "m" can be very useful in understanding the value and scope of a constant. In general, you should follow the same naming rules as for variables, although some programmers prefer to use all capitals for constant names.

Declaring Strings

Visual Basic uses two kinds of strings: variable-length and fixed-length. You declare a variable-length string this way:

```
Dim strVariableString As String
```

A variable-length string can contain up to approximately 2 billion characters, and it can grow or shrink to match the data you place in it.

You declare a fixed-length string this way, with a * character followed by the string's length:

```
Dim strFixedString As String * 20
```

Here, the fixed-length string has 20 characters. A fixed-length string can contain 1 to approximately 64K characters.

Converting Between Data Types

Now that you're using the various data types in Visual Basic, you may sometimes want to switch between data types. If you've programmed in other, strongly typed languages, you may be familiar with the idea of using "casts" to convert between variable types. In Visual Basic, the process is a little different—you use data-conversion functions to convert between data types (such as **Integer** to **Double**, and so on). The Visual Basic data-conversion functions appear in Table 2.9.

Table 2.9   *Data-conversion functions.*

Function	Result
Asc	Returns an Integer representing the character code corresponding to the first letter in a string.
CBool	Converts an expression to the Boolean data type.
CByte	Converts an expression to the Byte data type.
CCur	Converts an expression to the Currency data type.
CDate	Converts an expression to the Date data type.
CDec	Converts an expression to the Decimal data type.
CDbl	Converts an expression to the Double data type.
Chr	Returns a String containing the character associated with the specified character code.
CInt	Converts an expression to the Integer data type.
CLng	Converts an expression to the Long data type.
CSng	Converts an expression to the Single data type.
CStr	Converts an expression to the String data type.
CVar	Converts an expression to the Variant data type.
CVErr	Returns a Variant of subtype Error containing an error number specified by the user.
Format	Returns a Variant (String) containing an expression formatted according to instructions contained in a format expression.
Hex	Returns a String representing the hexadecimal value of a number.
Oct	Returns a Variant (String) representing the octal value of a number.
Str	Returns a Variant (String) representation of a number.
Val	Returns the numbers contained in a string as a numeric value of appropriate type.

Chapter 3

Organizing Your Data

In Brief

This chapter takes us beyond the simple variables we saw in the previous chapter, to start organizing data in more complex ways. In the last chapter, you learned how to work with the built-in data types in Visual Basic to create simple variables like **Integers**, **Doubles**, and so forth. In this chapter, we'll look at how to organize data into more complex structures: arrays, dynamic arrays, user-defined types, and collections.

Arrays

Let's start using arrays here, including all the built-in functions that work with arrays, as well as how to redimension arrays on the fly. Visual Basic offers extensive support for arrays—from declaring arrays to redimensioning them, from determining their bounds to setting up arrays with multiple dimensions—and we'll take a look at all of that support in this chapter.

Arrays are attractive because they provide you with an indexed way to store data. Unlike simple variables—which store individual data items—arrays let you store an entire set of data and access each item with an index. Using an index is a valuable ability, because you increment or decrement that index under program control. For example, if you've stored the test scores for a class of students in an array, you can add each successive value in that array to a running total, divide by the total number of students, and so find the average test score.

Visual Basic offers us a lot of power when working with arrays, and we'll put that power to work in this chapter.

User-Defined Types

We'll also examine how to work with the objects that are one step up from arrays: user-defined data types. By defining your own data types, you can structure your data into *fields*. To see how this works, consider an example in which you're creating records to store in a data file. Such records can hold names, phone numbers, and addresses, or item numbers, names, and inventory, or any number of such items—those items are called the record's fields. To create each record, you create a user-defined type made up of data items such as ID numbers, dates, and so on, and then create variables of that type. The variables of your user-defined type can therefore hold mixed data of many different formats, such as **String**s, **Integer**s, and **Double**s. You use these variables as the records in your data file. In this way, using user-defined types lets you collect different data types together, which can be invaluable if you're working with mixed data formats.

Collections

There's another way to group data items in Visual Basic: You can use *collections*. Collections are much like user-defined data types, in that they can support mixed-format data items, but they're actually Visual Basic objects, much like other objects you run across in Visual Basic (such as forms and controls).

As objects, collections can and do support methods and properties These methods and properties are very useful when it comes to managing your data—for example, you can use the **Add** method to add new items to the collection, or the **Count** property to determine the number of items in the collection.

You'll learn how to put all three of these techniques—arrays, user-defined types, and collections—to work organizing your data in this chapter. Chapter 2 gave you insight into working with built-in data types. In this chapter, you'll create your own.

Immediate Solutions

Declaring An Array

To declare an array, you can use several keywords:

- *Dim*—Creates a standard array.
- *ReDim*—Creates a dynamic array.
- *Static*—Creates an array that doesn't change between calls to the procedure it's in.
- *Private*—Creates an array that's private to the form or module it's declared in.
- *Public*—Creates an array that's global to the whole program.
- *Type*—Creates an array of user-defined types.

In this topic, we'll look at how to declare standard arrays of one dimension. To declare a standard array, use the **Dim** statement:

```
Dim [WithEvents] varname[([subscripts])] [As [New] type] _
    [, [WithEvents] varname[([subscripts])] [As [New] _
    type]] . . .
```

The **WithEvents** keyword is valid only in class modules. This keyword specifies that *varname* is an object variable used to respond to events triggered by an ActiveX object.

The *varname* identifier is the name of the variable you're declaring.

You use *subscripts* to declare the array. You set up the *subscripts* argument this way:

```
[lower To] upper [, [lower To] upper]
```

The **New** keyword enables creation of an object. If you use **New** when declaring the object variable, Visual Basic creates a new instance of the object on first reference to it.

The *type* argument specifies the data type of the variable: **Boolean**, **Byte**, **Currency**, **Date**, **Double**, **Integer**, **Long**, **Object**, **Single**, **String** (for variable-length strings), **String * length** (for fixed-length strings), **Variant**, a user-defined type, or an object type. If you don't specify a type, the default is **Variant**, which means the variable can act as any type.

Here are a few examples of standard array declarations:

```
Private Sub Command1_Click()
    Dim Data(30)
    Dim Strings(10) As String
End Sub
```

Declaring Arrays With Multiple Dimensions

Declaring arrays with multiple dimensions is almost as easy as declaring one-dimensional arrays in Visual Basic. In this topic, we'll take a look at declaring such arrays with the **Dim** keyword:

```
Dim [WithEvents] varname[([subscripts])] [As [New] type] _
    [, [WithEvents] varname[([subscripts])] [As [New] _
    type]] . . .
```

The **WithEvents** keyword is valid only in class modules. This keyword specifies that *varname* is an object variable used to respond to events triggered by an ActiveX object.

The *varname* identifier is the name of the variable you're declaring.

You use *subscripts* to declare the array. You set up the *subscripts* argument this way:

```
[lower To] upper [, [lower To] upper]
```

The **New** keyword enables creation of an object. If you use **New** when declaring the object variable, Visual Basic creates a new instance of the object on first reference to it.

The *type* argument specifies the data type of the variable: **Boolean**, **Byte**, **Currency**, **Date**, **Double**, **Integer**, **Long**, **Object**, **Single**, **String** (for variable-length strings), **String * length** (for fixed-length strings), **Variant**, a user-defined type, or an object type. If you don't specify a type, the default is **Variant**, which means the variable can act as any type.

To create an array with multiple dimensions, just list the successive dimensions (separated with commas) when you dimension the array.

Here are a few examples of standard array declarations that create arrays with multiple dimensions:

```
Private Sub Command1_Click()
    Dim TwoDArray(20, 40) As Integer
    Dim Bounds(5 To 10, 20 To 100)
End Sub
```

Accessing The Data In Arrays

To access the data in an array, use an array index.

An example will make this clear; first, you set up a **Names** array in the (General) section of a form, to hold the names of 10 people:

```
Dim Names(10) As String
```

Now, you're free to place data in that array; here, the code fills the first three strings in the array when the form loads:

```
Dim Names(10) As String

Private Sub Form_Load()
    Names(0) = "Tom"
    Names(1) = "Dick"
    Names(2) = "Harry"
End Sub
```

You can access that data as necessary. For example, let's display the third name in the array when the user clicks on a button:

```
Dim Names(10) As String

Private Sub Form_Load()
    Names(0) = "Tom"
    Names(1) = "Dick"
    Names(2) = "Harry"
End Sub

Private Sub Command1_Click()
    Text1.Text = Names(2)
End Sub
```

You're free to assign new values to the array items in the same way—simply refer to the item you want to work with by index.

Creating Arrays With The **Array** Function

You can use the **Array** function to create a new **Variant** holding an array. Here's how you use **Array**:

```
Array(arglist)
```

The **_arglist_** argument is a list of values assigned to the elements of the array contained within the **Variant**.

The following example creates an array containing the values zero, one, and two:

```
Dim A As Variant
A = Array(0,1,2)
```

TIP: *If you don't specify any arguments, the **Array** function returns an array of zero length.*

Setting An Array's Default Lower Bounds

When you declare arrays in a Visual Basic program, the default lower bound (the lowest index value you can use in the array) is zero. However, you can use the **Option Base** statement at the form or module level to set the lower bound for all arrays.

You can use either of these two statements: **Option Base 0** to set the lower bound to 0, or **Option Base 1** to set the lower bound to 1.

For example, say you want to keep track of employee names by ID number, and the ID number varies from 1 to 1000. In that case, starting the array of names at 0 like this is inappropriate:

```
Dim EmployeeNames(1000) As String

Private Sub Form_Load()
    EmployeeNames(0) = "Tom"
    EmployeeNames(1) = "Dick"
    EmployeeNames(2) = "Harry"
    .
    .
    .
End Sub
```

Instead, you can specify that arrays start with the index 1 this way, to better match the employee ID numbers:

```
Option Base 1
Dim EmployeeNames(1000) As String

Private Sub Form_Load()
    EmployeeNames(1) = "Tom"
    EmployeeNames(2) = "Dick"
    EmployeeNames(3) = "Harry"
    .
    .
    .
End Sub
```

The **Option Base** statement affects only the lower bound of arrays in the module where the statement is located.

TIP: *The* **To** *clause in the* **Dim**, **Private**, **Public**, **ReDim**, *and* **Static** *statements provides a more flexible way to control the range of an array's subscripts.*

Redimensioning Arrays

Using the **Dim** statement to set up an array with empty parentheses declares a *dynamic array*. You can dimension or redimension dynamic arrays as you need them, with the **ReDim** statement (which you must also call the first time you use a dynamic array). Here's how you use **ReDim**:

```
ReDim [Preserve] varname(subscripts) [As type] _
  [, varname(subscripts) [As type]] . . .
```

You use the **Preserve** keyword to preserve the data in an existing array when you change the size of the last dimension.

The *varname* argument holds the name of the array to (re)dimension.

The *subscripts* term specifies the dimensions of the array using this syntax:

```
[lower To] upper [,[lower To] upper].
```

The *type* argument specifies the type of the array. The type may be **Boolean**, **Byte**, **Currency**, **Date**, **Double**, **Integer**, **Long**, **Object**, **Single**, **String** (for variable-length strings), **String *length** (for fixed-length strings), **Variant**, a user-defined type, or an object type.

This is a topic that's made easier with an example. The following code uses dynamic arrays; it declares an array, dimensions it, and then redimensions it:

```
Option Base 1
Private Sub Command1_Click()
    Dim DynaStrings() As String
    ReDim DynaStrings(10)
    DynaStrings(1) = "The first string"
    'Need more data space!
    ReDim DynaStrings(100)
    DynaStrings(50) = "The fiftieth string"
End Sub
```

Checking If It's An Array

Visual Basic lets you check whether a variable is an array with the **IsArray** function. You may think such a function isn't very useful— if you've declared an array, presumably you'll *know* it's an array. In practice, you'll generally use **IsArray** when you use the **Array** function, because that function actually returns a **Variant** that contains an array.

IsArray returns **True** if the variable is an array; otherwise, it returns **False**.

Here's an example that shows how to put **IsArray** to work. First, you set up a **Variant** named **arData** that holds an array as returned from the **Array** function:

```
Private Sub Form_Load()
    Dim arData As Variant

    arData = Array(1, 2, 3)
    .
    .
    .
```

Next, you test **arData** with the **IsArray** function, indicating in a text box whether **arData** is an array:

```
Private Sub Form_Load()
    Dim arData As Variant

    arData = Array(1, 2, 3)

    If IsArray(arData) Then
        Text1.Text = "It's an array."
    Else
        Text1.Text = "It's not an array."
    End If
End Sub
```

Determining Array Bounds

You can determine the bounds of an array using two Visual Basic functions: **LBound** to determine the array's lower bound, and **UBound** to determine its upper bound. It might seem odd not to know the bounds of an array in your program, but in fact it's quite common. For example, you may be writing a utility function that needs to work with arbitrary arrays passed to it, or you may redimension an array in code and need to check its bounds at some later time.

Let's look at an example. Here, you declare an array named **arValues**, making its lower bound 4 and its upper bound 10:

```
Private Sub Form_Load()

    Dim arValues(4 To 10) As Integer
    .
    .
    .
End Sub
```

Next, you report the array's lower bound in a text box—**Text1**—using **LBound**:

```
Private Sub Form_Load()

    Dim arValues(4 To 10) As Integer

    Text1.Text = "Array lower bound = " & LBound(arValues)
```

```
    .
    .
    .
End Sub
```

Finally, you report the array's upper bound in another text box—
Text2—using **UBound**:

```
Private Sub Form_Load()

    Dim arValues(4 To 10) As Integer

    Text1.Text = "Array lower bound = " & LBound(arValues)

    Text2.Text = "Array upper bound = " & UBound(arValues)

End Sub
```

The result of this program appears in Figure 3.1.

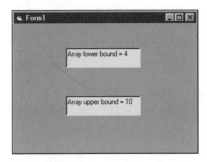

Figure 3.1   *Determining the upper and lower bounds of an array.*

Array-Handling Techniques Summary

Visual Basic provides a number of statements and functions for working with arrays; they appear in overview in Table 3.1, for easy reference.

Table 3.1   *Array-handling techniques.*

To do this:	Use this:
Verify an array.	IsArray
Create an array.	Array
Change default lower limit.	Option Base

(continued)

Table 3.1   Array-handling techniques (continued).

To do this:	Use this:
Declare and initialize an array.	Dim, Private, Public, ReDim, Static
Find the limits of an array.	LBound, UBound
Reinitialize an array.	Erase, ReDim

Creating A User-Defined Type

You can create your own variable types in Visual Basic using the **Type** keyword. This technique is useful if, for instance, you want to create a record type for storing data in files, or you want to associate data items of different types together.

To create a user-defined type, you must use the **Type** keyword in a standard (BAS) module. Here's how to use **Type**:

```
[Private | Public] Type varname _
  elementname [([subscripts])] As type _
  [elementname [([subscripts])] As type]
  .
  .
  .
End Type
```

The **Type** statement has these parts:

- *Public*—Declares user-defined types that are available to all procedures in all modules in all projects.

- *Private*—Declares user-defined types that are available only within the module containing the declaration.

- *varname*—Name of the user-defined type; follows standard variable-naming conventions.

- *elementname*—Name of an element of the user-defined type. Element names also follow standard variable-naming conventions, but you can use keywords.

- *subscripts*—Dimensions of an array element. Use parentheses only when declaring an array whose size can change. The *subscripts* argument uses the following syntax:

```
[lower To] upper [,[lower To] upper] . . .
```

- *type*—Data type of the element: **Boolean**, **Byte**, **Currency**, **Date**, **Decimal** (not currently supported), **Double**, **Integer**, **Long**, **Object**, **Single**, **String** (for variable-length strings), **String** * **length** (for fixed-length strings), **Variant**, another user-defined type, or an object type.

For example, here's how to create a new user-defined type named **Record**; this type has two fields—**Name** and **Number**—each of which is a fixed-length string of 50 characters:

```
Type Record
    Name As String * 50
    Number As String * 50
End Type
```

Related solution:	Found in:
Adding Or Removing Form, Standard, And Class Modules	Chapter 1

Declaring Variables Of A User-Defined Type

After you've set up a user-defined data type, you can declare variables of that type with the **Dim** statement. For example, after setting up a user-defined type named **Record** in a standard module, like this

```
Type Record
    Name As String * 50
    Number As String * 50
End Type
```

you can declare variables and arrays of that type in code using **Dim**:

```
Type Record
    Name As String * 50
    Number As String * 50
End Type

Dim WriteData(1 To 50) As Record
Dim ReadData(1 To 50) As Record
```

Accessing Members In A User-Defined Type

After setting up a user-defined type and creating variables of that type, you can access the fields in that user-defined variable with the dot (.) operator.

Let's look at an example to make this technique clearer. First, you declare a user-defined type named **Record** with two fields in it—**Name** and **Number**:

```
Type Record
    Name As String * 50
    Number As String * 50
End Type
```

Next, you declare two arrays—**WriteData** and **ReadData**—of type **Record**:

```
Type Record
    Name As String * 50
    Number As String * 50
End Type

Dim WriteData(1 To 50) As Record
Dim ReadData(1 To 50) As Record
    .
    .
    .
```

Now, you're able to access the data in each member of the array using the dot operator. For example, here's how to reach the **Name** and **Number** fields in the **WriteData(1)** record when the user clicks on a button:

```
Type Record
    Name As String * 50
    Number As String * 50
End Type

Dim WriteData(1 To 50) As Record
Dim ReadData(1 To 50) As Record

Private Sub Command1_Click()
    WriteData(1).Name = Text1.Text
    WriteData(1).Number = Text2.Text
End Sub
```

As you can see, you use the dot operator to reach the data in the fields of a user-defined variable: *variable.field*.

Creating A Collection

A *collection* is much like a user-defined variable; however, it's a Visual Basic object, and as such has built-in properties and methods. You usually use collections to group different types of data items, much as you would with a user-defined data type. However, with a collection, you can use the built-in methods and properties to manage its internal data items.

Here are some of the keywords you use with collections:

- *Collection*—Creates a Collection object.
- *Add*—Adds an object to a collection.
- *Remove*—Removes an object from a collection.
- *Item*—References an item in a collection.

To create a collection, you use the **Collection** keyword. This example creates a new collection named **PhoneBook**:

```
Dim PhoneBook As New Collection
```

That's all it takes to create a new collection. In the following topics, we'll see how to add data items (called *data members*) to the collection and manipulate them.

Adding Members To A Collection

You can use the **Add** method to add a member to a collection:

```
object.Add item, key, before, after
```

The **Add** method has the following arguments:

- *item*—An expression of any type that specifies the member to add to the collection.
- *key*—A unique string expression that specifies a key string that you can use instead of a positional index to access a member of the collection.

- *before*—An expression that specifies a relative position in the collection. You place the member to be added in the collection before the member identified by the *before* argument. In a numeric expression, *before* must be a number from one to the value of the collection's **Count** property. In a string expression, *before* must correspond to the *key* specified when the member being referred to was added to the collection.

- *after*—An expression that specifies a relative position in the collection. You place the member to be added in the collection after the member identified by the *after* argument. If *after* is numeric, it must be a number from one to the value of the collection's **Count** property. If *after* is a string, it must correspond to the *key* specified when the member referred to was added to the collection.

Let's look at an example. First, you declare a new collection:

```
Dim PhoneBook As New Collection
```

Next, you set up a few data items to add to the collection:

```
Dim PhoneBook As New Collection

Private Sub Form_Load()
    Dim strPhoneNumber As String
    Dim strAddress As String
    Dim intID As Integer

    strPhoneNumber = "555-1212"
    strAddress = "102 Boylston"
    intID = 299
    .
    .
    .
```

Finally, you add those items to the collection using the **Add** method:

```
Dim PhoneBook As New Collection

Private Sub Form_Load()
    Dim strPhoneNumber As String
    Dim strAddress As String
    Dim intID As Integer

    strPhoneNumber = "555-1212"
```

```
        strAddress = "102 Boylston"
        intID = 299

        PhoneBook.Add strPhoneNumber
        PhoneBook.Add strAddress
        PhoneBook.Add intID

    End Sub
```

In the next topic, you'll see how to reach the members of a collection.

Accessing Members In A Collection

To reach a member of a collection, use the **Item** method:

```
object.Item(index)
```

The **Item** method has one argument—*index*—that's an expression specifying the position of a member of the collection. If *index* is a numeric expression, it must be a number from one to the value of the collection's **Count** property. If *index* is a string expression, it must correspond to the *key* argument specified when the member referred to was added to the collection.

Let's look at an example that creates a new collection and adds a few data items to it:

```
    Dim PhoneBook As New Collection

Private Sub Form_Load()
    Dim strPhoneNumber As String
    Dim strAddress As String
    Dim intID As Integer

    strPhoneNumber = "555-1212"
    strAddress = "102 Boylston"
    intID = 299

    PhoneBook.Add strPhoneNumber
    PhoneBook.Add strAddress
    PhoneBook.Add intID

End Sub
```

When the user clicks on a command button, you can display, for instance, the item with index number 3 this way (the index values start at 1, so index 3 refers to the value in the **intID** member):

```
Private Sub Command1_Click()
    Text1.Text = "ID value = " & Val(PhoneBook.Item(3))
End Sub
```

Removing An Item From A Collection

You use the **Remove** method to remove an item from a collection:

```
object.Remove index
```

The **Remove** method has one argument—*index*—that's an expression specifying the position of a member of the collection. If *index* is a numeric expression, it must be a number from one to the value of the collection's **Count** property. If *index* is a string expression, it must correspond to the *key* argument specified when the member referred to was added to the collection.

Determining The Number Of Items In A Collection

You can determine the number of items in a collection with the collection's **Count** property. This property is a read-only long integer that holds the number of items in the collection. For example, this code displays a value of three for the three data members of the **PhoneBook** collection:

```
Dim PhoneBook As New Collection

Private Sub Form_Load()
    Dim strPhoneNumber As String
    Dim strAddress As String
    Dim intID As Integer

    strPhoneNumber = "555-1212"
    strAddress = "102 Boylston"
    intID = 299
```

3: Organizing Your Data

```
      PhoneBook.Add strPhoneNumber
      PhoneBook.Add strAddress
      PhoneBook.Add intID

      Text1.Text = Str(PhoneBook.Count)

End Sub
```

Operators And String Handling

In Brief

In the previous chapters, we've seen how to declare variables and how to assign values to those variables—now it's time to start working with those values. In this chapter, you'll learn how to use Visual Basic operators to manipulate the data you've stored in variables and arrays.

The Assignment Operator

Perhaps the most fundamental Visual Basic operator is the assignment operator (=) You use this operator to store values in variables as in the following code, which assigns the value 12 to the variable **NumberFiles**:

```
Private Sub Form_Load()
    Dim NumberFiles As Integer
    NumberFiles = 12
End Sub
```

As you can see, this operator is of paramount importance in Visual Basic—without it, you couldn't assign values even to simple variables.

Arithmetic Operators

Next in importance come the arithmetic operators. Using these operators, you can add, subtract, multiply, divide, and so forth. For example, here's how you use the addition operator (+) to add two numbers and store the result in a variable named **intSum**:

```
Private Sub Form_Load()
    Dim intValue1, intValue2, intSum As Integer
    intValue1 = 1
    intValue2 = 2
    intSum = intValue1 + intValue2
End Sub
```

We'll examine the available arithmetic operators in this chapter and see how to put them to work.

Comparison Operators

The Visual Basic comparison operators let you compare values by returning a **True** or **False** value. These operators form the basis of program-flow statements such as the **If** statement you'll see in the next chapter (we'll also discuss how to make use of program-flow statements in that chapter). For example, the following code compares the values in **intValue1** and **intValue2** using the greater-than operator (**>**), which returns a value of **True** if the first operand is greater than the second operand:

```
Private Sub Form_Load()
    Dim intValue1, intValue2 As Integer
    intValue1 = 1
    intValue2 = 2
    If intValue1 > IntValue2 Then
        MsgBox "intValue1 is greater than intValue2"
    End If
End Sub
```

We'll look at the available comparison operators in this chapter.

Logical Operators

Logical operators work on values of **True** and **False** and also return values of **True** and **False**. For example, you pass the **And** logical operator two values, and if both those values are **True**, the operator returns a value of **True**; otherwise, this operator returns **False**. In this way, the **And** operator returns **True** only if both operands are **True**.

Let's look at an example to make this explanation clearer. This code checks to be sure that **intValue1** is less than **intValue2** *and* that **intValue3** is less than **intValue4**, using the less-than operator (**<**) and the **And** logical operator:

```
Private Sub Form_Load()
    Dim intValue1, intValue2, intValue3, intValue4 As Integer
    intValue1 = 1
    intValue2 = 2
    intValue3 = 3
    intValue4 = 4
    If intValue1 < intValue2 And intValue3 < intValue4 Then
        MsgBox "Data values compare OK."
    End If
End Sub
```

You'll generally use logical operators to influence program flow, just like comparison operators; we'll see them at work in the next chapter.

Math Functions

Besides the built-in arithmetic operators, Visual Basic supports a wide variety of math functions, such as sine and cosine; we'll examine them in this chapter. We'll also see how to derive some higher math functions using the built-in Visual Basic math functions.

String Handling

Finally, we'll take a look at handling text strings in this chapter. Visual Basic has an excellent reputation for the way it works with strings—we'll see how it got that reputation as we discuss how to compare, concatenate, search, divide, and otherwise manipulate strings. Visual Basic's string-handling arsenal is very powerful, and we'll put it to work.

That's all the introduction you need—it's time to turn to the Immediate Solutions part of this chapter.

Immediate Solutions

Assigning Values To Variables

You use the assignment operator (=) to assign values to variables. For example, this code declares a variable named **NumberFiles** and then uses the assignment operator to assign the variable a value of 12:

```
Private Sub Form_Load()
    Dim NumberFiles As Integer
    NumberFiles = 12
End Sub
```

Besides immediate values (such as 12), you can also assign values to a variable from other variables or constants by using the assignment operator.

Using Arithmetic Operators

You use arithmetic operators to handle simple math operations, such as addition, subtraction, and multiplication. Visual Basic's arithmetic operators are listed in Table 4.1.

We'll see each of these operators at work in the following few topics.

Table 4.1   Arithmetic operators.

Operator	Definition
^	Exponentiation
*	Multiplication
/	Division
\	Integer division
Mod	Modulus
+	Addition
-	Subtraction

Addition

You use the addition operator (+) to add two operands. This operator adds the operands and returns the sum. For example, here's how you add the variables **intValue1** and **intValue2** using the addition operator and display the result:

```
Private Sub Form_Load()
    Dim intValue1, intValue2 As Integer
    intValue1 = 6
    intValue2 = 4
    MsgBox "intValue1 + intValue2 = " & intValue1 + intValue2
End Sub
```

Subtraction

You use the subtraction operator (-) to subtract one operand from another. This operator subtracts the operands and returns the difference. For example, here's how you subtract **intValue2** from **intValue1** using the subtraction operator and display the result:

```
Private Sub Form_Load()
    Dim intValue1, intValue2 As Integer
    intValue1 = 6
    intValue2 = 4
    MsgBox "intValue1 - intValue2 = " & intValue1 - intValue2
End Sub
```

Multiplication

You use the multiplication operator (*) to multiply two operands. This operator multiplies the operands and returns the product. For example, here's how you multiply **intValue1** by **intValue2** using the multiplication operator and display the result:

```
Private Sub Form_Load()
    Dim intValue1, intValue2 As Integer
    intValue1 = 6
    intValue2 = 4
    MsgBox "intValue1 * intValue2 = " & intValue1 * intValue2
End Sub
```

Division

You use the division operator (*/*) to divide two operands. This operator divides the operands and returns the result. For example, here's how you divide **intValue1** by **intValue2** using the division operator and then display the result:

```
Private Sub Form_Load()
    Dim intValue1, intValue2 As Integer
    intValue1 = 6
    intValue2 = 4
    MsgBox "intValue1 / intValue2 = " & intValue1 / intValue2
End Sub
```

Integer Division

You use the integer-division operator (\) to perform integer division on two operands. This operator divides the operands and returns the integer result. For example, here's how you divide **intValue1** by **intValue2** using the integer-division operator and then display the result:

```
Private Sub Form_Load()
    Dim intValue1, intValue2 As Integer
    intValue1 = 6
    intValue2 = 4
    MsgBox "intValue1 \ intValue2 = " & intValue1 \ intValue2
End Sub
```

This code returns a value of 1, whereas if you had used the division operator (*/*), the result would have been 1.5.

Exponentiation

You use the exponentiation operator (^) to raise one operand to the power of another. For example, here's how you raise **intValue1** to the power **intValue2** using the exponentiation operator and display the result:

```
Private Sub Form_Load()
    Dim intValue1, intValue2 As Integer
```

```
            intValue1 = 6
            intValue2 = 4
        MsgBox "intValue1 ^ intValue2 = " & intValue1 ^ intValue2
End Sub
```

In this case, the result is 6 raised to the power 4, or 1,296.

Modulus

You use the modulus operator (**Mod**) to find the modulus of two numbers (the *modulus* is the remainder after one operand is divided by the other). For example, here's how you find the modulus of **intValue1** and **intValue2** using the modulus operator and display the result:

```
Private Sub Form_Load()
        Dim intValue1, intValue2 As Integer
        intValue1 = 6
        intValue2 = 4
        MsgBox "intValue1 Mod intValue2 = " & intValue1 Mod intValue2
End Sub
```

In this case, the result is the remainder of 6 divided by 4, or 2.

Using Comparison Operators

As their name indicates, you use comparison operators to compare two operands. Comparison operators return a value of **True** or **False**; for example, using the greater-than operator (**>**) in the statement **1 > 4** will return a value of **False**.

The Visual Basic comparison operators are listed in Table 4.2.

Table 4.2   Comparison operators.

Operator	Definition
<	Less than
<=	Less than or equal to
>	Greater than
>=	Greater than or equal to
=	Equal to
<>	Not equal to

Table 4.3   Examples of true, false, and null expressions using the comparison operators.

Operator	True if	False if	Null if
<	*expression1* < *expression2*	*expression1* >= *expression2*	*expression1* or *expression2* = Null
<=	*expression1* <= *expression2*	*expression1* > *expression2*	*expression1* or *expression2* = Null
>	*expression1* > *expression2*	*expression1* <= *expression2*	*expression1* or *expression2* = Null
>=	*expression1* >= *expression2*	*expression1* < *expression2*	*expression1* or *expression2* = Null
=	*expression1* = *expression2*	*expression1* <> *expression2*	*expression1* or *expression2* = Null
<>	*expression1* <> *expression2*	*expression1* = *expression2*	*expression1* or *expression2* = Null

You can see how the comparison operators work by examining Table 4.3.

For example, the following code compares the values in **intValue1** and **intValue2** using the greater-than operator (**>**); this operator returns a value of **True** if the first operand is greater than the second operand:

```
Private Sub Form_Load()
    Dim intValue1, intValue2 As Integer
    intValue1 = 1
    intValue2 = 2
    If intValue1 > intValue2 Then
        MsgBox "intValue1 is greater than intValue2"
    End If
End Sub
```

In this case, the value in **intValue1** isn't greater than the value in **intValue2**, so the message box doesn't appear.

Using Logical Operators

You use logical operators to work on values that are **True**, **False**, or **Null** to produce other values. For example, the result of the expression *expression1* **And** *expression2*—which uses the logical **And** operator—is **True** if (and only if) both *expression1* and *expression2* are **True**. Here's an example to make this clearer; in this case, the code checks to be sure that **intValue1** is less than **intValue2** *and* that **intValue3** is less than **intValue4**, by using the less-than operator (**<**) and the **And** operator:

```
Private Sub Form_Load()
    Dim intValue1, intValue2, intValue3, intValue4 As Integer
    intValue1 = 1
    intValue2 = 2
    intValue3 = 3
    intValue4 = 4
    If intValue1 < intValue2 And intValue3 < intValue4 Then
        MsgBox "Data values compare OK."
    End If
End Sub
```

The Visual Basic logical operators are listed in Table 4.4.

We'll take a look at all these operators in this topic.

The **And** Operator

Both operands must be **True** to give a **True** result with the **And** operator. Table 4.5 shows the possible results of the expression *expression1* **And** *expression2*.

The **Eqv** Operator

The **Eqv** operator compares two logical values and returns **True** if they're the same. Table 4.6 shows the result of the expression *expression1* **Eqv** *expression2*.

Table 4.4   Logical operators.

Operator	Definition
And	Performs And operations
Eqv	Compares two logical values
Imp	Performs a logical implication on two values
Not	Flips its operand's logical value
Or	Performs Or operations
Xor	Performs exclusive Or operations

Table 4.5   The And operator.

If *expression1* is	And *expression2* is	The result is
True	True	True
True	False	False
True	Null	Null
False	True	False
False	False	False
False	Null	False
Null	True	Null
Null	False	False
Null	Null	Null

Table 4.6   The Eqv operator.

If *expression1* is	And *expression2* is	The result is
True	True	True
True	False	False
False	True	False
False	False	True

The **Imp** Operator

The **Imp** operator performs a logical implication on two operands. Table 4.7 shows the result of the expression *expression1* **Imp** *expression2*.

Table 4.7   The Imp operator.

If *expression1* is	And *expression2* is	The result is
True	True	True
True	False	False
True	Null	Null
False	True	True
False	False	True
False	Null	True
Null	True	True
Null	False	Null
Null	Null	Null

The **Imp** operator performs a bitwise comparison of identically positioned bits in two numeric expressions and sets the corresponding bit in the result, according to Table 4.8.

The **Not** Operator

The **Not** operator simply reverses the logical value of the operand you pass to it. If you use **Not** on a value of **True**, the result is **False**; if you use **Not** on a value of **False**, the result is **True**. The only value **Not** doesn't change is **Null**.

The **Or** Operator

The **Or** operator returns **True** if either of its operands is **True**. Table 4.9 shows the result of the expression *expression1* **Or** *expression2*.

The **Xor** Operator

The **Xor** operator returns **True** if either—but not both—of its operands is **True**, unless **Null** is one of its operands. In that case (i.e., if either operand is **Null**), it returns **Null**. Table 4.10 shows the result of the expression *expression1* **Xor** *expression2*.

Table 4.8   The Imp operator's bitwise operations.

If bit in *expression1* is	And bit in *expression2* is	The result is
0	0	1
0	1	1
1	0	0
1	1	1

Table 4.9   The Or operator.

If *expression1* is	And *expression2* is	The result is
True	True	True
True	False	True
True	Null	True
False	True	True
False	False	False
False	Null	Null
Null	True	True
Null	False	Null
Null	Null	Null

Table 4.10   The Xor operator.

If *expression1* is	And *expression2* is	The result is
True	True	False
True	False	True
False	True	True
False	False	False
Null	True	Null
Null	False	Null
True	Null	Null
False	Null	Null

Determining Operator Precedence

Suppose you're finished teaching your computer class and it's time to calculate the average grade on the final exam. Nothing could be easier, you think, and you put together the following program:

```
Private Sub Command1_Click()
    Dim intGrade1, intGrade2, inGrade3, NumberStudents As _
    Integer
    intGrade1 = 60
    intGrade2 = 70
    intGrade3 = 80
    NumberStudents = 3
    MsgBox ("Average grade = " &_
        Str(intGrade1 + intGrade2 + intGrade3 / NumberStudents))
End Sub
```

But when you run the program, it informs you that the average score is 156.66666667. That doesn't look so good—what's wrong?

The problem lies in this expression:

```
Str(intGrade1 + intGrade2 + intGrade3 / NumberStudents)
```

Visual Basic evaluates the expression in parentheses from left to right, using pairs of operands and their associated operators. In this case, Visual Basic adds the first two grades—but then, instead of adding the final grade, it first divides that grade by **NumberStudents**, because the division operation has higher precedence than addition. The result is 60 + 70 + (80/3) = 156.66666667.

The solution here is to use parentheses to group the values you want to add:

```
Str((intGrade1 + intGrade2 + intGrade3)/ NumberStudents)
```

Incorporating this new expression into the code gives you an average grade of 70, as it should.

This example points out the need to understand how Visual Basic evaluates expressions involving operators. In general, such expressions are evaluated left to right; when it comes to a contest between two operators (such as **+** and **/** in the last term of the previous original program), the operator with the higher precedence is used first.

Visual Basic's operator precedence appears in Table 4.11. The table's columns arrange the operators by category. The table's rows arrange the operators by precedence (except for the Comparison column, in which all the operators have equal precedence).

When expressions contain operators from only one category—either Arithmetic or Logical—Visual Basic evaluates them in the order listed. When expressions contain operators from only one category— Comparison—they are evaluated in the left-to-right order in which they appear in the expression.

When expressions contain operators from more than one category, Visual Basic evaluates arithmetic operators first, comparison operators next, and logical operators last.

Table 4.11   Operators and operator precedence.

Arithmetic (In Order Of Precedence)	Comparison (All Of Equal Precedence)	Logical (In Order Of Precedence)
Exponentiation (^)	Equality (=)	Not
Negation (−)	Inequality (<>)	And
Multiplication and division (*, /)	Less than (<)	Or
Integer division (\ )	Greater than (>)	Xor
Modulus arithmetic (Mod)	Less than or equal to (<=)	Eqv
Addition and subtraction (+, −)	Greater than or equal to (>=)	Imp
String concatenation (&)		

When in doubt, use parentheses—operations within parentheses are always performed before those outside. Within parentheses, however, Visual Basic maintains operator precedence.

Using The Math Functions

Visual Basic provides you with a substantial library of math functions, such as **Cos**, **Abs**, **Log**, and many more. The built-in Visual Basic math functions appear in Table 4.12.

Handling Higher Math

How do you calculate a hyperbolic cosecant, anyway? Can Visual Basic do it? Yes, although not directly. Consult Table 4.13, which shows how to calculate other results using the built-in Visual Basic math functions.

Table 4.12   The Visual Basic math functions.

Function	Calculates This
Abs	Absolute value
Atn	Arctangent
Cos	Cosine
Exp	Exponentiation
Fix	Fix decimal places
Int	Integer value
Log	Log
Rnd	Random number between 0 and 1
Sgn	Sign
Sin	Sine
Sqr	Square root
Tan	Tangent

Table 4.13   Calculated math functions.

Result	Calculation
Secant	$Sec(X) = 1 / Cos(X)$
Cosecant	$Cosec(X) = 1 / Sin(X)$
Cotangent	$Cotan(X) = 1 / Tan(X)$

(continued)

Table 4.13   Calculated math functions (continued).

Result	Calculation
Inverse sine	Arcsin(X) = Atn(X / Sqr(-X * X + 1))
Inverse cosine	Arccos(X) = Atn(-X / Sqr(-X * X + 1)) + 2 * Atn(1)
Inverse secant	Arcsec(X) = Atn(X / Sqr(X * X − 1)) + Sgn((X) − 1) * (2 * Atn(1))
Inverse cosecant	Arccosec(X) = Atn(X / Sqr(X * X - 1)) + (Sgn(X) − 1) * (2 * Atn(1))
Inverse cotangent	Arccotan(X) = Atn(X) + 2 * Atn(1)
Hyperbolic sine	HSin(X) = (Exp(X) − Exp(-X)) / 2
Hyperbolic cosine	HCos(X) = (Exp(X) + Exp(-X)) / 2
Hyperbolic tangent	HTan(X) = (Exp(X) − Exp(-X)) / (Exp(X) + Exp(-X))
Hyperbolic secant	HSec(X) = 2 / (Exp(X) + Exp(-X))
Hyperbolic cosecant	HCosec(X) = 2 / (Exp(X) − Exp(-X))
Hyperbolic cotangent	HCotan(X) = (Exp(X) + Exp(-X)) / (Exp(X) − Exp(-X))
Inverse hyperbolic sine	HArcsin(X) = Log(X + Sqr(X * X + 1))
Inverse hyperbolic cosine	HArccos(X) = Log(X + Sqr(X * X − 1))
Inverse hyperbolic tangent	HArctan(X) = Log((1 + X) / (1 − X)) / 2
Inverse hyperbolic secant	HArcsec(X) = Log((Sqr(-X * X + 1) + 1) / X)
Inverse hyperbolic cosecant	HArccosec(X) = Log((Sgn(X) * Sqr(X * X + 1) + 1) / X)
Inverse hyperbolic cotangent	HArccotan(X) = Log((X + 1) / (X − 1)) / 2
Logarithm to base N	LogN(X) = Log(X) / Log(N)

Handling Strings

Visual Basic offers a great deal of string-handling power, and you'll get an overview of string handling in this topic. Specifically, you use string-handling functions to manipulate strings in Visual Basic. For example, you use **Left**, **Mid**, and **Right** to divide a string into substrings; you find the length of a string with **Len**; and so on.

For reference, the Visual Basic string-handling functions appear in Table 4.14.

Searching Strings

You use the **InStr** function to find the position of the first occurrence of one string within another. This function returns a **Variant** (**Long**) giving that position:

Table 4.14   String-handling functions.

Function(s)	Description
StrComp	Compare two strings
StrConv	Convert strings
Format, Lcase, Ucase	Convert to lowercase or uppercase
Space, String	Create a string of a repeating character
Len	Find the length of a string
Format	Format a string
LSet, Rset	Justify a string
InStr, Left, LTrim, Mid, Right, RTrim, Trim	Manipulate strings
Option Compare	Set string-comparison rules
Asc, Chr	Work with ASCII and ANSI values

```
InStr([start, ]string1, string2[, compare])
```

The **InStr** function has these arguments:

- *start*—Numeric expression that sets the starting position for each search. (If omitted, the search begins at the first character position.) The *start* argument is required if compare is specified.

- *string1*—String expression being searched.

- *string2*—String expression you're searching for.

- *compare*—Type of string comparison. If you omit *compare*, the **Option Compare** setting determines the type of comparison.

Finding The Length Of A String

You use the **Len** function to determine the length of a string or the number of bytes needed to store a variable. This function returns a **Long** value:

```
Len(string | varname)
```

Concatenating Strings

You can use either the **+** or the **&** operator to concatenate (that is, join together) strings, but Microsoft recommends you use the **&** operator. Here's an example that uses the **&** operator to concatenate two strings to create one string, **"Hello there!"**:

```
Private Sub Form_Load()
    Dim strHello, strThere, strHelloThere As String
    strHello = "Hello "
```

```
        strThere = "there!"

        strHelloThere = strHello & strThere

        MsgBox strHelloThere
End Sub
```

Creating Substrings

You can use the functions **Left**, **LTrim**, **Mid**, **Right**, **RTrim**, and **Trim** to create substrings from a string.

LTrim, **RTrim**, and **Trim** each return a **Variant** (**String**) containing a copy of a specified string without leading spaces (**LTrim**), trailing spaces (**RTrim**), or both leading and trailing spaces (**Trim**):

```
LTrim(string)
RTrim(string)
Trim(string)
```

The **Left** function returns a **Variant** (**String**) containing a specified number of characters from the left side of a string:

```
Left(string, length)
```

The **Left** function has these arguments:

- *string*—String expression from which the leftmost characters are returned.

- *length*—Numeric expression indicating how many characters to return. If zero, a zero-length string ("") is returned. If greater than or equal to the number of characters in *string*, the entire string is returned.

The **Mid** function returns a **Variant** (**String**) containing a specified number of characters from a string:

```
Mid(string, start[, length])
```

The **Mid** function has these arguments:

- *string*—String expression from which characters are returned.

- *start*—Character position in *string* at which the part to be returned begins. If *start* is greater than the number of characters in *string*, **Mid** returns a zero-length string ("").

- *length*—Number of characters to return. If omitted, or if there are fewer than *length* characters in *string* (including the character at *start*), all characters from the start position to the end of the string are returned.

The **Right** function returns a **Variant** (**String**) containing a specified number of characters from the right side of a string:

```
Right(string, length)
```

The **Right** function has these arguments:

- *string*—String expression from which the rightmost characters are returned.

- *length*—Numeric expression indicating how many characters to return. If zero, a zero-length string ("") is returned. If greater than or equal to the number of characters in *string*, the entire string is returned.

Converting Strings To Numbers And Back Again

In Visual Basic, you often have to convert values from numbers to strings or from strings to numbers—and doing so is easy. You can use the **Str** function to return a string representation of a number, and you can use **Val** to convert a string to a number. That's all there is to it.

Besides **Str** and **Val**, you can also use the **Format** function, which lets you format an expression into a string this way:

```
Format(expression[, format[, firstdayofweek[, _
    firstweekofyear]]])
```

The **Format** function has these arguments:

- *expression*—The expression to format into the string

- *format*—A valid named or user-defined format expression

- *firstdayofweek*—A constant that specifies the first day of the week

- *firstweekofyear*—A constant that specifies the first week of the year

Chapter 5

Program Flow

In Brief

In this chapter, we're going to take a look at *program flow*—that is, we'll see how to make decisions based on data values and alter the course of program execution accordingly. In previous chapters, we've been working largely with data in Visual Basic programs. Here, we'll begin creating programs that can make decisions based on that data, using the computer's unique ability to interpret values and process information.

We'll examine two primary types of control structures: conditional statements and loops.

Conditional Statements

Visual Basic's conditional statements influence program flow based on decisions those statements make on data. The prime example of a Visual Basic conditional—and undoubtedly the most popular one—is the **If** statement. You use the **If** statement to test a value or values using the comparison and logical operators (discussed in Chapter 4) and then execute code statements accordingly. Here's a sample **If** statement that tests the value in a text box—**Text1**—and displays a message box if that value is less than zero:

```
Private Sub Command1_Click()
    If Text1.Text < 0 Then
        MsgBox "The value you entered is negative."
    End If
End Sub
```

The *body* of an **If** statement consists of the code between the **If** statement and the **End If** statement (you use **End** statements to terminate code blocks in Visual Basic). The program executes the body of the **If** statement if the condition in the **If** statement is **True** (in the previous example, if the number in the text box **Text1** is less than 0).

You can elaborate the **If** statement to include an **Else** clause; Visual Basic executes the body of this clause if the condition in the **If** statement is **False**:

```
Private Sub Command1_Click()
    If Text1.Text < 0 Then
        MsgBox "The value you entered is negative."
```

```
        Else
            MsgBox "The value you entered is zero or positive."
        End If
End Sub
```

Here, the code in the **Else** clause is executed only if the number in the text box **Text1** is *not* less than zero.

In this way, you can see how conditionals work: Visual Basic executes selected code statements depending on decisions made using data values.

Besides the **If** statement, Visual Basic provides a number of other conditionals (such as the **Select Case** statement) and special functions (such as **Switch** and **Choose**)—we'll investigate them all here.

Looping

Loops work in a way that's both similar to and different from conditionals. Loops have a conditional part, but their utility comes from the fact that they can execute a block of code a number of times under program control.

Loops are especially useful when you're working with data structures like arrays. Arrays store data in an indexed way, and you can increment (or decrement) the array's index using a loop—doing so allows you to handle all the items in the array conveniently.

For example, the following code uses the most popular type of loop— the **For** loop—to add all the items in an array named **arData**. Note the structure of the loop: a **For** statement followed by the loop's body (which Visual Basic executes each time the loop iterates) and a **Next** statement:

```
Option Base 1

Private Sub Command1_Click()
    Dim arData(5), intSum As Integer

    arData(1) = 1
    arData(2) = 2
    arData(3) = 3
    arData(4) = 4
    arData(5) = 5

    intSum = 0

    For intLoopIndex = 1 To UBound(arData)
```

```
        intSum = intSum + arData(intLoopIndex)
    Next intLoopIndex

    MsgBox "The total is:" & intSum
End Sub
```

Loops like this one use computers to perform the tasks computers are especially good at: working on large amounts of data repetitively.

Nested Loops

Like the other types of Visual Basic loops, you can nest **For** loops inside each other. Here's an example that adds all the values in a two-dimensional array, using two **For** loops and two loop indices:

```
Option Base 1

Private Sub Form_Load()

    Dim arData(2, 5), intSum As Integer

    arData(1, 1) = 1
    arData(1, 2) = 2
    arData(1, 3) = 3
    arData(1, 4) = 4
    arData(1, 5) = 5

    arData(2, 1) = 1
    arData(2, 2) = 2
    arData(2, 3) = 3
    arData(2, 4) = 4
    arData(2, 5) = 5

    intSum = 0

    For intLoopIndex1 = 1 To UBound(arData, 1)
        For intLoopIndex2 = 1 To UBound(arData, 2)
            intSum = intSum + arData(intLoopIndex1, intLoopIndex2)
        Next intLoopIndex2
    Next intLoopIndex1

    MsgBox "The total is:" & intSum
End Sub
```

Visual Basic includes other types of loops—such as **Do** loops and **While** loops—which we'll cover in this chapter.

That's all the introduction we need; let's turn to the Immediate Solutions part of the chapter now.

Immediate Solutions

Using The **If** Statement

The **If** statement is the bread and butter of Visual Basic conditionals. You use this statement to test a condition (which is made up of comparison and, possibly, logical operators, as well as their operands) and then execute code if the condition is **True**. You can also add **Else** clauses that are executed if the condition turns out to be **False**. In fact, you can even use **ElseIf** clauses to add conditional statements to **Else** clauses; the **ElseIf** clause functions as an **Else** clause coupled with a new **If** statement.

Here's how the **If** statement works, in all its detail:

```
If condition Then

[statements]
[ElseIf condition-n Then

[elseifstatements] ...
[Else

[elsestatements]]]
End If
```

The following example shows how to use the various parts of this statement:

```
Dim intInput
intInput = -1

While intInput < 0
    intInput = InputBox("Enter a positive number")
Wend

If intInput = 1 Then
    MsgBox ("Thank you.")
ElseIf intInput = 2 Then
    MsgBox ("That's fine.")
ElseIf intInput >= 3 Then
    MsgBox ("Too big.")
End If
```

5: Program Flow

If statements are very popular in Visual Basic, and you're going to see a lot of them in this book.

Using The **Select Case** Structure

Suppose you need to get a value from the user and respond in several different ways, but you don't look forward to writing a long, tangled series of **If...Then...Else** statements. What can you do?

If your program can handle multiple values for a particular variable and you don't want to stack up a lot of **If ElseIf** statements to handle them, you should consider **Select Case**. You use **Select Case** to test an expression, see which of several *cases* it matches, and execute the corresponding code. Here's the syntax:

```
Select Case testexpression

[Case expressionlist-n

[statements-n]] ...

[Case Else

[elsestatements]]
End Select
```

Let's look at an example that reads a positive value from the user and tests it, responding according to its value. Note that the code uses the **Select Case Is** keyword to check if the value read in is greater than a certain value; it also uses **Case Else** to handle values for which there's no explicit code. Here's the example:

```
Dim intInput
intInput = -1

While intInput < 0
    intInput = InputBox("Enter a positive number")
Wend

Const intMax = 10

Select Case intInput
    Case 1:
        MsgBox ("Thank you.")
```

5: Program Flow

```
Case 2:
    MsgBox ("That's fine.")
Case 3:
    MsgBox ("Your input is getting pretty big now...")
Case 4 To 10:
    MsgBox ("You are approaching the maximum!")
Case Is > intMax:
    MsgBox ("Too big, sorry.")
Case Else:
    MsgBox ("Please try again.")
```

Using The **Switch** Function

The **Switch** function evaluates a list of expressions and returns a **Variant** value or an expression associated with the first expression in the list that is **True**. Here's the syntax:

```
Switch(expr-1, value-1[, expr-2, value-2 ... [, expr-n, _
    value-n]])
```

In this case, *expr-1* is the first expression to evaluate; if it's **True**, **Switch** returns *value-1*. If *expr-1* isn't true but *expr-2* is, **Switch** returns *value-2*, and so on.

Here's an example that asks the user to enter a number and uses **Switch** to calculate the absolute value of that value (assume that we've temporarily forgotten how to use the built-in Visual Basic absolute-value function, **Abs**):

```
Dim intValue

intValue = InputBox("Enter a number")

intAbsValue = Switch(intValue < 0, -1 * intValue, _
    intValue >= 0, intValue)

MsgBox "Absolute value = " & Str(intAbsValue)
```

Using The **Choose** Function

You use the **Choose** function to return one of a number of choices based on an index. Here's the syntax:

```
Choose(index, choice-1[, choice-2, ... [, choice-n]])
```

If the *index* value is 1, the first choice is returned; if *index* equals 2, the second choice is returned; and so on.

Let's look at an example involving three employees—Bob, Denise, and Ted—with employee IDs 1, 2, and 3. This code snippet accepts an ID value from the user and uses **Choose** to display the corresponding employee name:

```
Dim intID
intID = -1

While intID < 0 Or intID > 3
    intID = InputBox("Enter employee's ID")
Wend

MsgBox "Employee name = " & Choose(intID, "Bob", "Denise", _
    "Ted")
```

Using The **For** Loop

The **For** loop is the most popular Visual Basic loop. Using this loop, you increment a loop index a set number of times, executing the code statements in the body of the loop that many times, as well. You can terminate loop execution before the specified number of iterations is exhausted by using the **Exit For** statement, which ends the loop at once.

Here's the syntax for the **For** loop:

```
For index = start To end [Step step]

[statements]

[Exit For]

[statements]
Next [index]
```

And here's how to put it to work:

```
Dim intLoopIndex, Total
Total = 0
```

```
For intLoopIndex = 1 To 10
    Total = Total + 1
Next intLoopIndex
```

Note that you can use the **Step** keyword to specify the value added to the index in each loop iteration. For example, this code chooses a step of -1 and works from a loop index of 10 down to 1, which gives the same result as the previous example:

```
Dim intLoopIndex, Total
Total = 0
```

```
For intLoopIndex = 10 To 1 Step -1
    Total = Total + 1
Next intLoopIndex
```

For loops are especially useful when you're working with arrays, because you can address the data in the array using the loop index as the array index, and so iterate through all the data in the array. For example, this code finds the average of a set of values in an array using a **For** loop:

```
Option Base 1

Private Sub Command1_Click()
    Dim arValues(5), intSum As Integer

    arValues(1) = 1
    arValues(2) = 2
    arValues(3) = 3
    arValues(4) = 4
    arValues(5) = 5

    intSum = 0

    For intLoopIndex = 1 To UBound(arValues)
        intSum = intSum + arValues(intLoopIndex)
    Next intLoopIndex

    MsgBox "The average is:" & intSum / UBound(arValues)
End Sub
```

TIP: *Although it's been common practice to use a loop index after a loop completes (to see how many loop iterations were executed), that practice is now discouraged by people who write about good and bad programming practices.*

5: Program Flow

Using The **Do** Loop

The **Do** loop has two versions. You can evaluate a condition either at the beginning

```
Do [{While | Until} condition]

[statements]

[Exit Do]

[statements]
Loop
```

or at the end

```
Do
[statements]
[Exit Do]

[statements]
Loop [{While | Until} condition]
```

TIP: *Note that the second form of the **Do** loop ensures that Visual Basic executes the body of the loop at least once.*

You can loop *while* a condition is **True** by using the **While** keyword, or *until* a condition is **True** by using the **Until** keyword.

Let's look at an example that reads from a file, looping until it reaches the end of the file. The code checks with the end-of-file function—**EOF**—using the **Do Until** form of the **Do** loop:

```
Do Until EOF(1)
    Line Input #1, Data$
    Form1.TextBox1.Text = Form1.TextBox1.Text + Data$
Loop
```

TIP: *Many Visual Basic functions—such as **EOF**—are explicitly constructed to return values of **True** or **False**. So, you can use them to control loops such as **Do** and **While** loops.*

Here's another example, which uses the **Do While** form of the **Do** loop to get a positive number from the user—in this case, the code keeps looping while the input value is less than or equal to zero:

```
Dim intInput
intInput = -1

Do While intInput <= 0
    intInput = InputBox("Enter a positive number")
Loop
```

As you can see, you use **Do** loops when you want to loop until some condition becomes **True** or **False**, and **For** loops when you want to loop a specific number of times.

Using The **While** Loop

You can use a **While** loop if you have a condition that becomes **False** when you want to stop looping. To use this loop, enclose the statements you want to execute between a **While** statement and a **Wend** statement. Here's the syntax:

```
While condition
[statements]
Wend
```

If *condition* in the **While** statement is **True**, Visual Basic executes all statements until it encounters the **Wend** statement. Control then returns to the **While** statement, and *condition* is checked again. If *condition* is still **True**, the process repeats; if it isn't **True**, execution skips to the statement following the **Wend** statement. Here's an example that puts **While** to work:

```
Dim intInput
intInput = -1

While intInput <= 0
    intInput = InputBox("Enter a positive number")
Wend
```

You can nest loops to any level (note that each **Wend** matches the most recent **While**).

TIP: *In general, the **Do** loop provides a more structured and flexible way to perform looping than the **While** loop.*

Using The **For Each** Statement

The **For Each** loop is similar to a **For** loop, but it repeats a group of statements for each element in a collection of objects (or in an array) rather than repeating the statements a given number of times. This kind of loop is useful if you don't know how many elements are in an array or collection.

Here's the **For Each** statement's syntax:

```
For Each element In group

[statements]

[Exit For]

[statements]
Next [element]
```

You can see this loop in action with an example like the following, which displays all the elements of an array in message boxes:

```
Dim IDArray(1 To 3)
IDArray(1) = 1
IDArray(2) = 2
IDArray(3) = 3

For Each ArrayItem In IDArray
    MsgBox (Str(ArrayItem))
Next ArrayItem
```

Some restrictions apply to the use of **For Each**:

- Used with collections, **_element_** must be a **Variant** variable, a generic **Object** variable, or an object listed in the Visual Basic Object Browser.
- Used with arrays, **_element_** must be a **Variant** variable.
- You can't use a **For Each** loop with an array of user-defined types (because a **Variant** can't contain a user-defined type).

Using The **With** Statement

The **With** statement isn't really a loop, but it can be as useful as a loop—and, in fact, many programmers think of it as a loop. You use the **With** statement to execute statements using a particular object. In the body of the **With** statement, all the properties and methods you use with just the dot (.) operator are assumed to belong to the object you've specified. In this way, the **With** statement can save you the trouble of having to specify the object you're using each time you make use of it.

Here's the syntax for the **With** statement:

```
With object

[statements]
End With
```

The following example shows how to put **With** to work; in this case, the code sets several of the **Text1** text box's properties in the body of the **With** statement:

```
With Text1
    .Height = 1000
    .Width = 3000
    .Text = "Welcome to Visual Basic"
End With
```

This code uses the **With** statement to set the **Height**, **Width**, and **Text** properties of **Text1**.

Using The **Exit** Statement

You can use the **Exit** statement to influence program flow; in particular, this statement causes control to exit a block of code in a **Do** loop, **For** loop, **Function**, or **Sub**. Here are the various forms of this statement:

```
Exit Do
Exit For
Exit Function
Exit Sub
```

Let's take a look at each of these forms in turn:

- *Exit Do*—Provides a way to exit a **Do** loop. Using **Exit Do** transfers control to the statement following the **Loop** statement. Note that when you use an **Exit Do** statement within nested **Do** loops, it transfers control to the loop one nested level *above* the loop containing the **Exit Do** statement.

- *Exit For*—Provides a way to exit a **For** loop. You can use an **Exit For** statement only in a **For** or **For Each** loop. It transfers control to the statement following the **Next** statement. When you use **Exit For** within nested **For** loops, it transfers control to the loop one nested level *above* the loop containing the **Exit For** statement.

- *Exit Function*—Exits the **Function** in which it appears. Execution continues with the statement following the statement that called the **Function**.

- *Exit Sub*—Exits the **Sub** procedure in which it appears. Execution continues with the statement following the statement that called the **Sub** procedure.

Using The **End** Statement

The **End** statement ends a procedure or a block of code. Although most programmers are familiar with statements like **End If** and **End Sub**, you can also use **End** by itself to end the program.

Here are the various forms of the **End** statement:

```
End
End Function
End If
End Select
End Sub
End Type
End With
```

Let's go through these forms one by one:

- *End*—Ends program execution immediately. You may place **End** anywhere in a procedure to end code execution, close files opened with the **Open** statement, and clear all variables.
- *End Function*—Required to end a **Function** statement.
- *End If*—Required to end a block **If**...**Then**...**Else** statement.
- *End Select*—Required to end a **Select Case** statement.
- *End Sub*—Required to end a **Sub** statement.

- *End Type*—Required to end a user-defined type definition in a **Type** statement.

- *End With*—Required to end a **With** statement.

When executed by itself, the **End** statement resets all module-level variables and all static local variables in all modules; to preserve the value of these variables, use the **Stop** statement instead.

Note that using the **End** statement by itself stops code execution abruptly, without firing the **Unload**, **QueryUnload**, or **Terminate** event—or, for that matter, any other Visual Basic code. Objects created from class modules are destroyed, files opened using the **Open** statement are closed, and memory used by your program is freed. Your program closes as soon as no other programs hold references to objects created from your public class modules and no code is executing. If you want to use **End** to simulate normal program termination, be sure you unload all forms by using their **Unload** method.

Using The **Stop** Statement

You can use **Stop** statements anywhere in procedures to suspend execution. In fact, using the **Stop** statement is similar to setting a breakpoint in the code—if you execute your program by choosing Visual Basic's Run|Start menu item, the debugger will open when execution encounters the **Stop** statement.

The **Stop** statement suspends execution. However, unlike **End**, **Stop** doesn't close any files or clear any variables, unless it's in a compiled EXE file.

5: Program Flow

Chapter 6

Creating Procedures

In Brief

In this chapter, we're going to group lines of code into procedures. A *procedure* is a block of code that's executed when called. You *call* a procedure in code simply by using its name (or alternatively, with a **Call** statement), as we'll see in this chapter. The values you pass to a procedure are called the procedure's *arguments*.

Divide And Conquer

Dividing your code into procedures can be an invaluable part of programming. As your programs become longer, it becomes more important to apply that famous programming dictum, "divide and conquer." Large tasks are most easily handled when you can cut them up into at least semiautonomous parts and tackle each one in turn—and that's what procedures let you do. Each procedure handles (ideally) one discrete task; after it's written, you can forget the code details and just remember the procedure by the task it performs. In this way, a program 10,000 lines long can be broken up into many smaller procedures—and easily handled.

In fact, the "divide and conquer" idea lies behind object-oriented programming (OOP) as well. By combining not only procedures but also the data they work on into *objects*, you can further divide a program into manageable, semiautonomous parts. OOP was created to handle larger programs, and in this book we'll see the OOP support Visual Basic provides.

Subroutines And Functions

Visual Basic uses two kinds of procedures: *subroutines* and *functions*. Their primary difference is that subroutines can accept data values passed to them but don't return a value, whereas functions not only accept data values but also return a value. For example, to use Visual Basic's built-in **Abs** function to get the absolute value of a variable, you can pass that variable—**intData**—to the **Abs** function and store the returned value in the variable **intAbsData**:

```
Private Sub Command1_Click()
    Dim intData, intAbsData As Integer
```

```
    intData = Val(Text1.Text)

    intAbsData = Abs(intData)

    Text2.Text = Str(intAbsData)
End Sub
```

We've already covered how to add comments to your procedures (see the "Adding Comments To Your Code" topic in the Immediate Solutions section of Chapter 1). In this chapter, you'll learn more about subroutines and functions, including:

- How to declare them
- How to call them
- How to pass values to them
- How to pass optional arguments
- How to set up default arguments
- How to return a value from a function
- How to preserve the values of variables in a procedure between calls to that procedure

You'll become a procedure expert by familiarizing yourself with the topics in the Immediate Solutions part of this chapter, next.

6: Creating Procedures

Immediate Solutions

Declaring Subroutines

Everyone knows about subroutines—these handy blocks of code organize your programs into single-purposed sections and make writing applications easier. Unlike functions, subroutines don't return values; but, like functions, you can pass values to subroutines in an argument list.

Here's how you declare a subroutine:

```
[Private | Public | Friend] [Static] Sub name [(arglist)]
    .
    .
    .
[statements]
    .
    .
    .
[Exit Sub]
    .
    .
    .
[statements]
    .
    .
    .
End Sub
```

The subroutine's parts work as follows:

- ***Private** keyword*—Makes a procedure accessible only to other procedures in the module or form in which it's declared.

- ***Public** keyword*—Makes a procedure accessible to all other procedures in all modules and forms.

- ***Friend** keyword*—Used only in class modules; specifies that the procedure is visible throughout the project, but not visible to a controller of an instance of an object.

- ***Static** keyword*—Specifies that the procedure's local variables should be preserved between calls.

- ***name** identifier*—The name of the procedure.

- ***arglist** identifier*—Stands for a list of variables representing arguments that are passed to the procedure when it's called; multiple variables should be separated with commas.

- **statements** *identifier*—Stands for the group of statements to be executed within the procedure.

- **Exit Sub** *keywords*—Cause an immediate exit from a **Sub** procedure.

- **End Sub** *keywords*—End the procedure definition.

The **arglist** identifier has this syntax:

```
[Optional] [ByVal | ByRef] [ParamArray] varname[( )] [As type] _
    [= defaultvalue]
```

In **arglist**, the parts have these meanings:

- **Optional** *keyword*—Means that an argument isn't required.

- **ByVal** *keyword*—Means that the argument is passed by value.

- **ByRef** *keyword*—Means that the argument is passed by reference (**ByRef** is the default in Visual Basic).

- **ParamArray** *keyword*—Used as the last argument in **arglist**, to indicate that the final argument is an array of **Variant** elements.

- **varname** *identifier*—The name of the variable passed as an argument.

- **type** *identifier*—The data type of the argument.

- **defaultvalue** *identifier*—Any constant or constant expression, used as the argument's default value if you've used the **Optional** keyword.

TIP: *When you use **ByVal**, you pass a copy of a variable to a procedure. When you use **ByRef**, you pass a reference to the variable—if you make changes to that reference, the original variable is changed as well.*

You call a **Sub** procedure using the procedure name followed by the argument list. Here's an example of a subroutine:

```
Sub CountFiles(Optional intMaxFile As Variant)
    If IsMissing(intMaxFile) Then
        'intMaxFiles was not passed
        MsgBox ("Did you forget something?")
    Else
    .
    .
    .
    End If
End Sub
```

Declaring Functions

Subroutines can take arguments passed in parentheses, but they don't return a value; functions also take arguments, but they do return a value (which you can discard, if you choose). A function is a block of code that you call and pass arguments to; using functions breaks your code into manageable parts.

Here's how you declare a function:

```
[Private | Public | Friend] [Static] Function name _
    [(arglist)] [As type]
    .
    .
    .
[statements]
    .
    .
[name = expression]


    .
    .
[Exit Function]
    .
    .
[statements]
    .
    .
End Function
```

The function's parts work as follows:

- **Private** *keyword*—Makes a procedure accessible only to other procedures in the module or form in which it's declared.

- **Public** *keyword*—Makes a procedure accessible to all other procedures in all modules and forms.

- **Friend** *keyword*—Used only in class modules; specifies that the procedure is visible throughout the project, but not visible to a controller of an instance of an object.

- **Static** *keyword*—Specifies that the procedure's local variables should be preserved between calls.

- **name** *identifier*—The name of the procedure.

- **arglist** *identifier*—Stands for a list of variables representing arguments that are passed to the procedure when it's called; separate multiple variables with commas.

- ***type*** *identifier*—The data type returned by the function.

- ***statements*** *identifier*—Stands for the group of statements to be executed within the procedure.

- ***Exit Function*** *keywords*—Cause an immediate exit from a **Function** procedure.

- ***End Function*** *keywords*—End the procedure definition.

The ***arglist*** identifier has the following syntax:

```
[Optional] [ByVal | ByRef] [ParamArray] varname[( )] _
    [As type] [= defaultvalue]
```

In ***arglist***, the parts have these meanings:

- ***Optional*** *keyword*—Means that an argument isn't required.

- ***ByVal*** *keyword*—Means that the argument is passed by value.

- ***ByRef*** *keyword*—Means that the argument is passed by reference (**ByRef** is the default in Visual Basic).

- ***ParamArray*** *keyword*—Used as the last argument in ***arglist***, to indicate that the final argument is an array of **Variant** elements.

- ***varname*** *identifier*—The name of the variable passed as an argument.

- ***type*** *identifier*—The data type of the argument.

- ***defaultvalue*** *identifier*—Any constant or constant expression, used as the argument's default value if you've used the **Optional** keyword.

TIP: *When you use **ByVal**, you pass a copy of a variable to a procedure. When you use **ByRef**, you pass a reference to the variable—if you make changes to that reference, the original variable is changed as well.*

You call a **Function** procedure using the function name, followed by the argument list in parentheses. You return a value from a function by assigning to the function's name the value you want to return, like this: ***name = expression***.

Here's an example that shows how to use a function:

```
Private Sub Command1_Click()
    Dim intResult As Integer
    intResult = Add1(5)
    MsgBox ("Result = " & Str$(intResult))
End Sub
```

```
Function Add1(intAdd1ToMe As Integer) As Integer
    Add1 = intAdd1ToMe + 1
End Function
```

Calling Subroutines

A call to a subroutine is a standalone statement—unlike a function, you can't call a subroutine by using its name within an expression. In addition, a subroutine doesn't return a value in its name, as does a function. However, like a function, a subroutine can modify the values of any variables passed to it.

You can call a subroutine two ways. Either use the **Call** statement or just use the subroutine's name, listing its arguments this way:

```
Call Circle (intXLocation, intYLocation)
Circle intXLocation, intYLocation
```

When you use the **Call** statement, its arguments must be enclosed in parentheses. If you don't use the **Call** keyword, omit the parentheses.

Calling Functions

You can call a function by using its name in an expression and assigning its return value to a variable. This example passes the **Abs** function a variable named **intData** and stores its return value in a variable named **intAbsData**:

```
Private Sub Command1_Click()
    Dim intData, intAbsData As Integer

    intData = Val(Text1.Text)

    intAbsData = Abs(intData)

    Text2.Text = Str(intAbsData)
End Sub
```

It's also possible to call a function just as you'd call a subroutine. The following statements both call the same function:

```
Call StoreData(intData)
StoreData intData
```

Note that calling a function this way is legal, but Visual Basic throws away the return value.

Calling A Procedure In Another Module

Procedures in other modules can be called from anywhere (within a project), if they've been declared **Public**. Note that you might need to specify which module contains the procedure you're calling, and that the ways of doing so differ, depending on whether the procedure is located in a form, a standard module, or a class module.

Calling A Procedure In A Form

If you call a procedure that's located in another form module, you must specify the other form's name. For example, here's how to call a **ChessGame** subroutine located in **Form2**:

```
Form2.ChessGame
```

Calling A Procedure In A Standard Module

To call a procedure that's located in a standard module, you don't need to include the module name in the call. However, if two or more modules contain a procedure with the same name, you may need to qualify that name with the module name, like this:

```
Module2.PlayMovie
```

Calling A Procedure In A Class Module

When you call a procedure that's located in a class module, your call must be qualified with a variable that points to an instance of the class. For example, **VideoObject** is an instance of a class named **ScreenClass**:

```
Dim VideoObject as New ScreenClass
VideoObject.ShowStartupScreen
```

Specifying Argument Types In Calls To Procedures

The arguments you pass to procedures are of the **Variant** type by default. You can declare other data types as you please, however, when you declare the procedure.

For example, the following function accepts two integers and returns an integer:

```
Function intSum(intValue1 As Integer, intValue2 As Integer) _
   As Integer
      intSum = intValue1 + intValue2
End Function
```

The list of variables in the parentheses following the function name is called the *parameter list*.

Passing Arguments By Value

When you pass an argument to a procedure by value, only a copy of a variable is passed to the procedure. You use the **ByVal** keyword in the procedure's parameter list to indicate that an argument is passed by value.

Here's an example in which the variable **intEmployeeID** is passed by value to the subroutine **CalculatePension**:

```
Sub CalculatePension(ByVal intEmployeeID as Integer)
   .
   .
   .
End Sub
```

If the procedure changes the value, the change affects only the copy— not the variable itself. Note that by default in Visual Basic, arguments are passed by reference, not by value.

Passing Arguments By Reference

When you pass an argument to a procedure by reference, you pass the location of the variable to the procedure; this gives the procedure access to the actual variable contents. As a result, the variable's value can be changed by the procedure to which you pass it. Passing by reference is the default in Visual Basic.

TIP: If a procedure specifies a data type for an argument passed by reference, you must pass a value of that type. You can get around this requirement by passing an expression rather than a data type. The simplest way to turn a variable into an expression is to enclose it in parentheses.

Preserving A Variable's Value Between Calls To Procedures

Suppose you've written a **Counter** function to keep track of the number of times the user clicks on a particular button. Each time the user clicks on the button, you call the **Counter** function to increment the count of button clicks and then display the result in a message box. But, the counter never seems to be incremented; instead, it always returns one. Why?

Let's look at the code:

```
Private Sub Command1_Click()
    Dim intResult As Integer
    intResult = Counter()
    MsgBox ("Result = " & Str$(intResult))
End Sub

Function Counter() As Integer
    Dim intCountValue As Integer
    intCountValue = intCountValue + 1
    Counter = intCountValue
End Function
```

The problem here is that the counter variable—**intCountValue**—in the **Counter** function is reinitialized each time the **Counter** function is called. Each time you call a procedure, Visual Basic allocates new copies of all the variables local to that procedure.

The solution is to declare **intCountValue** as *static*—doing so will make it retain its value between calls to the **Counter** function. Here's the working code:

```
Private Sub Command1_Click()
    Dim intResult As Integer
    intResult = Counter()
    MsgBox ("Result = " & Str$(intResult))
End Sub

Function Counter() As Integer
    Static intCountValue As Integer
    intCountValue = intCountValue + 1
    Counter = intCountValue
End Function
```

In fact, you could declare the whole function static, which would make all the variables in it static:

```
Private Sub Command1_Click()
    Dim intResult As Integer
    intResult = Counter()
    MsgBox ("Result = " & Str$(intResult))
End Sub

Static Function Counter() As Integer
    Dim intCountValue As Integer
    intCountValue = intCountValue + 1
    Counter = intCountValue
End Function
```

Besides declaring variables with **Static**, then, you can also use the **Static** keyword when declaring functions or subroutines.

Returning A Value From A Function

How can you return a value from a function? You do that by assigning the value you want to return to the function's name in code.

For example, the following **intDifference** function accepts two arguments and returns their difference:

```
Function intDifference(intValue1 As Integer, intValue2 As _
    Integer) As Integer
    intDifference = intValue1 - intValue2
End Function
```

Using Optional Arguments

You can make arguments passed to a procedure *optional*, so you don't have to pass values for those arguments when you call the procedure. You make arguments optional by placing the **Optional** keyword in front of them in the parameter list.

Note that if you specify an optional argument, all following arguments in the parameter list must also be optional and declared as such with the **Optional** keyword.

Let's look at an example that uses a subroutine named **DrawBox** to draw a rectangle starting at the upper-left corner of a form—(0, 0), measured in twips (1/1440 of an inch). **DrawBox** uses the Visual Basic **Line** method to draw a rectangle (passing that method the argument **B** makes it draw a rectangle); the optional **color** argument specifies the color of the rectangle:

```
Sub DrawBox(x As Integer, y As Integer, Optional color As _
    Long)

        Line (0, 0)-(x, y), color, B

End Sub
```

You can also call this subroutine when the form loads. For instance, this code draws the box from (0, 0) to (1000, 1000), using Visual Basic's **vbRed** constant to make the box red (to draw from the form load event, you must also set the form's **AutoRedraw** property to **True**):

```
Private Sub Form_Load()
    DrawBox 1000, 1000, vbRed
End Sub
```

Note that although this code works, it relies on Visual Basic to give a value of zero to undefined variables—you still call the **Line** method with the variable **color**, which is undefined if no value is passed for it:

```
Sub DrawBox(x As Integer, y As Integer, Optional color As _
    Long)

        Line (0, 0)-(x, y), color, B

End Sub
```

There's a better way to do this: You can use the **IsMissing** function to determine if a value has been passed for a specific optional argument.

Using The **IsMissing** Function

The **IsMissing** function returns a value of **True** if the optional variable you pass it was *not* passed to a procedure. So, you can modify the **DrawBox** subroutine to check whether the optional argument **color** was indeed passed; if not, you can call the **Line** method without passing the **color** argument, like this:

```
Sub DrawBox(x As Integer, y As Integer, Optional color As _
    Long)

    If IsMissing(color) Then
        Line (0, 0)-(x, y), , B
    Else
        Line (0, 0)-(x, y), color, B
    End If

End Sub


Private Sub Form_Load()
    DrawBox 1000, 1000, vbRed
End Sub
```

Giving An Optional Argument A Default Value

You can give the optional arguments passed to a procedure *default values*. In case no value is passed for those arguments, Visual Basic will use the default values.

For example, you can give the optional **color** argument the default value **vbBlue** (a Visual Basic predefined constant) this way:

```
Sub DrawBox(x As Integer, y As Integer, Optional _
    color As Long = vbBlue)

    If IsMissing(color) Then
        Line (0, 0)-(x, y), , B
    Else
        Line (0, 0)-(x, y), color, B
    End If
```

```
End Sub

Private Sub Form_Load()
    DrawBox 1000, 1000
End Sub
```

Now, when you call the **DrawBox** subroutine without passing a value for the color argument, **vbBlue** is used for that value automatically.

Passing An Indefinite Number Of Arguments

You can construct procedures that take a variable number of arguments using the **ParamArray** keyword. You use the **ParamArray** keyword in the procedure's argument list, preceding an array name. Inside the procedure, you can loop over the elements of that array with a **For Each** loop.

For example, here's a function named **intProduct** that multiplies as many arguments as you pass to it and returns the product of all passed arguments; notice the **ParamArray** keyword in the parameter list:

```
Function intProduct(ParamArray intNumbers())
    Dim intMultiplyBy As Variant
    Dim intRunningProduct As Integer

    intRunningProduct = 1

    For Each intMultiplyBy In intNumbers
        intRunningProduct = intRunningProduct * intMultiplyBy
    Next intMultiplyBy

    intProduct = intRunningProduct
End Function
```

Now you can pass arguments to **intProduct** as you like:

```
Private Sub Command1_Click()
    Text1.Text = intProduct(1, 2, 3, 4, 5)
End Sub
```

Related solution:	Found in:
Using The **For Each** Statement	Chapter 5

6: Creating Procedures

Using **GoSub**

You can use the **GoSub** statement to branch to and return from a code block within a procedure. **GoSub** is included in Visual Basic mostly for historical reasons—it was in Basic before Basic even supported subroutines or functions. However, its use is discouraged by nearly every writer who discusses good coding practices.

You use **GoSub** with line labels (that is, a name followed by a colon) or a line number:

```
GoSub line
     .
     .
     .
line
     .
     .
     .
Return
```

Execution transfers to *line* and then returns when the **Return** statement is encountered.

TIP: *Writing procedures that you can call is a more structured way of performing the same task as **GoSub**.*

Chapter 7

Forms, Controls, And The Event Model

In Brief

At this point, we're ready to put Visual Basic programs together, which means working with forms (that is, windows), controls (such as buttons or text boxes), and events. In this chapter, we'll see how event-driven programming works, how to use forms and controls, and—most important—how to interact with the user.

From a programming point of view, this means that we're going to start working with Visual Basic *objects*, because both forms and controls are objects.

Visual Basic Objects

There's a lot going on when you start working with forms and controls in Visual Basic. For example, you must now take into consideration the location of controls, the size of the form, the text in a control, how to respond when the user clicks on a button or resizes a form, and so forth. Visual Basic handles these factors by making forms and controls into *objects* that have properties, methods, and events. By creating these objects, Visual Basic lets you handle these tasks (and much more) in a conveniently packaged way. Let's take a look at how properties, methods, and events can work for you.

Properties

When you start working with windows (called *forms* in Visual Basic), you've got a lot to keep track of. For example, you can select a window's background color, foreground color, title bar text, size, location, and more. In Visual Basic, such attributes are called *properties*.

An example of a property is **BackColor**, which allows you to set the background color of a form. You can access that property with the dot operator (.) using this general format: *object.property*. Here's how to set **Form1**'s background color to red when the user clicks on a command button (**Command1**), using the predefined Visual Basic constant **vbRed**:

```
Private Sub Command1_Click()

    Form1.BackColor = vbRed

End Sub
```

Visual Basic includes several types of properties:

- Properties you work with when you're designing a program in the Integrated Development Environment (IDE)

- Properties you work with when you're running a program

- Properties you can work with both when you're designing a program and when you're running it

- Properties you can only write to

- Properties you can only read from

- Properties that you can both write to and read from

We'll look at a variety of properties in this chapter.

Methods

Besides properties, Visual Basic objects support *methods*. Methods are procedures built into an object. For example, you can use a form object's **Show** method to display the form. As with properties, you use the dot operator (.) to invoke an object's methods. Here's how to use the **Show** method of a form named **Form2** to make that form visible:

```
Private Sub Command1_Click()

    Form2.Show

End Sub
```

You can also pass arguments to methods, just as you can to any procedure. For example, the following code uses the form method **Circle** to draw a circle on a form at (1000, 1000) with a radius of 1000 (all measurements are in Visual Basic's default measurement, twips—1/1440 of an inch):

```
Private Sub Command1_Click()

    Form1.Circle (1000, 1000), 1000

End Sub
```

Events

In addition to properties and methods, Visual Basic objects can support *events*. A non-Windows program can set the course of program execution, but things work differently in Windows—the user can determine the course your program takes by using program controls, such as buttons, menus, list boxes, and more. When the user under-takes some action—such as moving the mouse, clicking on a control, or resizing a form—an event is generated. You can make your program respond to an event by setting up an *event-handling procedure* (also called an *event handler*) for the event. The event handler is called when the event occurs.

To create an event handler for a form or control event, you use the code editor (see the "Entering Code" topic in Chapter 10). Here's how the process works in overview. First, you open the code editor window by clicking on its icon in the Project window or by double-click-ing on the form or control you want to work with in the Visual Basic IDE. Now, select the object you want to work with (such as **Form1** or **Command1**) in the code editor's left list box and click on the event you want to work with (such as **Click** or **Resize**) in the code editor's right list box. Visual Basic will automatically add to your program the event handler you chose, and you can add code to it in the code editor.

We've already seen event handlers for command buttons; when the user clicks on a command button, a **Click** event is generated. You can then catch that event in the event handler **Command1_Click**, which is called when the **Click** event occurs:

```
Private Sub Command1_Click()


End Sub
```

You can add code to this procedure, and it will execute when the event occurs. In a previous example, we saw that this code draws a circle:

```
Private Sub Command1_Click()

    Form1.Circle (1000, 1000), 1000

End Sub
```

Forms also have events—such as the **Resize** event—that occur when the form is resized. This code, in a form's resize event handler (**Form_Resize**), keeps a command button (**Command1**) in the middle of a form when the form is resized:

```
Private Sub Form_Resize()
    Command1.Move ScaleWidth / 2 - Command1.Width / 2, _
```

```
        ScaleHeight / 2 - Command1.Height / 2
End Sub
```

Now that you've had an overview of how to work with Visual Basic objects, let's take a look at the two types of objects we'll work with in this chapter: forms and controls.

Visual Basic Forms

Form is the name for a window in Visual Basic. (Originally, you called a design-time window a *form* and the runtime result a *window*, but common usage now refers to both as *forms*.) You add controls to forms in the IDE.

Figure 7.1 shows a form being designed in the Visual Basic IDE. At the top of the form is the *title bar*, which displays the form's title (in this case, *Form1*). At right in the title bar is the control box, which includes the minimize/maximize buttons and the close button. The user takes these controls for granted in most windows, although we'll see that they're inappropriate in some cases (such as in dialog boxes).

Under the title bar is the *menu bar*, if there is one; in Figure 7.1, the form has only a File menu. Under the menu bar, forms can have *toolbars*, as you see in the IDE itself.

The main area of a form—the area in which everything takes place—is called the *client area*. In general, Visual Basic code works with controls in the client area and leaves the rest of the form to Visual

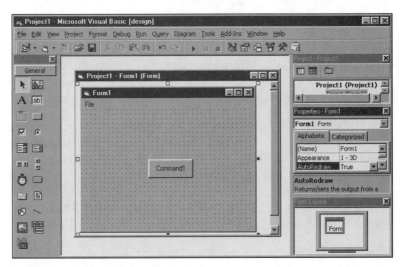

Figure 7.1 *A form under design.*

Basic (in fact, the client area is itself a window). In Figure 7.1, we've added a control—a command button—to the form.

Finally, the whole form is surrounded by a *border*. You can use several types of borders, as we'll see in this chapter.

When you create a new project in Visual Basic, that project includes a form by default. To add new forms, you can use the Project|Add Form menu item. You use the Properties Window in the Visual Basic IDE to set form properties at design time. This chapter assumes that you're familiar with basic techniques for handling forms in the Visual Basic IDE—for more information, see Chapter 10.

Visual Basic Controls

Visual Basic controls are the buttons, list boxes, menus, picture boxes, checkboxes, and so on, with which the user interacts. Like forms, controls are Visual Basic objects that support properties, methods, and events. (In fact, like forms, controls are themselves windows.)

Controls are the foundation of the user interface in Visual Basic. Each control has a set of events—such as a button's **Click** event—that allow you to respond to user events. For example, when the user clicks on a button, you can add code to that button's **Click** event handler to place text in text box **Text1**, using that text box's **Text** property:

```
Private Sub Command1_Click()

    Text1.Text = "Hello, world!"

End Sub
```

In this chapter, you'll learn a great deal about handling controls in Visual Basic programs, such as how to move and size controls, how to respond to user events, how to show or hide controls, and more.

You add controls to forms using the Visual Basic toolbox, which appears at left in Figure 7.1. To add a control, just click on that control's tool in the toolbox and draw the control on the form using the mouse. To set a control's properties, use the Properties window, which appears at right in the IDE. This chapter assumes that you're familiar with basic techniques for handling controls in the Visual Basic IDE—for more information, see Chapter 10.

That's it for our overview—it's time to turn to the Immediate Solutions part of this chapter.

Immediate Solutions

Setting Title Bar Text

How can you change the text in the title bar of a form? This task stymies many Visual Basic programmers, because the title bar text seems like something that Windows itself, not the program, manages. In fact, the program determines this text, and setting it couldn't be easier. At design time, you simply change the form's **Caption** property.

You can also set the **Caption** property at runtime in code, like this (note that the code uses the **Me** keyword to refer to the current form—see the "Referring To The Current Form In Code" topic later in this chapter):

```
Private Sub Command1_Click()
    Me.Caption = "Hello from Visual Basic!"
End Sub
```

Adding Or Removing Min/Max Buttons

Forms usually include minimize and maximize buttons, as well as a close box in the upper-right corner. However, these buttons aren't appropriate in all cases; to remove them, you can set the form's **ControlBox** property to **False**.

You can also specify which buttons appear on a form by setting the form's border type. For example, if you set the border style to a fixed type (see the next topic), the minimize and maximize buttons will disappear.

Setting A Form's Border

You set a form's border style with its **BorderStyle** property; here are the possible values for that property:

- *0*—None
- *1*—Fixed single

- *2*—Sizable
- *3*—Fixed dialog
- *4*—Fixed tool window
- *5*—Sizable tool window

Sizing And Moving A Form

To move and size a form, use the **Move** method:

```
form.Move left, [top, [width, [height]]]
```

The **Move** method has these arguments:

- *left*—Indicates the horizontal coordinate (x-axis) for the left edge of an object.
- *top*—Indicates the vertical coordinate (y-axis) for the top edge of an object.
- *width*—Indicates the new width of an object.
- *height*—Indicates the new height of an object.

For standalone forms, these measurements are in screen coordinates; for Multiple Document Interface (MDI) child forms, they're with respect to the upper-left corner of the MDI form's client area. For example, here's how to move a standalone form to the upper-left corner of the screen:

```
Private Sub Command1_Click()

    Me.Move 0, 0

End Sub
```

Measurements In Forms

The default measurement units for forms are twips (1/1440 of an inch), but can you use other measurement systems? Yes, you can; we'll take a look at that and other measurement issues here.

You can get the dimensions of a form's client area with these properties:

- *ScaleWidth*—Width of the client area

- *ScaleHeight*—Height of the client area

- *ScaleLeft*—Horizontal coordinate of the upper-left corner of the client area

- *ScaleTop*—Vertical coordinate of the upper-left corner of the client area

And you can get the overall dimensions of the form using these properties:

- *Width*—Width of the form

- *Height*—Height of the form

- *Left*—Horizontal coordinate of the upper-left corner of the form

- *Top*—Vertical coordinate of the upper-left corner of the form

You can also use the **ScaleMode** property to set a form's coordinate system units—you don't have to use twips. Here are the possible values for **ScaleMode**:

- *0*—User-defined

- *1*—Twips (1/1440 of an inch)

- *2*—Points (1/72 of an inch)

- *3*—Pixels

- *4*—Characters (120 twips horizontally, 240 twips vertically)

- *5*—Inches

- *6*—Millimeters

- *7*—Centimeters

User-Defined Coordinates

To make life easier for yourself, you can set up a *user-defined coordinate system*: Simply set the **ScaleWidth** and **ScaleHeight** properties.

For example, if you want to plot data on a 1000×1000 grid, set **ScaleWidth** and **ScaleHeight** to 1000. Then, to draw a scatter plot of your data, you could use **PSet** to set individual pixels directly. If one of the points to graph was (233, 599), you could draw that dot this way: **PSet(233, 599)**.

Referring To The Current Form In Code

Let's say you've written a subroutine—**GreenWindow**—to change a form's color to green:

```
Sub GreenWindow(FormToColor As Form)
    FormToColor.BackColor = vbGreen
End Sub
```

Now, you want to color all the forms in your project when the user clicks on a button. That's easy to do using the **Me** keyword, which refers to the current object. For example, this code passes the current form to the **GreenWindow** subroutine:

```
Private Sub Command1_Click()
    ColorWindow Me
End Sub
```

Me is an implicit variable that's always available. It stands for the current object, which comes in handy when you want to pass the current object to a procedure.

TIP: The **Me** keyword is very useful in class modules when more than one instance of a class can occur, because it always refers to the current instance.

Redrawing The Contents Of A Form

Let's assume you've written some code to draw an X across a form, like this:

```
Private Sub Command1_Click()
    Line (0, 0)-(ScaleWidth, ScaleHeight)
    Line (0, ScaleHeight)-(ScaleWidth, 0)
End Sub
```

You try it out and it looks good—but when you minimize and then maximize the program, the X is gone. What happened?

One of the biggest headaches for Windows programmers is refreshing the window when required, because doing so involves redrawing the entire form's contents. To make matters worse, redrawing is a common occurrence—in Windows, the user is constantly covering and uncovering windows, minimizing and maximizing them, and changing their size, all of which means that your program has to keep redrawing itself.

Fortunately, Visual Basic provides an easy fix (one of the things that made Visual Basic so popular in the first place): the **AutoReDraw** property.

When you set the **AutoReDraw** property to **True**, the graphics displayed on the form are stored and redisplayed as needed. All the window refreshes are done for you. Now, when you minimize and then maximize your X program, the X will reappear as it should. (Note that when you want to draw on the form from the form load event, you must first set **AutoRedraw** to **True**.)

Working With Multiple Forms

Let's say you need a second form (**Form2**) in your program, and that form has a text box on it (**Text1**). How can you specify that text box from code in **Form1**, the program's main form?

In multiple-form programs, you have to specify the form you want to work with if it isn't the current form. For example, to place the text *Hello from Visual Basic* in **Form2**'s **Text1** text box from code in **Form1**, you can refer to that text box as **Form2.Text1** as follows:

```
Private Sub Command1_Click()
    Form2.Text1.Text = "Hello from Visual Basic"
End Sub
```

In this way, you can work with multiple forms in a Visual Basic program. Just remember that you have to specify what form you want to work with if it's not the current form—that's all there is to it.

Loading, Showing, Hiding, And Unloading Forms

Sometimes, you might want to work with a form to initialize it (with graphics and so on) before displaying it on screen. In such a case, you can load the form into memory using the **Load** statement.

TIP: You don't need to load or unload forms to show or hide them—the loading and unloading processes are automatic. You usually load forms explicitly only to work on them before displaying them; this is what Visual Basic recommends when you want to work with a form before showing it. But, it turns out that you don't really need to use **Load** even then, because referring to a form makes Visual Basic load it automatically. As a result, you don't have to load forms to use the **Show** or **Hide** methods with them.

To show the form on screen, use the **Show** method. Here's an example that loads a new form (**Form2**) and then shows it:

```
Private Sub Command1_Click()
    Load Form2
    Form2.Show
End Sub
```

TIP: If you load an MDI child window without having loaded its associated MDI frame, the MDI frame is also loaded automatically.

After displaying a form, you can hide it with the **Hide** method and unload it (although doing so isn't necessary) with the **Unload** statement. You usually unload forms if you have many of them and you're concerned about memory use. This example hides **Form2** and then unloads it:

```
Private Sub Command2_Click()
    Form2.Hide
    Unload Form2
End Sub
```

If you hide all the windows in a Visual Basic program that has no **Main** procedure in a module, the program will end.

Creating New Forms In Code

New forms are simply new objects in Visual Basic. To declare a new form based on a form you already have—say, **Form1**—you just use **Dim**:

```
Private Sub NewForm_Click()
    Dim NewForm As Form1
```

```
        .
        .
        .
End Sub
```

Next, you create the new form with the **New** keyword:

```
Private Sub NewForm_Click()
    Dim NewForm As Form1
    Set NewForm = New Form1
        .
        .
        .
End Sub
```

Finally, you show the new form:

```
Private Sub NewForm_Click()
    Dim NewForm As Form1
    Set NewForm = New Form1
    NewForm.Show
End Sub
```

Calling this subroutine will add as many new forms as you want to a program.

Note that you don't need to keep track of the new form's name (**NewForm** is a local variable in **NewForm_Click**, and you can't use it after returning from that procedure). You might want to save any new forms in an array so you can close them under program control.

Creating Multiple Document Interface (MDI) Programs

MDI frame windows can display multiple child windows—in fact, the Visual Basic IDE is an MDI frame window. For example, if you already have a program based on a single form, **Form1** (the usual starting point for a new project), and you want to make that form into an MDI child window inside an MDI frame, follow these steps:

1. Add a new MDI form to the project by choosing the Project|Add MDI Form menu item.

2. Set the **MDIChild** property of the form you want to use as the MDI child form to **True**.

3. Run the program; the form you've made into the MDI child form will appear in the MDI form.

TIP: *In Visual Basic, you can use all kinds of MDI children in an MDI form, as long as their **MDIChild** property is set to **True**. You can also use **Show** and **Hide** on those windows to manage them.*

Setting Control Tab Order

In Visual Basic, you can make controls accessible to the keyboard by setting their *tab order*. The user can move from control to control, highlighting the currently selected control, by using the Tab key. But, it's up to you to set the order in which focus moves from control to control, and even whether or not a control can be reached with the Tab key.

To set the tab order of the controls in your program, follow these steps:

1. Select a control whose tab order you want to set.

2. Make sure the control's **TabStop** property is set to **True**. If this property is **False**, the user can't reach the control using the Tab key.

3. Set the control's position in the tab order by setting its **TabIndex** property. The first control in the **Tab** order has a **TabIndex** of 0, the next has a **TabIndex** of 1, and so on.

When you run the program, the first control is highlighted. When a user presses the Tab key, the focus moves to the second control in the tab order; when Tab is pressed again, focus moves to the third control; and so on.

You can also set the **TabStop** and **TabIndex** properties in code, as in this example, which sets a command button's **TabIndex** property to 0 (the lowest possible value):

```
Private Sub Command1_Click()
    Command2.TabIndex = 0
End Sub
```

Moving And Sizing Controls In Code

All controls have these properties available at design time or runtime to set their location and dimensions:

- *Left*—The x coordinate of the control's upper-left corner
- *Top*—The y coordinate of the control's upper-left corner
- *Width*—The width of the control
- *Height*—The height of the control

You can change all these settings interactively to move or resize a control on a form.

Note that all measurements are in twips (1/1440 of an inch) by default, and that the origin—(0, 0)—in a form is at its upper-left corner.

You can also use a control's **Move** method to move a control to a new location:

```
object.Move left, [top, [width, [height]]]
```

Let's look at an example. In this case, when the user clicks on a button, **Command1**, the code doubles the button's width and height and moves it 1000 twips to the left:

```
Private Sub Command1_Click()
    Const intIncrement = 1000
    Command1.Width = 2 * Command1.Width
    Command1.Height = 2 * Command1.Height
    Command1.Move (Command1.Left + intIncrement)
End Sub
```

TIP: *One way of creating simple animation is to use an image control to display an image and use its **Move** method to move it around a form.*

Showing And Hiding Controls On A Form

Showing and hiding a control is easy: Simply use the control's **Visible** property. Setting this property to **True** displays the control, whereas setting it to **False** hides the control. Here's an example that makes a button disappear (probably much to the user's surprise) when the user clicks on it:

```
Private Sub Command1_Click()
    Command1.Visible = False
End Sub
```

Setting Up A Control Array

If you have many of the same type of controls to work with, you might consider setting up a control array. Rather than name and handle the controls separately, a control array lets you refer to all the controls in the array with an index.

Let's look at an example. Use the Visual Basic toolbox to add a command button to a form and give it the name **Command** (to do so, set its **Name** property in the Properties window). Now, add another button and name it **Command**, as well. When you set the second button's name, Visual Basic will display a message box (see Figure 7.2) that asks if you want to set up a control array.

Click on Yes. Now you've set up a control array consisting of the two buttons and any additional buttons you add that are named **Command**. The event handler for these buttons will be passed an index value so you can determine which button the current event is for:

```
Private Sub Command_Click(Index As Integer)

End Sub
```

If the **Index** argument is 0, the first button was clicked; if **Index** is 1, the second button was clicked; and so forth.

If you want to specify a particular button in code, you can refer to it as part of the control array: **Command(0)** for the first button, **Command(1)** for the second button, and so on. In this way, you can work with the controls in a control array.

Figure 7.2   Visual Basic asks whether you want to set up a control array.

Adding Controls To A Form

You can use the Visual Basic toolbox to add controls to a form at design time, but is there a way to add controls to a Visual Basic program at runtime? Yes, there is. You can use the **Load** statement to load new controls if they're part of a control array.

To see how this works, add a new button to a form and give it the name **Command** (to do so, set its **Name** property in the Properties window). To make it the first member of a control array, set its **Index** property to 0. Now, when the user clicks on this button, you can add a new button of the same type to the form by using **Load**. The following code loads **Command(1)**, because **Command(0)** is already on the form:

```
Private Sub Command_Click(Index As Integer)
    Load Command(1)
    .
    .
    .
End Sub
```

Because the new button is a copy of the original one—including the original button's position—you need to move the new button so it doesn't cover the original one:

```
Private Sub Command_Click(Index As Integer)
    Load Command(1)
    Command(1).Move 0, 0
    .
    .
    .
End Sub
```

Finally, make the new button visible by setting its **Visible** property to **True**:

```
Private Sub Command_Click(Index As Integer)
    Load Command(1)
    Command(1).Move 0, 0
    Command(1).Visible = True
End Sub
```

And that's it—you've added a new button to the program at runtime.

7: Forms, Controls, And The Event Model

TIP: *You can also remove buttons at runtime by unloading them with **Unload**.*

Chapter 8

Working With Files

In Brief

In this chapter, we'll take a look at file handling in Visual Basic. We'll see how to use the common dialog control to access the File Open and File Save As dialog boxes, as well as how to create a file, open a file, read from a file, write to a file, close a file, and more.

In Visual Basic, you can work with a file in three main ways: as a sequential file, a random-access file, or a binary file (you set the way you'll treat a file when you open it). We'll get an overview of these types of files before turning to the Immediate Solutions part of this chapter.

Using Sequential-Access Files

Sequential files are often organized into text strings in Visual Basic. These files are like tape cassettes: You read data from them in a sequential manner. If you want data from the end of the file, you have to read all the intervening data first.

You use the following Visual Basic statements and functions with sequential files (the # symbol refers to an open file number, as we'll see):

- **Open**
- **Line Input #**
- **Print #**
- **Write #**
- **Input$**
- **Input #**
- **Close**

If you have a text file full of variable-length strings, you usually treat that file as sequential.

Using Random-Access Files

Random-access files are organized into records (usually of the same length). You can read a particular record in a file without having to read all the intervening data—you can move to that record directly. That is, whereas sequential files are like cassettes, random-access files are more like CDs.

Here are the Visual Basic statements and functions you use with random-access files:

- **Type...End Type** (to create and format records)
- **Open**
- **Put #**
- **Len**
- **Seek**
- **Loc**
- **Get #**
- **Close**

If you want to create your own database files and format them as you like, you'll organize them into records. In fact, any file that you want to organize into records is best formatted as a random-access file.

Using Binary Files

Binary files are simply unformatted binary data. Visual Basic doesn't interpret (for example, by looking for text strings) or organize the contents (into records) of such files—to Visual Basic, these files are just bytes. You'll generally use these statements and functions with binary files:

- **Open**
- **Get**
- **Put**
- **Seek**
- **Close**

Binary files include EXE files, graphics files, and so on.

That's it for the overview of files and file handling—it's time to turn to the Immediate Solutions part of this chapter.

Immediate Solutions

Using The File Open And Save As Dialog Boxes

You usually start working with files by getting a file name from the user via the File Open or File Save As dialog box.

You display the File Open and File Save As dialog boxes with the common dialog control's **ShowOpen** and **ShowSave** methods. These methods need no arguments passed to them—to set various options, you set the common dialog control's **Flags** property. You can also set the **Filter** property so the dialog box displays only certain types of files, such as text files.

To find out what file the user wants to work with, check the common dialog box's **FileName** property after the user clicks on OK in the dialog box. That property holds the fully qualified (that is, with path) name of the file to open. If you only want the file's name, use the **FileTitle** property. For example, here's how to get the name of a file to open when the user clicks on a command button (**Command1**):

```
Private Sub Command1_Click()
    On Error GoTo Cancel
    CommonDialog1.ShowOpen
    MsgBox "File to open: " & CommonDialog1.FileName
Cancel:
End Sub
```

Creating And Opening Files

How do you create or open a file in Visual Basic? You use the **Open** statement. The **Open** statement works like this:

```
Open pathname For mode [Access access] [lock] As _
    [#]filenumber [Len=reclength]
```

Here are the meanings of the various arguments:

- *pathname*—A file name (may include the directory or folder, and drive).

- *mode*—A keyword specifying the file mode: **Append**, **Binary**, **Input**, **Output**, or **Random** (if unspecified, the file is opened for **Random** access).

- *access*—A keyword specifying the operations permitted on the open file: **Read**, **Write**, or **Read Write**.

- *lock*—A keyword specifying the operations restricted on the open file by other processes: **Shared**, **Lock Read**, **Lock Write**, or **Lock Read Write**.

- *filenumber*—A valid file number in the range 1 to 511, inclusive. Use the **FreeFile** function to obtain the next available file number.

- *reclength*—A number less than or equal to 32,767 (bytes). For files opened for random access, this value is the record length. For sequential files, this value is the number of characters buffered.

If the file is already open and the specified type of access isn't allowed, the **Open** operation fails and an error occurs. Also note that the **Len** clause is ignored if *mode* is **Binary**.

If the file specified by *pathname* doesn't exist, Visual Basic creates it when a file is opened for **Append**, **Binary**, **Output**, or **Random** mode. If you open an existing file for **Output**, it's overwritten; if you open it for **Append**, Visual Basic adds new data to the end of the file.

After you've created the file, refer to it using the file number.

For example, the following code opens a file named *file.txt* and writes the contents of a text box (**Text1**) to that file:

```
Private Sub Command1_Click()
    On Error GoTo FileError
    Open "c:\file.txt" For Output As #1
    Print #1, Text1.Text
    Close #1
    Exit Sub

FileError:
    MsgBox "File Error!"
End Sub
```

Sequential Files: Writing

Sequential files are often text strings in Visual Basic, but they can also be mixtures of text and numbers. You generally use these standard statements to write to sequential files in Visual Basic:

```
Print # number, expressionlist
Write # number, expressionlist
```

Here, **number** is an open file number and **expressionlist** is a list of variables to write, separated by commas.

The **Print #** Statement

If you want to store your data in text format, use **Print #**. As an example, let's store the text in a text box to a file named *file.txt* using **Print #**. Begin by checking for errors with the **On Error** statement:

```
Private Sub Command1_Click()
    On Error GoTo FileError
    .
    .
    .
FileError:
    MsgBox "File Error!"
End Sub
```

Then, open a file for output:

```
Private Sub Command1_Click()
    On Error GoTo FileError
    Open "c:\file.txt" For Output As #1
    .
    .
    .
FileError:
    MsgBox "File Error!"
End Sub
```

Now, print the text in text box **Text1** to the file:

```
Private Sub Command1_Click()
    On Error GoTo FileError
    Open "c:\file.txt" For Output As #1
    Print #1, Text1.Text
    .
    .
    .
FileError:
    MsgBox "File Error!"
End Sub
```

Finally, close the file:

```
Private Sub Command1_Click()
    On Error GoTo FileError
    Open "c:\file.txt" For Output As #1
    Print #1, Text1.Text
    Close #1
    Exit Sub

FileError:
    MsgBox "File Error!"
End Sub
```

Now the user can write the contents of a text box to disk.

The **Write #** Statement

You can also use the **Write #** statement to write text and other types of data to a file. You use this statement with a file number and a comma-delimited list of the variables you want to write to that file.

For example, the following code opens a file—data.dat—and writes to that file three numbers that the user has entered in the text boxes **Text1**, **Text2**, and **Text3**:

```
Private Sub Command1_Click()
    Open "c:\data.dat" For Output As #1
    Write #1, Val(Text1.Text), Val(Text2.Text), Val(Text3.Text)
    Close #1
End Sub
```

To see how to read those values back in, take a look at the next topic, which addresses reading from sequential files.

Sequential Files: Reading

To read from a sequential file, you can use these standard statements:

```
Input # number, expressionlist
Line Input # number, string
Input$ (numberbytes, [#] number)
```

Here, **number** is a file number, **expressionlist** is a list of variables the data will be stored in, **string** is a string variable to store data in, and **numberbytes** is the number of bytes you want to read.

The **Input #** Statement

You can use the **Input #** statement to read text and numbers from a sequential file. For example, when the user clicks on **Command1**, you can write three integers the user has entered in **Text1, Text2**, and **Text3** to the file data.dat using **Write #**:

```
Private Sub Command1_Click()
    Open "c:\data.dat" For Output As #1
    Write #1, Val(Text1.Text), Val(Text2.Text), Val(Text3.Text)
    Close #1
End Sub
```

Then, when the user clicks on **Command2**, you can read those integers using **Input #**:

```
Private Sub Command2_Click()
    Dim int1, int2, int3 As Integer

    Open "c:\data.dat" For Input As #1
    Input #1, int1, int2, int3
    Text4.Text = Str(int1)
    Text5.Text = Str(int2)
    Text6.Text = Str(int3)
    Close #1

End Sub
```

The result appears in Figure 8.1. When the user enters three integers in the top text boxes and clicks on the Write Data button, you write the integers to disk. When the user clicks on the Read Data button, you read them back in using **Input #**. In that way, you're able to write and read a sequential file.

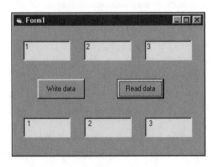

Figure 8.1   *Using **Write #** and **Input #** to save and restore integers.*

The **Line Input** # Statement

Using the **Line Input** # statement, you can read lines (text strings that end with a carriage return or carriage return/line feed pair) from a file. For example, suppose you have this set of lines—separated by carriage return/line feed pairs—in a file named *file.txt*:

```
This is the
multiple line text
that our program
is going to read in.
```

When the user clicks on a button, you can read this text line by line using **Line Input #**. Open the file like this:

```
Private Sub Command1_Click()

    On Error GoTo FileError
    Open "c:\file.txt" For Input As #1
    .
    .
    .
FileError:
    MsgBox "File Error!"
End Sub
```

Now, loop over all the lines in the file using the Visual Basic **EOF** (end of file) function, which returns **True** when you reach the end of the file:

```
Private Sub Command1_Click()

    On Error GoTo FileError
    Open "c:\file.txt" For Input As #1
    Do Until EOF(1)
    .
    .
    .
    Loop

    Exit Sub

FileError:
    MsgBox "File Error!"
End Sub
```

Finally, use **Line Input #** to read lines of text from the file and append the lines to a multiline text box (that is, a text box whose **MultiLine** property is set to **True**) named **Text1**, along with a carriage return/line feed pair:

```
Private Sub Command1_Click()
    Dim NewLine As String

    On Error GoTo FileError
    Open "c:\file.txt" For Input As #1
    Do Until EOF(1)
        Line Input #1, NewLine
        Text1.Text = Text1.Text + NewLine + vbCrLf
    Loop

    Exit Sub

FileError:
    MsgBox "File Error!"
End Sub
```

The **Input$** Statement

The **Input$** statement lets you read a string of a specified length. It might seem odd to have to know a string's length before reading it, but **Input$** does have one very useful aspect—if you use it together with the **LOF** (length of file) function, you can read an entire text file at once.

For example, this code reads the file.txt file from the previous example all at once, without having to work line by line:

```
Private Sub Command1_Click()
    Dim NewLine As String

    On Error GoTo FileError
    Open "c:\file.txt" For Input As #1

    Text1.Text = Input$(LOF(1), #1)

    Exit Sub

FileError:
    MsgBox "File Error!"
End Sub
```

This example produces the same result as the previous example, which used **Line Input #**.

Random-Access Files: Writing Records

You usually write records to random-access files using the **Put** statement:

```
Put [#]filenumber, [recnumber], varname
```

Here, *filenumber* is the number of a file to write to, *recnumber* is the number of the record to write (you set the record size when you open the file), and *varname* is the name of the variable that holds the data to write to the file.

To work with records in a random-access file, first define a record type. For example, let's see how to write three strings from the text boxes **Text1**, **Text2**, and **Text3** to a random-access file.

To start, define a new type named **Record** in a module (you can only define types in modules; to add a new module to a program, choose the Project|Add Module menu item):

```
Type Record
    Name As String * 50
    Number As String * 50
    ID As String * 50
End Type
```

Note that you use fixed-length strings to make all your records the same size. Now, declare 50 such records in the **(General)** section of the program and declare a variable named **TotalRecords** to keep track of the total number of records you've filled:

```
Dim WriteData(1 To 50) As Record
Dim TotalRecords As Integer
```

The **Command1** button has the caption *Write Data*. When the user clicks on this button, the program starts the file-writing process by entering the strings the user has written in **Text1**, **Text2**, and **Text3** into the first record in the array of records:

```
Sub Command1_Click()
    WriteData(1).Name = Text1.Text
    WriteData(1).Number = Text2.Text
    WriteData(1).ID = Text3.Text
    TotalRecords = 1
    .
    .
    .
```

Next, set up error checking and open the file records.dat for writing:

```
Sub Command1_Click()
    WriteData(1).Name = Text1.Text
    WriteData(1).Number = Text2.Text
    WriteData(1).ID = Text3.Text
    TotalRecords = 1

    On Error GoTo FileError
    Open "c:\records.dat" For Random As #1 Len = Len(WriteData(1))
        .
        .
        .
    Exit Sub

FileError:
    MsgBox "File Error!"

End Sub
```

Finally, loop over your records (in this case, that's only one record), use **Put** to write them to the file, and then close the file:

```
Sub Command1_Click()
    WriteData(1).Name = Text1.Text
    WriteData(1).Number = Text2.Text
    WriteData(1).ID = Text3.Text
    TotalRecords = 1

    On Error GoTo FileError
    Open "c:\records.dat" For Random As #1 Len = Len(WriteData(1))
    For loop_index = 1 To TotalRecords
        Put #1, , WriteData(loop_index)
    Next loop_index
    Close #1
    Exit Sub

FileError:
    MsgBox "File Error!"

End Sub
```

Now you've written the record to the file records.dat on disk. In the next topic, you'll read that record back in.

Random-Access Files: Reading Records

You use **Get** to read records from a random-access file. **Get** works like this:

```
Get [#]filenumber, [recnumber], varname
```

Here, *filenumber* is the number of the file to read from, *recnumber* is the number of the record to read, and *varname* is the name of the variable that should hold the data that's read.

In the previous topic, we saw how to write records to a random-access file, records.dat. You set up a new type named **Record** in a module:

```
Type Record
    Name As String * 50
    Number As String * 50
    ID As String * 50
End Type
```

Now, let's set up a form-wide array of records—**ReadData**—to hold the records you read from records.dat (these variables are stored in the **(General)** section of the form):

```
Dim WriteData(1 To 50) As Record
Dim ReadData(1 To 50) As Record
Dim TotalRecords As Integer
```

You'll read the records when the user clicks on a command button, **Command2**. First, open the file records.dat for random access, setting the record size to the length of each array element:

```
Sub Command2_Click()
    Dim intLoopIndex As Integer

    Open "c:\records.dat" For Random As #1 Len = Len(ReadData(1))
    .
    .
    .
```

Now, read the number of records in records.dat (which you find by dividing the length of the file by the length of a record) and store the record in the **ReadData** array (the result appears in Figure 8.2):

```
Sub Command2_Click()
    Dim intLoopIndex As Integer
```

```
Open "c:\records.dat" For Random As #1 Len = Len(ReadData(1))

For intLoopIndex = 1 To LOF(1) / Len(ReadData(1))
    Get #1, , ReadData(intLoopIndex)
Next intLoopIndex

Close #1
  .
  .
  .
```

Finally, display the record in the text boxes **Text4**, **Text5**, and **Text6**:

```
Sub Command2_Click()
    Dim intLoopIndex As Integer

    Open "c:\records.dat" For Random As #1 Len = Len(ReadData(1))

    For intLoopIndex = 1 To LOF(1) / Len(ReadData(1))
        Get #1, , ReadData(intLoopIndex)
    Next intLoopIndex

    Close #1

    Text4.Text = ReadData(1).Name
    Text5.Text = ReadData(1).Number
    Text6.Text = ReadData(1).ID

    Exit Sub

FileError:
    MsgBox "File Error!"
End Sub
```

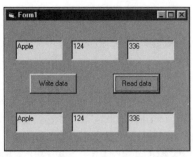

Figure 8.2   *Writing and reading a random-access record.*

Random-Access Files: Accessing Any Record

When you've set up a file to hold records (by creating it in **Random** mode with the **Open** statement and passing the length of the records you want to open), you can use **Get** to get any record in the file by record number:

```
Get #1, recordnumber, variablename
```

In this case, you're reading record number *recordnumber* from file 1 and placing the data read into a variable named *variablename*. In the same way, you can write any record with **Put**:

```
Put #1, recordnumber, variablename
```

TIP: Besides **Get** and **Put**, you can use the **Seek** function to set the position at which a record will next be read or written in a file—called the read/write position—and the **Loc** function to determine the current read/write position.

Binary Files: Writing Data

You usually write records to binary files using the **Put** statement:

```
Put [#]filenumber, [recnumber], varname
```

Here, *filenumber* is the number of the file to write to; *recnumber* is the number of the record to write for random files, or the byte at which to start writing for binary files; and *varname* is the name of the variable that holds the data to write to the file.

Let's look at an example that shows how to use **Put**. Suppose you've read a binary bitmap file—hello.bmp—into an array named **bytFile** and stored the length of that file in a **Long** variable named **lngLength** (we'll see how to do this in the next topic). Now, you'll write that file out to a new file named *hello2.bmp*. All you have to do is to open the file for binary operations and use **Put** to write to the file, like this:

```
Dim bytFile() As Byte
Dim lngLength, lngLoopIndex As Long
```

```
Private Sub Command2_Click()

    On Error GoTo FileError

    ' Open "c:\lvbbb\binary\hello2.bmp" For Binary As #1

    For lngLoopIndex = 0 To lngLength - 1
        Put #1, , bytFile(lngLoopIndex)
    Next lngLoopIndex

    Close #1

    Text1.Text = "File written out."
    Exit Sub

FileError:
    MsgBox "File Error!"
End Sub
```

To find out how to read the bitmap file in the first place, see the next topic.

Binary Files: Reading Data

How do you read raw data from files that have been opened in **Binary** format with the **Open** statement? You generally use **Get** to read data from a binary file (although you can use **Input #** as well):

```
Get [#]filenumber, [recnumber], varname
```

Here, *filenumber* is the number of the file to read from; *recnumber* is the number of the record to read for random files, or the byte at which to start reading for binary files; and *varname* is the name of the variable that will hold the read-in data.

Let's look at an example. In this case, you'll read a bitmap file named *hello.bmp* and then place its data in an array named **bytFile** and its length in a long variable named **lngLength**. You start by opening the file for binary operations, getting its length, and redimensioning the **bytFile** array to match that length:

```
Dim bytFile() As Byte
Dim lngLength, lngLoopIndex As Long
```

```
Private Sub Command1_Click()

    On Error GoTo FileError
    Open "c:\lvbbb\binary\hello.bmp" For Binary As #1

    lngLength = LOF(1)

    ReDim bytFile(lngLength)
    .
    .
    .
```

Now, loop over the bytes in the file and store them in your array; then, close the file:

```
Dim bytFile() As Byte
Dim lngLength, lngLoopIndex As Long

Private Sub Command1_Click()

    On Error GoTo FileError
    Open "c:\lvbbb\binary\hello.bmp" For Binary As #1

    lngLength = LOF(1)

    ReDim bytFile(lngLength)

    For lngLoopIndex = 0 To lngLength -1
        Get #1, , bytFile(lngLoopIndex)
    Next lngLoopIndex

    Close #1

    Text1.Text = "File read in."
    Exit Sub

FileError:
    MsgBox "File Error!" & Err.Description

End Sub
```

And that's it—now you're reading binary files from disk.

8: Working With Files

Closing Files

How do you close a file in Visual Basic? It's simple—just use the **Close** statement:

```
Private Sub Command1_Click()
    On Error GoTo FileError
    Open "c:\file.txt" For Output As #1
    Print #1, Text1.Text
    Close #1
    Exit Sub

FileError:
    MsgBox "File Error!"
End Sub
```

Closing a file writes all the data stored in Visual Basic's internal buffers to disk.

TIP: *If you want to close all the files your application has open, use the* **Close** *statement without any arguments.*

Chapter 9

Programming The Windows API

In Brief

In this chapter, we're going to take a look at connecting Visual Basic to the Windows Application Programming Interface (API). All the Windows procedures that Windows programs use are available through Visual Basic, and we'll see how to reach them in this chapter—often, those functions can do things the functions built into Visual Basic just can't do.

Core Windows DLLs

You can connect to the Windows API because the procedures that make up that API are in dynamic link libraries (DLLs) in the windows\system directory; you call them directly from those DLLs. Here's a list of the kind of core Windows DLLs we'll be using in this chapter:

- *Advapi32.dll*—Advanced API services library supporting numerous APIs, including many security and Registry calls

- *Comdlg32.dll*—Common dialog API library

- *Gdi32.dll*—Graphics Device Interface (GDI) API library

- *Kernel32.dll*—Core Windows 32-bit base API support

- *Lz32.dll*—32-bit compression routines

- *Mpr.dll*—Multiple Provider Router (MPR) library

- *Netapi32.dll*—32-bit network API library

- *Shell32.dll*—32-bit shell API library

- *User32.dll*—Library for user-interface routines

- *Version.dll*—Version library

- *Winmm.dll*—Windows multimedia library

In this chapter, we'll see how to put these DLLs to work as we connect to the functions in them, how to determine what functions are available, and how to use them in code. One quick note: if you're using Windows NT or Windows 2000 and you get integer overflow errors with the code in this chapter, try switching from using integers to using long integers. That's all the overview we need for connecting to Windows—now it's time to turn to the Immediate Solutions part of this chapter.

Immediate Solutions

What Procedures Are Available In The Windows API?

Although thousands of functions are available in the Windows API, they won't do you any good unless you know what's there.

You'll find the procedures, constants, and types used in the Windows API in the file win32api.txt, which is in the Visual Basic tools\winapi directory. You can open that file in a word processor (such as Windows WordPad) and copy and paste the declarations you need into your Visual Basic program, as you'll do in this chapter.

Note that the win32api.txt file includes only the raw declarations for procedures, constants, and types—it doesn't tell you what all the variables mean. To find reference information on the Windows API set, refer to the Microsoft Win32 Software Development Kit (SDK), which (depending on your version of Visual Basic) may be included on the Microsoft Developer Network Library CD.

You can also use the Visual Basic API Viewer add-in tool to work with win32api.txt; this tool appears on Visual Basic's Add-Ins menu. (If the API Viewer doesn't appear on your Add-Ins menu, you can add it to Visual Basic with the Add-Ins|Add-In Manager menu item.) You can open win32api.txt in the API Viewer, as shown in Figure 9.1.

How To Use The Windows API Procedures In Visual Basic

Thousands of Windows API functions are available for your use. For example, let's say you want to play sounds directly (without using the Visual Basic multimedia control). You can do that with the Windows API **PlaySound** function. To let Visual Basic know where to find this function (it's stored in the winmm.dll dynamic link library), what arguments it takes, and what arguments it returns, you declare that function like this in the (General) declarations section of a form:

9: Programming The
Windows API

153

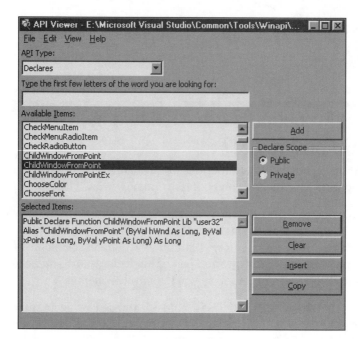

Figure 9.1   *The Visual Basic API Viewer.*

```
Private Declare Function PlaySound Lib "winmm.dll" Alias _
    "PlaySoundA" (ByVal lpszName As String, ByVal hModule As _
    Long, ByVal dwFlags As Long) As Long
```

You declare this function as *private* so you can declare it in a form. If you omit the **Private** keyword, you must make declarations in a module. After you've declared the function, you're free to use it. For example, this code plays the file c:\windows\media\Ding.wav (one of the files that come with Windows):

```
Private Sub Command1_Click()
    retVal = PlaySound("c:\windows\media\Ding.wav", _
    0&, &H20000)
End Sub
```

You should notice a number of points here. Because most Windows procedures are functions, you have to provide a way to handle the return value; the previous example stores it in the **retVal** variable. Alternatively, you can use the Visual Basic **Call** statement and omit the return value. You'll discard most of these return values, but Visual Basic will give you an error unless you handle functions as you've seen here.

For subroutines (which don't return a value), use the **Call** statement, like this:

```
Call MoveMemory(hMemoryPointer, outbuffer, DataLength)
```

Now, look at this declaration for **PlaySound**:

```
Private Declare Function PlaySound Lib "winmm.dll" Alias _
   "PlaySoundA" (ByVal lpszName As String, ByVal hModule _
   As Long, ByVal dwFlags As Long) As Long
```

This declaration comes from a file named *win32api.txt* that comes with Visual Basic (in the tools\winapi directory); you can find more about this file in the topic "What Procedures Are Available In The Windows API?" earlier in this chapter. In this case, the declaration indicates to Visual Basic that this function is to be found in the winmm.dll file (which is in the windows\system directory).

The **Alias** clause (if there is one) gives the actual name of the Windows function—in this example, what Visual Basic declares as **PlaySound** is actually the Windows function **PlaySoundA**. This **PlaySoundA** function uses ANSI text strings, the format you need in order to work with Visual Basic (as opposed to other versions of **PlaySound**, which can use other text formats, such as Unicode). In general, you should use the Windows functions as declared in the win32api.txt file, because the designers of Visual Basic have already selected the functions that will work with Visual Basic in that file.

That's how to declare the Windows API functions with the **Declare** statement. To see how to pass data to Windows API functions, take a look at the next topic.

Passing Arguments To The Windows API Functions

In the previous topic, we saw how to declare Windows API functions. Here, we'll see how to pass arguments to them. The first thing to note is that the argument names in the API calls use *Hungarian* prefix notation. For example, in this API declaration, the prefix of the variable name **lpszName**—*lpsz*—means the variable is a **Long** pointer to a zero-terminated string:

```
Private Declare Function PlaySound Lib "winmm.dll" Alias _
   "PlaySoundA" (ByVal lpszName As String, ByVal hModule _
   As Long, ByVal dwFlags As Long) As Long
```

What do these prefixes mean? You'll find a list of them in Table 9.1 to help you unravel the variable types in Windows API calls.

Note that the arguments to **PlaySound** are also passed with the **ByVal** keyword. What does this mean?

The standard Windows calling convention is actually the Pascal calling convention—which isn't the same as the Visual Basic calling convention. When you pass a variable to a procedure in Visual Basic, Visual Basic usually passes a *reference* to the variable; the called procedure

Table 9.1   Windows Hungarian notation.

Prefix	Means This
a	Array
b	Bool (Int)
by	Unsigned Char (Byte)
c	Char
cb	Count of bytes
cr	Color reference value
cx, cy	Short (count of x, y length)
dw	Unsigned Long (Dword)
fn	Function
h	Handle
i	Integer
m_	Data member of a class
n	Short or Int
np	Near pointer
p	Pointer
l	Long
lp	Long pointer
s	String
sz	String terminated with zero
tm	Text metric
w	Unsigned Int (Word)
x, y	Short (x or y coordinate)

then uses that reference to read (and possibly write) the value in the passed variable. This process is called *passing arguments by reference*. On the other hand, when you pass variables to the Windows API, you should often pass the variable's *value* directly, not a reference to the variable. This process is called *passing arguments by value*. You specify which way to pass variables using the **ByRef** and **ByVal** keywords.

As you can see, you must deal with a few interface issues when connecting to the Windows API. Take a look at the first argument in **PlaySound**: **lpszName**. This is a **Long** pointer to a zero-terminated string buffer—how do you construct one of those in Visual Basic, which doesn't even use pointers? It turns out that all you have to do is to pass a standard Visual Basic string for this argument when you call **PlaySound**, as follows:

```
retVal = PlaySound("c:\windows\media\Ding.wav", O&, &H20000)
```

In fact, you can handle the data types needed when you use the Windows API by using Visual Basic data types, as shown in Table 9.2. It may look complex, but don't worry—you'll get practical experience passing variables using the conversions in Table 9.2 in the examples throughout this chapter. Doing so is easier than you think—for example, when you need to pass a long integer variable to the Windows API, you just use a Visual Basic **Long** variable, passing it by value.

In addition, sometimes you need to pass a special Windows-defined variable—see the next topic for more information.

Table 9.2   The Windows and Visual Basic variable types.

Windows Type	Passed As
char	ByVal String
handle	ByVal Long
int	ByVal Integer
long	ByVal Long
lpint	ByRef Integer
lplong	ByRef Long
lpstr	ByVal String
lpsz	ByVal String
lpvoid	ByRef Any

Related solutions:	*Found in:*
Passing Arguments By Value	Chapter 6
Passing Arguments By Reference	Chapter 6

9: Programming The Windows API

157

Passing Windows-Defined Variables

Sometimes, a Windows API procedure takes an argument of a Windows-defined type. For example, the **MoveToEx** function—which moves the current drawing position—takes an argument of type **POINTAPI**:

```
Private Declare Function MoveToEx Lib "gdi32" (ByVal hdc _
    As Long, ByVal x As Long, ByVal y As Long, lpPoint As _
    POINTAPI) As Long
```

You'll find the declarations of types like **POINTAPI** in the win32api.txt file; you can copy them and put them in a module in your own program (data types need to be declared in a module):

```
Type POINTAPI
        x As Long
        y As Long
End Type
```

Now you're free to use that type in your Visual Basic programs, like this:

```
Dim ptPoint As POINTAPI

ptPoint.x = 0
ptPoint.y = 0

lngRetVal = MoveToEx(intHandle, intX, intY, ptPoint)
```

In this way, you can handle the data types and data structures needed by Windows procedures.

Launching Another Program

This chapter's first Windows API example will be an easy one—you'll use the Windows function **WinExec** to launch another program. For example, you can launch the Windows calculator program, calc.exe (see Figure 9.2).

To use **WinExec**, first get its declaration from win32api.txt and place that declaration in a form:

```
Private Declare Function WinExec Lib "kernel32" (ByVal _
    lpCmdLine As String, ByVal nCmdShow As Long) As Long
```

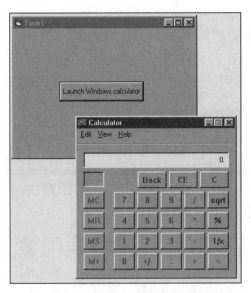

Figure 9.2   *Launching a Windows program.*

You only have to pass the path and name of the program you want to launch, as well as a constant value that indicates *how* you want to show the launched program: maximized, minimized, and so on. As with the other constant values you pass to Windows API functions, you'll find the possible values for this constant value in win32api.txt (these constants are actually defined for the function **ShowWindow**, which is why they have the prefix *SW*):

```
Const SW_HIDE = 0
Const SW_SHOWNORMAL = 1
Const SW_NORMAL = 1
Const SW_SHOWMINIMIZED = 2
Const SW_SHOWMAXIMIZED = 3
Const SW_MAXIMIZE = 3
Const SW_SHOWNOACTIVATE = 4
Const SW_SHOW = 5
Const SW_MINIMIZE = 6
Const SW_SHOWMINNOACTIVE = 7
Const SW_SHOWNA = 8
Const SW_RESTORE = 9
Const SW_SHOWDEFAULT = 10
Const SW_MAX = 10
```

After adding these declarations to your form, you're ready to use the **WinExec** function to launch the Windows calculator. You might do so when the user clicks on a button (**Command1**) labeled Launch Windows Calculator:

```
Private Sub Command1_Click()
    Call WinExec("c:\windows\calc.exe", SW_NORMAL)
End Sub
```

That's all it takes. Run the program and click on the button to make the Windows calculator appear (refer back to Figure 9.2). Now you're launching Windows programs.

Getting Windows Device Contexts— Including The Entire Screen

Before you can draw with the Windows API graphics functions, you need a device context. Visual Basic controls like picture boxes have an **hDC** property, which holds their device context, but you can get device contexts for any window.

To get a device context for a window, you can use **GetDC**, which returns a handle to a device context or 0 if unsuccessful:

```
Declare Function GetDC Lib "user32" Alias "GetDC" _
    (ByVal hwnd As Long) As Long
```

GetDC's hwnd parameter is a handle to the window for which you want a device context.

You can also get a device context for a particular device with the **CreateDC** function, which returns a handle to a device context or 0 if unsuccessful:

```
Declare Function CreateDC Lib "gdi32" Alias "CreateDCA" _
    (ByVal lpszDriverName As String, ByVal lpszDeviceName _
    As String, ByVal lpszOutput As String, lpInitData As _
    DEVMODE) As Long
```

Here are the parameters for **CreateDC**:

- *lpszDriverName*—String that specifies the file name (without extension) of the device driver (for example, **"EPSON"**).

- *lpszDeviceName*—String that specifies the name of the specific device to be supported (for example, **"EPSON LQ-80"**). Use the **lpszDeviceName** parameter if the module supports more than one device.

- *lpszOutput*—String that specifies the file or device name for the physical output medium (file or output port).

- *lpInitData*—A **DEVMODE** structure containing device-specific initialization data for the device driver. The Windows **DocumentProperties** function retrieves this structure filled in for a given device. The **lpInitData** parameter must be **NULL** if the device driver is to use the default initialization (if any) specified by the user through the Control Panel.

The **CreateDC** function may seem a little abstract, but it has one very powerful use: You can get a device context for the entire screen using this function, which means you can then use Windows functions to draw anywhere on screen.

To get a device context for the screen, you declare the **DEVMODE** type (as declared in win32api.txt) in a standard module:

```
Type DEVMODE
        dmDeviceName As String * CCHDEVICENAME
        dmSpecVersion As Integer
        dmDriverVersion As Integer
        dmSize As Integer
        dmDriverExtra As Integer
        dmFields As Long
        dmOrientation As Integer
        dmPaperSize As Integer
        dmPaperLength As Integer
        dmPaperWidth As Integer
        dmScale As Integer
        dmCopies As Integer
        dmDefaultSource As Integer
        dmPrintQuality As Integer
        dmColor As Integer
        dmDuplex As Integer
        dmYResolution As Integer
        dmTTOption As Integer
        dmCollate As Integer
        dmFormName As String * CCHFORMNAME
        dmUnusedPadding As Integer
        dmBitsPerPel As Integer
        dmPelsWidth As Long
        dmPelsHeight As Long
        dmDisplayFlags As Long
        dmDisplayFrequency As Long
End Type
```

9: Programming The Windows API

161

You also need to declare these two constants, which are used in the above code:

```
Public Const CCHDEVICENAME = 32

Public Const CCHFORMNAME = 32
```

Next, you pass the string **"DISPLAY"** as the device type to **CreateDC**, to get a device context for the entire screen. The following code does so when a form loads:

```
Private Sub Form_Load()
    Dim devDevMode As DEVMODE
    Dim intHandleDisplay As Integer

    intHandleDisplay = CreateDC("DISPLAY", 0&, 0&, devDevMode)
End Sub
```

Now, you can draw anywhere on screen, using the screen device context and the Windows API drawing functions (see the next topic).

TIP: *When you're done with a device context, you can delete it and reclaim its memory with the **DeleteDC** function.*

Drawing In A Windows Device Context

After you get a Windows device context (see the previous topic), how do you draw in it? The Windows API includes many, many drawing functions. For example, you can use the **LineTo** function to draw lines; this function draws a line from the current drawing position to the position you specify.

To draw a line, you first set the current drawing position with the **MoveToEx** function:

```
Declare Function MoveToEx Lib "gdi32" Alias "MoveToEx" _
    (ByVal hdc As Long, ByVal x As Long, ByVal y As _
    Long, lpPoint As POINTAPI) As Long
```

The arguments to **MoveToEx** are as follows:

• *hdc*—The device context to draw in

• *x*—The x coordinate of the new position

- *y*—The y coordinate of the new position
- *lpPoint*—A **POINTAPI** variable that will be filled with the old location

After you set the current drawing position, use **LineTo** to draw a line to a new position:

```
Declare Function LineTo Lib "gdi32" (ByVal hdc As Long, _
  ByVal x As Long, ByVal y As Long) As Long
```

Here's what the arguments mean:

- *hdc*—The device context to draw in
- *x*—The x coordinate of the end of the line
- *y*—The y coordinate of the end of the line

Both **MoveToEx** and **LineTo** return a nonzero value if successful.

Let's see an example that draws a box made of four lines in a picture box. You start by adding a module to a program and declaring the **POINTAPI** type that **MoveToEx** needs:

```
Type POINTAPI
    x As Long
    y As Long
End Type
```

Next, you declare **MoveToEx** and **LineTo** as **Private** in the form's (General) section:

```
Private Declare Function MoveToEx Lib "gdi32" (ByVal hdc _
  As Long, ByVal x As Long, ByVal y As Long, lpPoint As _
  POINTAPI) As Long
```

```
Private Declare Function LineTo Lib "gdi32" (ByVal hdc As _
  Long, ByVal x As Long, ByVal y As Long) As Long
```

Add a picture box (**Picture1**) to the form (set the picture box's **ScaleMode** property to **Pixels** (3) so you can pass pixel values to **LineTo**), along with a command button (**Command1**); when the user clicks on the command button, you can draw the lines you want, forming a rectangle:

```
Private Sub Command1_Click()
    Dim ptPoint As POINTAPI
```

```
retval = MoveToEx(Picture1.hdc, Picture1.ScaleWidth / 4, _
    Picture1.ScaleHeight / 4, ptPoint)
retval = LineTo(Picture1.hdc, Picture1.ScaleWidth / 4, 3 * _
    Picture1.ScaleHeight / 4)
retval = LineTo(Picture1.hdc, 3 * Picture1.ScaleWidth / 4, _
    3 * Picture1.ScaleHeight / 4)
retval = LineTo(Picture1.hdc, 3 * Picture1.ScaleWidth / 4, _
    Picture1.ScaleHeight / 4)
retval = LineTo(Picture1.hdc, Picture1.ScaleWidth / 4, _
    Picture1.ScaleHeight / 4)
```

```
End Sub
```

The result of this code appears in Figure 9.3. Now you're drawing lines with the Windows API.

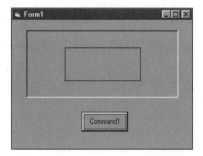

Figure 9.3   *Drawing a four-line box with the Windows API.*

Capturing And Using The Mouse Outside Your Window

In Visual Basic, sometimes you want to work with the mouse no matter where the pointer appears on the screen. To do that, you can use the **SetCapture** and **ReleaseCapture** functions:

```
Private Declare Function SetCapture Lib "user32" _
    (ByVal hwnd As Long) As Long

Private Declare Function ReleaseCapture Lib "user32" () _
    As Long
```

Here, **hwnd** is the handle of the window that the mouse should send mouse events to, no matter where the pointer is on the screen. As you might guess from their names, **SetCapture** captures the mouse and **ReleaseCapture** releases it.

Let's work through an example. In this case, you'll capture the mouse when the user clicks on a command button (**Command1**); when the user drags the pointer anywhere on the screen, you'll report its current x and y locations in a text box (**Text1**). (Note: Set the form's **ScaleMode** property to **Pixels** (3) so that you get your mouse locations in pixels.)

You'll use two **Boolean** flags here: **blnStartCapture**, which you set to **True** when the user clicks on the command button to capture the mouse; and **blnAmCapturing**, which you set to **True** when the user starts dragging the mouse. You should report the mouse location in the text box. Along with **SetCapture** and **ReleaseCapture**, then, you add all the declarations to the form's (General) section:

```
Dim blnStartCapture As Boolean
Dim blnAmCapturing As Boolean

Private Declare Function SetCapture Lib "user32" (ByVal _
   hwnd As Long) As Long
Private Declare Function ClientToScreen Lib "user32" _
   (ByVal hwnd As Long, lpPoint As POINTAPI) As Long
Private Declare Function ReleaseCapture Lib "user32" () _
   As Long
```

Note also that you include the **ClientToScreen** function; you use this function to translate coordinates from window coordinates to the whole screen. You'll need to do that, because the mouse coordinates passed to your mouse event handlers are in window coordinates—you need screen coordinates, because you're using the mouse with the whole screen.

You pass a variable of type **POINTAPI** to **ClientToScreen**, so you include that type's declaration in a new module you add to the program:

```
Type POINTAPI
     x As Long
     y As Long
End Type
```

To start the program, set your **Boolean** flags to **False** when the program's form loads:

```
Private Sub Form_Load()
```

```
    blnStartCapture = False
    blnAmCapturing = False

End Sub
```

Now, when the user clicks on command button **Command1**, you capture the mouse with **SetCapture** and set the **blnStartCapture** flag to **True**:

```
Private Sub Command1_Click()
    blnStartCapture = True
    intRetVal = SetCapture(hwnd)
    Command1.Caption = "Drag the mouse"
End Sub
```

When the user presses the mouse button again, set the **blnCapturing** flag to **True** and begin reporting the mouse location in the text box **Text1**:

```
Private Sub Form_MouseDown(Button As Integer, Shift As _
    Integer, x As Single, y As Single)
    Dim ptPoint As POINTAPI

    If blnStartCapture Then
        ptPoint.x = x
        ptPoint.y = y
        retval = ClientToScreen(hwnd, ptPoint)
        Text1.Text = "Mouse location: " & Str(ptPoint.x) & _
            ", " & Str(ptPoint.y)
        blnAmCapturing = True
    End If
End Sub
```

Similarly, in the **MouseMove** event, you check to see whether you're capturing the mouse. If so, display the pointer location in the text box:

```
Sub Form_MouseMove(Button As Integer, Shift As Integer, x _
    As Single, y As Single)
    Dim ptPoint As POINTAPI

    If blnAmCapturing Then

        ptPoint.x = x
        ptPoint.y = y
        retval = ClientToScreen(hwnd, ptPoint)
        Text1.Text = "Mouse location: " & _
            Str(ptPoint.x) & ", " & Str(ptPoint.y)
```

```
      End If
End Sub
```

Finally, when the user releases the mouse button, you release the mouse with **ReleaseCapture** and reset the **Boolean** flags:

```
Sub Form_MouseUp(Button As Integer, Shift As Integer, x As _
    Single, y As Single)

    If blnAmCapturing Then

        ReleaseCapture
        blnStartCapture = False
        blnAmCapturing = False
        Command1.Caption = "Start capture"

    End If
End Sub
```

That's it—now run the program (see Figure 9.4), click on the Drag The Mouse button, and drag the mouse. No matter where you move the mouse pointer, its location appears in the program's text box. You've captured the mouse! To release it, simply release the mouse button.

TIP: *You need to know about one peculiarity: Starting with Windows 95, you can capture the mouse for only one mouse operation—when you finish with the mouse, it's released. This means that if you begin a mouse drag by pressing the mouse button while inside the program's window, everything is fine—the program retains control of the mouse while you drag. On the other hand, if you press the mouse button outside the program's window and begin to drag, the mouse is released. You can remedy this problem by using the right mouse button for mouse operations. For example, you can have the user press the mouse button in the program's window and drag the mouse to the desired region of the screen, then press the right mouse button (while holding the left one down) to use the mouse.*

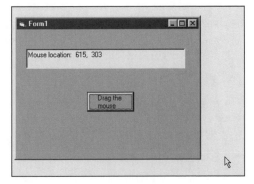

Figure 9.4 *Using the mouse outside a program.*

Setting Another Window's Title Text

In this topic's example, you'll set another window's title bar text by clicking on that window. To work with a window in the Windows API, you need a window handle. One way to get a handle for any window on screen is to use the **WindowFromPoint** function. You simply pass that function the x and y coordinates (in screen coordinates) of a point inside the window whose handle you want:

```
Private Declare Function WindowFromPoint Lib "user32" _
   (ByVal xPoint As Long, ByVal yPoint As Long) As Long
```

The example program includes a command button (**Command1**) with the caption *Click here and then click target window*. When the user clicks on this button, moves the mouse to any window's title bar on the screen, and then clicks on that window's title bar, you'll set that window's title to *Hello from Visual Basic*.

When the user clicks on the button, you set a form-wide **Boolean** variable—**blnChoose**—to **True**. By doing so, you'll know that the next mouse-click indicates which window the user wants to set the text in:

```
Dim blnChoose As Boolean
```

You set **blnChoose** to **False** when the form first loads:

```
Private Sub Form_Load()
    blnChoose = False
End Sub
```

To capture the mouse, you'll need **SetCapture** and **ReleaseCapture**; to convert from window to screen coordinates, you'll need **ClientToScreen**. Declare those functions, as well:

```
Private Declare Function SetCapture Lib "user32" (ByVal _
   hwnd As Long) As Long
Private Declare Function ReleaseCapture Lib "user32" () _
   As Long
Private Declare Function WindowFromPoint Lib "user32" _
   (ByVal xPoint As Long, ByVal yPoint As Long) As Long
Private Declare Function ClientToScreen Lib "user32" _
   (ByVal hwnd As Long, lpPoint As POINTAPI) As Long
```

In addition, set the **ScaleMode** property of the form to pixels. You also need to declare the **POINTAPI** type, because **ClientToScreen** uses that type; add that declaration to a module you add to the program:

```
Type POINTAPI
        x As Long
        y As Long
End Type
```

Now, when the user clicks on the command button, you capture the mouse and set the **blnChoose** flag to **True**:

```
Private Sub Command1_Click()
    blnChoose = True
    intRetVal = SetCapture(hwnd)
End Sub
```

When the user clicks on a window, the program's **MouseDown** event handler will be called. To determine the screen location at which the mouse button was pressed, you use **ClientToScreen**:

```
Private Sub Form_MouseDown(Button As Integer, Shift As _
  Integer, x As Single, y As Single)
    Dim ptPoint As POINTAPI

    If blnChoose Then

        ptPoint.x = x
        ptPoint.y = y
        retval = ClientToScreen(hwnd, ptPoint)
        .
        .
        .

    End If
End Sub
```

Now, you can get a window handle for the window the user clicked on with **WindowFromPoint**:

```
Private Sub Form_MouseDown(Button As Integer, Shift As _
  Integer, x As Single, y As Single)
    Dim window As Long
    Dim ptPoint As POINTAPI

    If blnChoose Then
```

```
        ptPoint.x = x
        ptPoint.y = y
        retval = ClientToScreen(hwnd, ptPoint)

        window = WindowFromPoint(ptPoint.x, ptPoint.y)
        .
        .
        .
    End If
End Sub
```

You now have a window handle for any window that the user wants to click on. Using that handle, you can perform all kinds of operations on the window—resize it, close it, change its style, and more, using API functions.

In this case, let's set the window's title bar text to *Hello from Visual Basic* when the user clicks on that title bar. To do that with **SetWindowText**, add this declaration to the program:

```
Private Declare Function SetWindowText Lib "user32" _
    Alias "SetWindowTextA" (ByVal hwnd As Long, ByVal _
    lpString As String) As Long
```

Now, you can set the clicked-on window's title this way:

```
Private Sub Form_MouseDown(Button As Integer, Shift As _
    Integer, x As Single, y As Single)
    Dim window As Long
    Dim buffer As String * 1024
    Dim ptPoint As POINTAPI

    If blnChoose Then

        ptPoint.x = x
        ptPoint.y = y
        retval = ClientToScreen(hwnd, ptPoint)

        window = WindowFromPoint(ptPoint.x, ptPoint.y)

        Call SetWindowText(window, "Hello from Visual _
            Basic.")
    End If
End Sub
```

That's it—the result of running this program is shown in the bottom window in Figure 9.5; the program changes the title bar text of WordPad to *Hello from Visual Basic* when you click on WordPad's title bar.

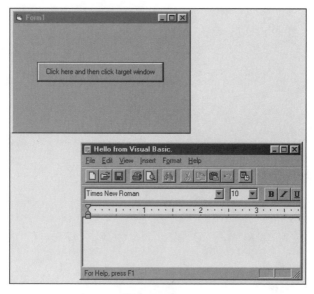

Figure 9.5   *Setting another window's title text.*

Part II

The Visual Basic Tools

The Integrated Development Environment

In Brief

In this chapter, we're going to start looking at the tools available in Visual Basic, beginning with the most essential tool of them all—the Integrated Development Environment (IDE). You see the IDE when you start Visual Basic, as shown in Figure 10.1. You do your Visual Basic programming in the IDE.

As a programmer with Visual Basic experience, you're probably quite familiar with the essentials of the IDE—how to add a control to a form, save a project, or run a program from the IDE. In this chapter, we'll not only cover tasks like these, but also see what the IDE is capable of as we take a look at its advanced options. The IDE has become more complex over time, but it's still a good tool, and Microsoft has designed the IDE so that using it is fairly intuitive.

In fact, the IDE was Visual Basic's original big selling point. Using the IDE, you could design your program in a way that was revolutionary for Windows—by simply drawing controls in a window. Until then, Windows programming was a very difficult process, but Visual Basic made it almost fun. That reputation has stuck with Visual Basic to this day.

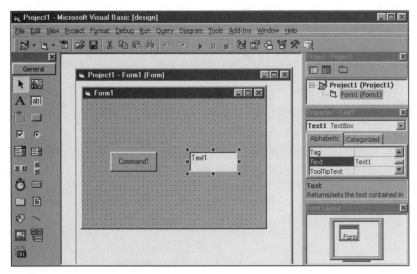

Figure 10.1 The Visual Basic Integrated Development Environment.

The Parts And States Of The IDE

The Visual Basic IDE has three distinct states: Design, Run, and De-bug. The current state appears in Visual Basic's title bar. We'll cover the Debug state in Chapter 12. In the Run state, Visual Basic is in the background while your program runs. This chapter concentrates on the Design state—the IDE's specialty—in which you design your program.

The IDE is composed of these parts: the menu bar, the toolbar, the Project Explorer, the Properties window, the Form Layout window, form designers, and code windows. The IDE works hard to be user-friendly: Almost all the windows in the IDE are *dockable*, which means you can drag them with the mouse and rearrange them as you like. The toolbars are also dockable; simply click on the double-upright bars at the left end of the toolbar (Visual Basic uses Explorer-style toolbars) and drag the toolbar to its new location—you can even place it above the menu bar. We'll take a look at all of these parts in this chapter, as we see how to use the IDE to create Visual Basic applications.

That's all the overview we need—let's turn to the Immediate Solutions part of this chapter now.

Immediate Solutions

Using The IDE Menu Bar

The IDE menu bar, which appears at the top of the IDE (refer back to Figure 10.1), holds the Visual Basic menus. Here's a list of those menus and what they do:

- *File*—Handles files and printing; also makes EXE files
- *Edit*—Performs standard editing functions, Undo, and searches
- *View*—Displays or hides windows and toolbars
- *Project*—Sets project properties, adds/removes forms and modules, and adds/removes references and components
- *Format*—Aligns or sizes controls
- *Debug*—Starts/stops debugging and stepping through programs
- *Run*—Starts a program, or compiles and starts it
- *Query*—Works with data queries
- *Diagram*—Diagrams data materials
- *Tools*—Adds procedures, starts the Menu Editor, and sets IDE options
- *Add-Ins*—Opens the Add-In Manager; lists add-ins such as the Application Wizard and API Viewer
- *Window*—Arranges or selects open windows
- *Help*—Handles help and the About dialog box

TIP: *The File menu lets you perform an important job: creating EXE files for your programs. When you run a program from the Run menu, no EXE file is created. But, if you want to run the program outside of Visual Basic, you must create that EXE file; you do so with the File menu's Make ProjectName.exe item (where ProjectName is the name you've set for the project).*

Using The IDE Toolbar

The main Visual Basic toolbar appears in Figure 10.2. This toolbar contains buttons matching popular menu items; clicking on a button is the same as selecting a menu item and can save you some time.

Besides the main toolbar, you can also display Visual Basic's other dockable toolbars: the Debug, Edit, and Form Editor toolbars. To display one of these toolbars, just select it using the View|Toolbars menu item; the toolbar appears free-floating at first, but you can dock it as you like in the IDE.

TIP: *If you're unsure what a particular toolbar tool does, just rest the mouse pointer over it. A tooltip (a small yellow window displaying text) will display the tool's purpose.*

Figure 10.2 *The main Visual Basic toolbar.*

Using The IDE Properties Window

The IDE Properties window appears in Figure 10.3. Here, you set an object's properties; for example, you can set the caption of a command button, the text in a text box, and literally hundreds of other properties.

When you select an object (such as a control) in Visual Basic by clicking on it with the mouse, that object's properties appear in the Properties window. To change or examine a property setting in the Properties window, find that property's name in that window (the

Figure 10.3 *The Properties window.*

properties appear on the left and their settings on the right). If you want to change a property value, nothing could be easier—just click on its current setting. For properties that you set yourself, the current property value is highlighted; simply type in the new setting (similar to placing new text in a text box). If the property can be set to only one of a specific range of values, a down arrow will appear in the property setting box; click on this button to see the property's possible values.

Note that Visual Basic includes two kinds of properties: *design-time* and *runtime* properties. For example, a control might have a runtime property to hold items the user has selected, because it doesn't make sense to set that property at design time. The properties that appear in the Properties window are design-time properties.

Using The IDE Project Explorer

The Project Explorer appears in Figure 10.4. All the files in a project appear in the Project Explorer, arranged in a tree view.

The Project Explorer can be very useful when you're working in a large project and the IDE is filled with design and code windows. To pick out the part of the project you want to work on, you only have to find it in the Project Explorer and double-click on it. Doing so brings the appropriate window to the foreground and—if you've clicked on a form—opens that form in the Properties window.

The icons at the top of the Project Explorer in Figure 10.4 allow you to switch between views. Clicking on the left icon displays an object's code window, the middle icon displays the object itself, and the right icon toggles folders open and closed in the Project Explorer as in a standard tree view (you can click on the folders themselves to do that, as well).

Figure 10.4   *The Visual Basic Project Explorer.*

Using The Mouse In The Project Explorer

You can add and remove files in a project by right-clicking on them with the mouse in the Project Explorer. In particular, you can add new forms, MDI forms, modules, class modules, and so on, just by right-clicking on the project's icon in the Project Explorer and selecting from the pop-up menu that appears. You can also remove forms or modules by right-clicking on them and selecting Remove from the pop-up menu.

The Project Explorer gives you a valuable overview of the entire project, which is useful when a project becomes large and contains many components.

TIP: *Like the other windows in the IDE, the Project Explorer is dockable—you can move it around with the mouse and size it as you like. In fact, you can rearrange all the windows in the IDE.*

Using The IDE Form Layout Window

How do you determine where your forms appear when your application starts? You use the Form Layout window, which appears in Figure 10.5. Using this window, you can position forms as you want them to appear on the screen when they're first displayed in your application.

To give a form a new initial location, just drag the form in the Form Layout window to that new location. You'll see the new screen position of the form's upper-left corner (in twips) displayed at the right end of the toolbar (it's the first set of numbers in the toolbar; refer back to Figure 10.2).

Figure 10.5 *The Form Layout window.*

Using IDE Form Designers

You design forms in IDE *form designers*. These are windows—such as the one in the center of Figure 10.6—that display the current form and the controls in it.

Form designers give you a visual indication of what your program's forms will look like when the program runs. To open a form designer for a form, just double-click on that form's entry in the Project Explorer. When you use the tools in the IDE toolbox to add controls to a form, you work with the form in its form designer.

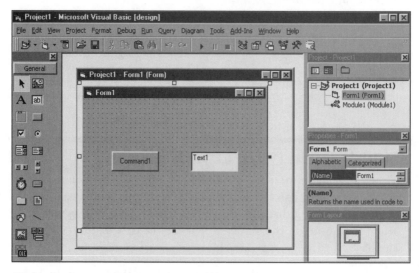

Figure 10.6   *An IDE form designer and code window.*

Using The IDE Toolbox

The Visual Basic IDE toolbox appears in Figure 10.7. This window is a mainstay of Visual Basic; it shows what was so revolutionary about Visual Basic in the first place. You use the toolbox to add controls to your projects, and you do so in a very easy way—simply click on a tool (such as the command button tool) and draw the new control on a form. That's all it takes. You can also double-click on a control's tool in the toolbox to create a new control of that type in the center of a form under design.

The toolbox is loaded with controls you can add to your forms—text boxes, labels, list boxes, image controls, checkboxes, timers, and much more. When you add a new ActiveX control to your project (using the

Figure 10.7 *The Visual Basic toolbox.*

Project|Components menu item), that control appears in the toolbox and you're ready to add it to your form.

Entering Code

To enter code in the Visual Basic IDE, you use a code window, which operates like a text editor and arranges the various code procedures and declarations in a module. You can see a Visual Basic code window in the center of Figure 10.8; the window displays the code you're working on.

To add code to an object in a module, you open a code window by double-clicking on the object (such as a control in a form) or by selecting the module in the Project Explorer and clicking on the code window icon at upper-left in the Project Explorer.

To attach code to an object in the code window, use the two dropdown list boxes at the top of the code window. The left list lets you select the object to add code to, and the right list lets you select the procedure to add (all the events the object supports appear in this list). When you've selected the event for which you want to add code, Visual Basic adds an empty event handler in the code window.

You don't need to add code to a particular object to work with code in the code window—you can create your own subroutines and functions with the Tools|Add Procedure menu item. Selecting this item opens the Add Procedure dialog box you see in Figure 10.9.

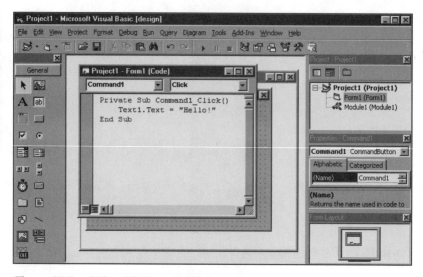

Figure 10.8   *A Visual Basic code window.*

Figure 10.9   *The Add Procedure dialog box.*

You can use the Add Procedure dialog box to add a new procedure to the currently open code window (or you can just type in the new procedure directly); doing so adds a new, empty procedure of the type you've selected, with the name you've specified.

When you're entering code, the code window supports all the standard Windows editing techniques: selecting, copying, cutting, pasting, and searching for text using the editing commands from the Edit menu, as well as standard shortcut keys like Ctrl+C for copying and Ctrl+X for cutting. Code windows provide you with powerful text-editing capabilities to write and revise your code.

Installing The Specialized IDE Toolbars

By default, Visual Basic displays one toolbar: the standard toolbar. However, other toolbars are available—the Debug, Edit, and Form Editor toolbars. If you want to use one of them, you can add it by opening the View|Toolbars submenu and clicking on the desired toolbar. You can remove one or all toolbars the same way.

The Debug toolbar has the following buttons:

- Start
- Break
- End
- Toggle Breakpoint
- Step Into
- Step Over
- Step Out
- Locals Window
- Immediate Window
- Watch Window
- Call Stack

The Edit toolbar includes these buttons:

- List Properties/Methods
- List Constants
- Quick Info
- Parameter Info
- Complete Word
- Indent
- Outdent
- Toggle Breakpoint
- Comment Block
- Uncomment Block
- Toggle Bookmark
- Next Bookmark
- Previous Bookmark
- Clear All Bookmarks

The Form Editor toolbar includes these buttons:

- Bring To Front
- Send To Back
- Align
- Center
- Width
- Lock Controls

Setting A Project's Startup Form

You might have a number of forms in a project—you specify which one is displayed first in the General tab of the Project Properties dialog box. Follow these steps:

1. Select the Project|Properties menu item to open the Project Properties dialog box (see Figure 10.10).
2. Click on the General tab.
3. Select the form you want to make the startup form from the Startup Object drop-down list, selected in Figure 10.10, and click on OK.

Now, when your program starts, the form you've selected will act as the startup form.

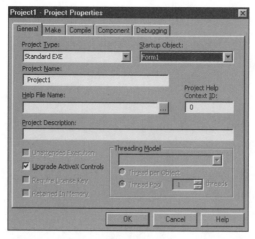

Figure 10.10   *The Project Properties dialog box.*

Setting A Project's Startup Procedure

To start a program from code that's not in any form, add a subroutine named **Main** to your program. When the program starts, Visual Basic runs the code in **Main** first, rather than displaying a form. Follow these steps to add a **Main** subroutine to your program:

1. Select the Project|Properties menu item to open the Project Properties dialog box.

2. Click on the General tab, select Sub Main from the Startup Object drop-down list, and click on OK.

3. Select the Project|Add Module menu item and double-click on the Module icon in the resulting Add Module dialog box.

4. Add this code to the new module's (General) section in the code window:

```
Sub Main()

End Sub
```

5. Place the code you want in the **Main** subroutine.

Aligning Multiple Controls Simultaneously

For a professional look, you can easily align and space multiple controls on a form using the IDE. To work with a number of controls at once, you have to select those controls; you do so this way:

1. Hold down the Ctrl key and click on all the controls you want to align.

2. Be sure that one control is in the correct position and click on that one last. *Sizing handles*—the eight small boxes that you can grasp with the mouse to resize a control—will appear around all the selected controls. The sizing handles will appear hollow around all but the last control you selected, as shown in Figure 10.11. The last control has solid sizing handles; it will act as the key control. Visual Basic will align the other controls based on this key control's position.

3. Select the Format|Align menu item to open the Align submenu.

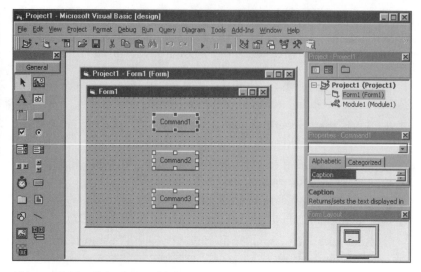

Figure 10.11   *Selecting multiple controls.*

4. From the Align submenu, select the type of alignment you want:
   You can align the left edges of the controls with the key control,
   or their centers, right edges, tops, middles, or bottoms.

5. While the controls are still collectively selected, you can also
   move them as a group to any new location.

Sizing Multiple Controls Simultaneously

To make selected controls the same size as one particular control,
follow these steps:

1. Hold down the Ctrl key and click on all the controls you want
   to resize.

2. Click last on the control that's already sized correctly.

3. Select the Format|Make Same Size menu item to open that
   submenu.

4. Choose the appropriate item in the Make Same Size submenu to
   size the controls as you want them: They can match the key
   control's width, height, or both.

Spacing Multiple Controls Simultaneously

To space multiple controls vertically or horizontally, follow these steps:

1. Hold down the Ctrl key and click on all the controls you want to space.

2. Select the Format|Horizontal Spacing or Format|Vertical Spacing menu item to open that submenu.

3. To space the controls horizontally or vertically, select one of the items in the corresponding submenu: Make Equal (sets the spacing to the average of the current spacing), Increase (increases by one grid line), Decrease (decreases by one grid line), or Remove.

Adjusting The Design-Time Grid

The design-time grid is the array of dots you see on a form at design time. This grid can help you place controls on a form; by default, Visual Basic aligns controls to the grid (they're sized to fit along vertical and horizontal lines of dots). You can change the grid units (in twips) in the Options dialog box—to open it, select the Tools|Options menu item. Click on the General tab, as shown in Figure 10.12, and type the design grid's new measurements in the Width and Height boxes.

TIP: *Besides setting the units of the grid, you can also specify that controls must be aligned to the grid by selecting the Align Controls To Grid checkbox.*

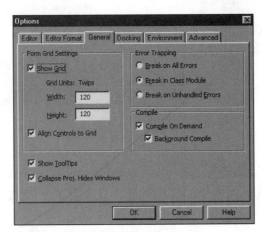

Figure 10.12   Resizing the design-time grid.

Managing Visual Basic IDE Add-Ins

Visual Basic comes with a wide variety of add-in tools, such as the Package And Deployment Wizard (which creates a setup program for your application), the API Viewer (which lets you access Windows API declarations), and more. These add-ins appear in the Add-Ins menu when they're installed.

You can use the Visual Basic Add-In Manager to install add-ins and to see which add-ins are available.

Here's how to use the Add-In Manager:

1. Select Visual Basic's Add-Ins|Add-In Manager menu item.
2. The Add-In Manager will open, as shown in Figure 10.13.
3. Select the add-in you want, indicate how you want to load it by checking the appropriate checkboxes in the Load Behavior box (see Figure 10.13), and click on OK.

Now you've added the add-in—you can invoke it by selecting its name in the Add-Ins menu. To remove the add-in, simply deselect its box in the Add-In Manager.

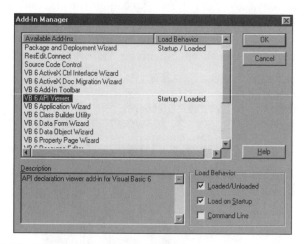

Figure 10.13   The Visual Basic Add-In Manager.

Adding ActiveX Controls To Your Project

Many of the controls available in Visual Basic are ActiveX controls, such as the toolbar control, the status bar control, progress bars, sliders and more. How do you add those controls to the toolbox so you can use them in forms? You do so as follows (note that the ActiveX control you want to add must be registered with Windows):

1. Select the Project|Components menu item.

2. The Visual Basic Components dialog box will open; click on the Controls tab.

3. Select the ActiveX control you want to add and click on OK to close the Components dialog box. The new control will appear in the toolbox.

TIP: *If the ActiveX control you want to add to a Visual Basic project doesn't appear in the Components dialog box, it may not have been registered with Windows properly. Try using the regsvr32.exe tool in the Windows\system directory to register the control again.*

Adding Insertable Objects To Your Project

You can add insertable objects—such as Microsoft Excel spreadsheets—to a Visual Basic project by using the Components dialog box this way:

1. Select the Project|Components menu item.

2. The Visual Basic Components dialog box will open; click on the Insertable Objects tab.

3. Select the object you want to add and then click on OK to close the Components dialog box. You can now use that object in your project.

Using Syntax Checking, Auto List Members, And Quick Info

Visual Basic includes a set of features designed to assist you as you work on your code. These features are:

• Auto List Members

• Quick Info

• Syntax Checking

The Auto List Members feature lists the members of an object as you're typing the object's name—actually, when you type the dot (.) after the object's name—as shown in Figure 10.14.

The Quick Info feature lets you know what parameters a procedure takes as you're typing the procedure's name, as shown in Figure 10.15. This useful feature can save you time looking up a procedure's parameter order or type.

You can guess what Syntax Checking does by its name—when you move the text insertion point away from a line of Visual Basic code while writing that code, Visual Basic will check the line's syntax and display an error box if appropriate. If you're the type of programmer who likes to move around in a file while writing code, you may get a lot of these messages and find them annoying.

You can turn all these features on and off by following these steps:

1. Select the Tools|Options menu item.

2. Select the Editor tab in the Options dialog box.

3. Select the options you want from the checkboxes: Auto Syntax Check, Auto List Members, Auto Quick Info, and Auto Data Tips.

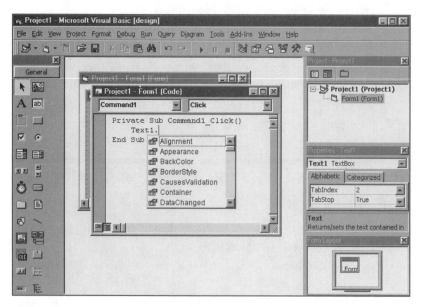

Figure 10.14   *The Visual Basic Auto List Members feature.*

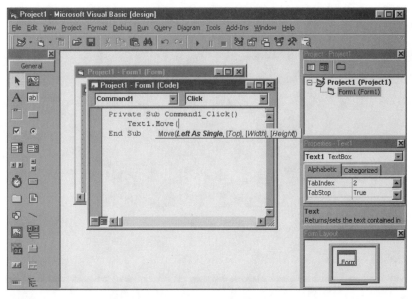

Figure 10.15   *The Visual Basic Quick Info feature.*

Customizing The IDE's Menus

You can move items between menus and toolbars in the Visual Basic IDE. Here's how:

1. Right-click on the menu bar to open the Customize dialog box, as shown in Figure 10.16.

2. Find the menu item you want to add to another menu or to a toolbar.

3. Using the mouse, drag the menu item from the Customize dialog box's Commands list to the new location in a menu or a toolbar.

4. Release the mouse button to add the menu item to its new location.

5. Click on Close in the Customize dialog box.

TIP: *If you use one particular menu item frequently, you might consider moving it directly into the menu bar (where it will appear among all the menu names). You can do that the same way you'd drag that item to a new menu—just drag it into the menu bar, instead.*

Figure 10.16   *Customizing Visual Basic menus.*

Customizing The IDE's Colors And Fonts

To help you program better and make clear at a glance what's in your program, the Visual Basic IDE comes with all kinds of preset colors—blue for keywords, green for comments, black for other code, and so on. You can adjust these colors as you prefer.

To change the default colors, open the Options dialog box by choosing the Tools|Options menu item and clicking on the Editor Format tab, as shown in Figure 10.17.

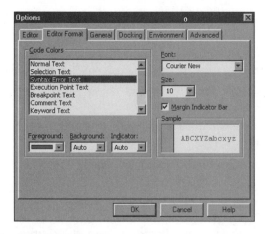

Figure 10.17   *Selecting IDE colors.*

Here are the text items whose colors you can select:

- Normal Text
- Selection Text
- Syntax Error Text
- Execution Point Text
- Breakpoint Text
- Comment Text
- Keyword Text
- Identifier Text
- Bookmark Text
- Call Return Text

To set the color and background color for a particular type of text, simply select the appropriate color(s) from the Foreground and Background drop-down lists and click on OK. You can set text fonts and font sizes the same way—specify the new setting(s) in the Font and Size dropdown lists and click on OK to customize the text.

Chapter 11

The Menu Editor

In Brief

If you're a Windows user, you know about menus. Menus are those useful controls that contain lists of items you can use to make selections—and they appear only when you want them. Menus hide their lists of selections out of the way until you need them, providing a way to compact the options a program offers. An application like Microsoft Word contains more than 100 menu items—imagine 100 buttons offering those options instead. You wouldn't have space left for anything else.

In this chapter, we're going to take a look at the Menu Editor. This tool lets you create and manage menus in your Visual Basic applications.

You may wonder why there is no menu control tool in the toolbox. The Menu Editor is an interesting tool because it's a rarity in Visual Basic: a non-toolbox tool you use to add controls to forms. To add other (non-menu) controls to a form, you use the tools in the toolbox. Beginning programmers sometimes search for a menu-control tool in the toolbox—but there's no such tool. Microsoft originally made the Menu Editor a separate tool because of the relative complexity of specifying all the information to create a menu; this process didn't fit in well with the simple properties of other controls at that time. However, many new controls have very complex setups, which you complete using property pages in Visual Basic. The Menu Editor is certainly simpler than a number of those controls, and it's fair to assume that if Microsoft was adding menu controls to Visual Basic today, it would use property pages rather than a new tool.

Let's start our chapter on the Visual Basic Menu Editor by taking a look at the parts of a menu.

The Parts Of A Menu

For reference, a menu—the Visual Basic Project menu—appears in Figure 11.1. Note how the Visual Basic menu system works in that figure: The menu names appear in the menu bar, usually just under the title bar; when the user selects a menu, that menu opens.

Each menu usually contains *items* arranged in a vertical list. The user makes a choice by selecting an item from that list. Menu items are often placed in functional groups with *menu separators*, which are the thin horizontal rules.

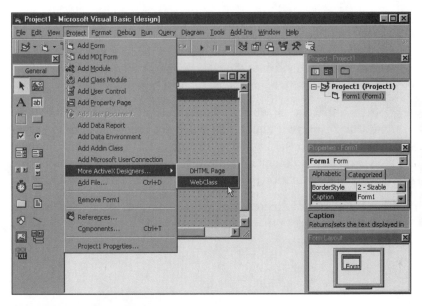

Figure 11.1 *The Visual Basic Project menu.*

When the user selects a menu item (using either the keyboard or the mouse), that item appears highlighted; pressing Enter or releasing the mouse button opens that item.

Menu items can also be *disabled* (or *grayed out*); see the Add User Document menu item in Figure 11.1 for an example. A disabled item isn't accessible to the user and does nothing if selected. Note that if your program presents the user with many disabled menu items, the user may feel locked out and frustrated. To avoid such situations, many programs add or remove menu items from menus at runtime.

Menu items can also have *submenus*. For instance, Figure 11.1 shows the submenu connected to the menu item More ActiveX Designers. A submenu is a mini-menu next to a parent menu; it allows the user to make immediate selections, as with any other kind of menu.

According to Microsoft, ideally each menu item should have a unique *access character* for users who choose commands with a keyboard. The user reaches the menu or menu item by pressing Alt and the access character. The access character should be the first letter of the menu or item title, unless another letter offers a link that is more easily remembered; no two menus or menu items at a given level should use the same access character.

Menu *shortcuts* are also handy for the user; for example, the shortcut for the Add File menu item in Figure 11.1 is Ctrl+D. These shortcuts are faster than access characters, because the user need only enter a single shortcut to execute the corresponding menu item (that is, the user doesn't have to open the menu itself first).

Note also that an ellipsis (...) should follow the name of any menu item that displays a dialog box when selected (Save As..., Preferences..., and so on). In addition, if a menu on the menu bar immediately executes a command instead of opening a menu, you should append an exclamation point to the menu's name (such as Collate!).

That completes our menu overview—it's time to turn to the Immediate Solutions part of this chapter to see how to use the Menu Editor to create menus.

Immediate Solutions

What Item Goes In Which Menu?

When you're designing your menu system, keep in mind that users expect to find certain standard items in certain menus (if your program supports those items).

Here are the kinds of items you'll find in the File menu:

- New
- Open
- Close
- Close All
- Save
- Save As
- Save All
- Properties
- Templates
- Page Setup
- Print Preview
- Print
- Print Using
- Send
- Update
- Exit

Note that even in programs that don't handle files, you'll often see a File menu for one reason: The user expects to find the Exit item there. Don't forget to add an Exit item to your menu system. You can end a Visual Basic program using the End statement, so this menu item is easy to implement.

The Edit menu usually holds items like these:

- Undo
- Redo

- Cut
- Copy
- Paste
- Paste Using
- Paste Special
- Clear
- Select All
- Find
- Replace
- Bookmark
- Insert Object (unless you have a separate Insert menu)

The View menu contains items like these:

- Toolbar
- Status Bar
- Refresh
- Options

The Window menu usually holds items like these:

- New Window
- Cascade
- Tile Windows
- Arrange All
- Split
- List Of Windows

The Help menu has items like these:

- Help
- Help Index
- Help Table of Contents
- Search for Help On
- Web Support
- About

Creating A New Menu With The Menu Editor

In this topic, we'll see how to add a menu to a form. Select a form in the IDE (that is, click on the form) and open the Menu Editor by selecting the Tools|Menu Editor menu item. You can also select its icon on the toolbar (the icon displays the tooltip *Menu Editor*). The Visual Basic Menu Editor appears in Figure 11.2.

You need to provide only two items to create a new menu: the caption of the menu and its name. The **Caption** property holds the title of the menu (such as File), and the **Name** property holds the name you'll use for that menu in code (such as **mnuFile**).

TIP: Note that **mnu** is the Microsoft-recommended prefix for menus and menu items in code: For example, **mnuFile** is the name of a File menu. You name menu items by combining the **mnu** prefix, the name of the menu the item is in, and the item name; for example, **mnuFileOpen** is the name of the Open item in the File menu.

Fill in the **Caption** and **Name** properties for your new menu now. Congratulations—you've created a new menu with the Menu Editor. Now it's time to add items to the menu; see the next topic for more information.

Creating A New Menu Item With The Menu Editor

To add an item to a newly created menu, click on Next in the Menu Editor to move the highlighted bar in the menu-list box at the bottom of the Menu Editor down one line. If you entered new **Caption** and

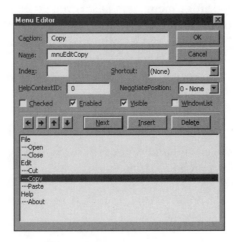

Figure 11.2   *The Visual Basic Menu Editor.*

Name values and left it at that, you'd create a new menu, not a new menu item. So, click on the right-arrow button in the Menu Editor to indent the next item four spaces in the menu-list box. Now, enter the **Caption** and **Name** values for the new menu item.

For example, if you've added an item named *New* to a File menu, the item you've just created appears in the Menu Editor indented like this:

```
File
....New
```

The Menu Editor displays your menu system as a series of indented items. For example, suppose your menu system includes a File menu with New and Open items and an Edit menu with Cut, Copy, and Paste items. This menu system would look like this in the Menu Editor:

```
File
....New
....Open
Edit
....Cut
....Copy
....Paste
```

Adding Code To Menu Items

You edit the code for a menu item just as you do for other controls—double-click on the menu item in the form you're designing (open the item's menu first, if necessary). Doing so opens the menu item's event handler, like this:

```
Private Sub mnuFileNew_Click()

End Sub
```

Now, add to the event-handler procedure the code you want to execute when the user chooses this menu item:

```
Private Sub mnuFileNew_Click()
    docCreateNewDocument
End Sub
```

And that's it—you're ready to code your menu items.

Creating Menu Separators

Menus themselves give you ways to group commands by function (File, Edit, and so on). But, it often helps the user if you group menu *items* by function within a menu (Print, Print Preview, Page Setup, and so on). You do that with *menu separators*.

A menu separator is a horizontal rule that has only one purpose—to divide menu items into groups. Using the Menu Editor, you can add separators to your menus.

To add a menu separator, select the menu item *before* which you want to add a separator, and then click on Insert to create a new item. To make this new item a menu separator, enter a hyphen (-) for its **Caption** property. You must give all menu items a name, even if they don't do anything, so give the separator a dummy **Name** property value, such as **mnuSeparator**.

When you run the program, you'll see the menu separators in place. See Figure 11.3 for an example of a menu with menu separator.

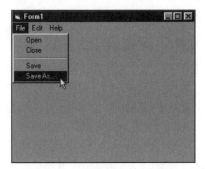

Figure 11.3   *A menu with menu separators.*

Rearranging Items In A Menu System

Using the Menu Editor, you can rearrange the items in a menu as you like. You use the four arrow buttons to move items up and down, as well as to indent or outdent (that is, remove one indent level) menu items. Here's what the arrows do:

- *Right arrow*—Indents a menu item
- *Left arrow*—Outdents a menu item

- *Up arrow*—Moves the currently selected item up one level
- *Down arrow*—Moves the currently selected item down one level

For example, to move the Save As item from the Edit menu to the File menu, you select that item and keep clicking on the up arrow until the item is positioned where you want it in the File menu.

Step By Step: Creating An Entire Menu System With The Menu Editor

Here's how to create a complete menu system in the Menu Editor:

1. Enter the first menu's **Caption** and **Name** properties.
2. Click on Next (or press Enter).
3. Click on the right arrow to indent one level, making this entry a menu item.
4. Enter the menu item's **Caption** and **Name** properties.
5. Click on Next (or press Enter).
6. Repeat Steps 4 and 5 for all the items in the first menu.
7. Click on Next (or press Enter).
8. Click on the left arrow to outdent, making this entry a menu.
9. Enter the next menu's **Caption** and **Name** properties.
10. Click on the right arrow to indent one level, making this entry a menu item.
11. Repeat Steps 4 and 5 for the items in the new menu.
12. Repeat Steps 7 through 11 for the rest of the menus in the program.
13. Click on OK to close the Menu Editor.
14. Edit the code.

Inserting Or Deleting Items In A Menu System

You can use the Menu Editor to add a new item to a menu or a new menu to the menu system. To do so, select the item *before* which you want to add a new item, and then click on Insert. This inserts a new, empty entry into the menu:

```
File
....New
....Open
....
Edit
....Cut
....Copy
....Paste
```

Now, enter the new item's **Caption** and **Name** properties, and you're all set.

To remove a menu or menu item, select that menu or item and click on Delete.

Inserting Access Characters With The Menu Editor

As their name implies, *access characters* give the user quick access to menu items. The user can use an access key combination to open the desired menu (such as Alt+F for the File menu) and then press Alt and the access character to select the associated menu item (such as Alt+O to select the Open item).

How do you connect an access character with a menu or menu item? In that menu or item's caption, you simply place an ampersand (&) in front of the character you want to make into the access character.

For example, suppose you had this menu system:

```
File
....New
....Open
Edit
....Cut
....Copy
....Paste
```

You could make the first letter of each menu or menu item into an access character by placing an ampersand in front of it:

```
&File
....&New
....&Open
&Edit
....&Cut
....C&opy
....&Paste
```

Note that two Edit menu items—Cut and Copy—begin with *C*. That's a problem, because an access character must be unique at its level (where the level is the menu bar for menus and a menu for menu items). To avoid confusion, you can make *O* (the second letter in *Copy*), the access character for that item.

The result of adding access characters to a menu appears in Figure 11.4.

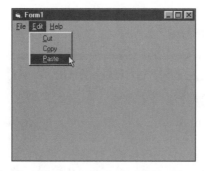

Figure 11.4   *Adding access characters to a menu.*

Inserting Shortcut Keys With The Menu Editor

Shortcut keys are single keys or key combinations that let the user execute a menu command immediately—without having to open the menu the command is in, as you must do with access keys.

You usually use function-key or Ctrl-key combinations for shortcut keys. For example, the standard shortcut key for Select All is Ctrl+A; entering that shortcut selects all the text in a document.

Giving a menu item a shortcut key is very easy in the Menu Editor. Open the Menu Editor, select the item to which you want to assign a shortcut key—such as the File menu's Open item in Figure 11.5—and select the shortcut key you want to use from the Shortcut box. In Figure 11.5, we assign the shortcut Ctrl+O to the Open item.

That's all it takes; now run the program, as shown in Figure 11.6. You can see *Ctrl+O* at right in the Open menu item—you've installed a new menu shortcut.

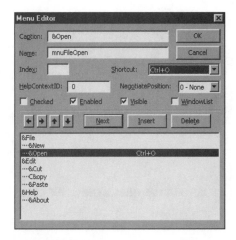

Figure 11.5   *Setting a shortcut key.*

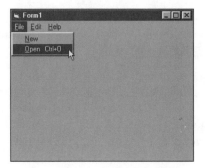

Figure 11.6   *A new shortcut key in a program's menu.*

Adding A Checkmark To A Menu Item

When you want to indicate toggling of an option in a program (such as Insert mode for entering text), it's easy to add or remove checkmarks in front of menu items. Displaying a checkmark gives the user visual feedback about the toggle state of the option.

To add a checkmark to a menu item at design time, you simply select the Checked box in the Menu Editor. For example, Figure 11.7 shows how to add a checkmark to the Edit menu's Overstrike item.

Now, when you first display the Edit menu at runtime, the Overstrike item will appear checked.

Figure 11.7   *Adding a checkmark to a menu item at design time.*

Creating Submenus With The Menu Editor

Submenus let you organize your menu system in a compact way. When a small arrow appears to the right of a menu item, this indicates that a submenu is attached to that menu item. Selecting the menu item opens the submenu, which appears as a menu attached to the main menu. As you can see in Figure 11.8, the small arrow next to the

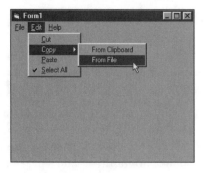

Figure 11.8   *A program with a submenu.*

Edit|Copy menu item indicates that a submenu is attached. Selecting the Edit|Copy menu item opens the submenu, which contains the items From Clipboard and From File.

Adding submenus to a program is simple; for example, let's say you started with From Clipboard and From File menu items in the Edit menu:

```
Edit
....Cut
....Copy
....From Clipboard
....From File
....Paste
...Select All
```

To put those items in a submenu, you indent them using the right arrow in the Menu Editor (note that they must appear just under the submenu's name):

```
Edit
....Cut
....Copy
........From Clipboard
........From File
....Paste
...Select All
```

That's it—now close the Menu Editor.

You add code to a submenu item the same way that you add code to a menu item—simply click on it to open the corresponding event-handler function and add the code you want. For instance, this code reports the user's submenu selection:

```
Private Sub mnuEditCopyFromClipboard_Click()
    MsgBox ("Copy made from clipboard")
End Sub

Private Sub mnuEditCopyFromFile_Click()
    MsgBox ("Copy made from file")
End Sub
```

Disabling Menu Items In The Menu Editor

To indicate to the user that a menu item isn't available at a particular time (such as the Copy item when the user hasn't selected any text), you can disable the menu item (also called *graying it out*).

To disable a menu item, deselect the Enabled box in the Menu Editor. For example, in Figure 11.9, the Copy menu item is disabled.

Now, when you first open the Edit menu, the Copy item will be disabled.

Figure 11.9   *Disabling a menu item.*

Creating Pop-Up Menus With The Menu Editor

Pop-up menus—menus that appear when you right-click on a form—have become very popular. To create a new pop-up menu, use the Menu Editor as shown in Figure 11.10. Here, we create a new menu named *Popup* that has two items in it: Message and Beep.

Note that setting this menu's **Visible** property to **False** ensures that this menu doesn't appear in the menu bar.

But, if the pop-up menu doesn't appear in the menu bar, how can you add code to its menu items?

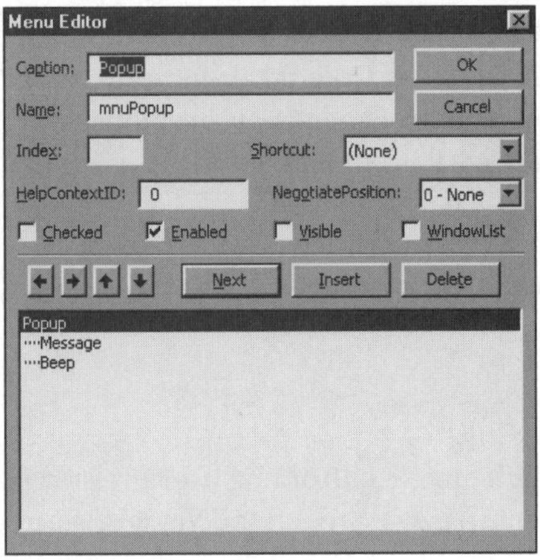

Figure 11.10 *Designing a pop-up menu.*

You can reach those two menu items—**mnuPopupMessage** and **mnuPopupBeep**—in the code window. Double-click on the form now to open the code window. The left drop-down list box in the code window lists all the objects on the form; find **mnuPopupMessage** and **mnuPopupBeep** and add event-handling functions to their **Click** events:

```
Private Sub mnuPopupBeep_Click()

End Sub


Private Sub mnuPopupMessage_Click()

End Sub
```

Let's make the Beep item beep and the Message item display a message box acknowledging the user's action:

```
Private Sub mnuPopupBeep_Click()
    Beep
End Sub

Private Sub mnuPopupMessage_Click()
    MsgBox ("You selected the Message item")
End Sub
```

That completes the design of the pop-up menu—but how do you display it when the user right-clicks on the form? See the next topic.

Displaying A Pop-Up Menu

When the user right-clicks the mouse, you can display a pop-up menu. In this case, you want to check for right-mouse-button events; to do so, add a **MouseDown** event handler to your program using the code window:

```
Private Sub Form_MouseDown(Button As Integer, Shift As _
    Integer, X As Single, Y As Single)

End Sub
```

You can tell which mouse button the user pressed by comparing the **Button** argument to these predefined Visual Basic constants:

- *vbLeftButton*—1
- *vbRightButton*—2
- *vbMiddleButton*—4

The following code checks for the right mouse button:

```
Private Sub Form_MouseDown(Button As Integer, Shift As _
    Integer, X As Single, Y As Single)
    If Button = vbRightButton Then
        .
        .
        .
    End If
End Sub
```

If the right mouse button was pressed, display the pop-up menu with the **PopupMenu** method:

```
[object.]PopupMenu menuname [, flags [,x [, y [, _
    boldcommand]]]]
```

Here, ***menuname*** is the name of the menu to open, ***x*** and ***y*** indicate a position for the menu, and ***boldcommand*** is the name of the one (but no more than one) menu item you want to appear bold. The possible values for the *flags* parameter appear in Table 11.1.

Here's how to use **PopupMenu**:

```
Private Sub Form_MouseDown(Button As Integer, Shift As _
    Integer, X As Single, Y As Single)
    If Button = vbRightButton Then
        PopupMenu mnuPopup
```

```
      End If
   End Sub
```

That's it—the result appears in Figure 11.11.

Table 11.1   PopupMenu constants.

Constant	Does This
vbPopupMenuLeftAlign	Default. The specified *x* location defines the left edge of the pop-up menu.
vbPopupMenuCenterAlign	The pop-up menu is centered around the specified *x* location.
vbPopupMenuRightAlign	The specified *x* location defines the right edge of the pop-up menu.
vbPopupMenuLeftButton	Default. The pop-up menu is displayed when the user clicks on a menu item with the left mouse button.
vbPopupMenuRightButton	The pop-up menu is displayed when the user clicks on a menu item with either the right or left mouse button.

Figure 11.11   A pop-up menu at work.

Chapter 12

The Debugger

In Brief

In this chapter, we'll look at debugging your programs. As a programmer, you know what you want a program to do, but sometimes it's hard to convince Visual Basic to do it correctly—and that's where the debugging process comes in.

Visual Basic provides programmers with a debugger that's hard to beat. You can debug programs interactively, working through your code line by line as the program runs. This powerful technique lets you work behind the scenes in a way that's invaluable when it comes to seeing what's going wrong.

You can also specify where to begin debugging a program by adding *breakpoints*—tags on lines of code that tell Visual Basic to halt your program and start debugging.

In this chapter, we'll see how to set and use breakpoints, execute code line by line, execute code up to a specified line, watch variables as they change, and more.

Catching Errors At Runtime

Visual Basic also lets you catch many errors at runtime—a process called *trapping*—and we'll look into that here. In addition, when we catch an error at runtime, we'll see how to recover from that error without crashing the program. Handling runtime errors is usually a part of any commercially released Visual Basic program, because Visual Basic handles such errors by displaying information that's useful only to the programmer. Visual Basic lets you handle runtime errors by trapping them with special code; these errors are referred to as *trappable* errors. In this chapter, we'll cover how to write code to trap such errors.

That's it for the overview—now it's time to turn to the Immediate Solutions part of this chapter.

Immediate Solutions

Stress-Test Your Programs

Before you release your programs for others to use, you'll probably want to test them. Doing so can involve a large investment of time—an investment many programmers are reluctant to make.

It helps if you're smart about how you approach the task. If your program operates on numeric data, you should test the bounds of variable ranges; for example, it's easy to forget that the limits of Visual Basic integers (which are only two-byte variables) are -32,768 to 32,767. Entering values like these, or values outside that range, can help test possible danger points. You can perform a bounds check for every crucial variable in your program.

Of course, you should check mid-range values as well, because it may turn out that some combination of values gives you unexpected errors.

File operations are notorious for generating errors—what if the disk is full and you try to write to it? What if the file the user wants to read in doesn't exist? What if the output file turns out to be read-only? You should address and check all these considerations.

Besides these kinds of programming checks, determining the logic danger points of a program is also very important. For example, if your program has an array of data and you let the user average sections of that data by entering the number of cells to average, what will happen if the user enters a value of 0? Or -100?

In addition, be wary of the perennial Visual Basic error: misspelling a variable name and, as a result, unintentionally declaring a new implicit variable.

Besides testing the software yourself, it's often a good idea to release beta versions of the software to be tested by other programmers or potential users.

If you do a lot of programming, you'll begin to feel that, inevitably, some user will come up with exactly the bad data set or operation that will crash your program. You might even dread the letters forwarded to you from your company's Customer Relations department.

It's far better to catch all possible problems before the program goes out the door—which is what stress-testing your software is all about.

The longer you test your program under usual—and unusual—operating circumstances, the more confidence you'll have that things are working as they should.

Debugging Without The Debugger

Want to save a little time debugging? Often, the crucial aspect of debugging is watching the values in your variables change as your program executes. Sometimes, doing that without the debugger is easy enough: Simply add some temporary text boxes or message boxes to your program and use them to display the values you want to watch. This is an expedient shortcut for simple bugs—but if it doesn't fit the bill for you, turn to the debugger.

Setting A Breakpoint

Breakpoints are the foundation of Visual Basic debugging. When you set breakpoints in a program and run that program, execution continues until a breakpoint is encountered. Then, program execution stops, making Visual Basic enter the Debug state.

You place a breakpoint in code by moving the text-insertion cursor to that line and either selecting the Debug|Toggle Breakpoint menu item or pressing F9. Breakpoints toggle, so to remove the breakpoint, select Debug|Toggle Breakpoint or press F9 again.

When you place a breakpoint in code, it appears at design time in red (see Figure 12.1).

When you run the program and reach the breakpoint, execution stops. Visual Basic now appears in the Debug state, as shown in Figure 12.2. You can see the breakpoint highlighted in that figure; the arrow in the left margin of the code window points to the current line of execution.

You can execute the lines following a breakpoint by single-stepping. We'll take a look at that process in the next topic.

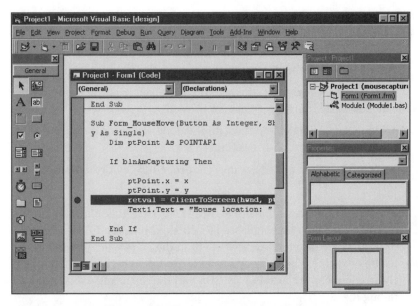

Figure 12.1 *Setting a breakpoint in code at design time.*

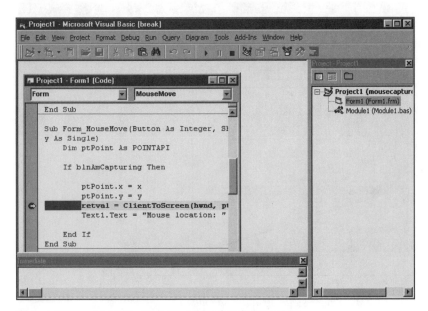

Figure 12.2 *A breakpoint in Visual Basic's Debug state.*

Debugging By Single-Stepping

When your code stops at a breakpoint, you can move through the code with these single-stepping options in the Debug menu:

- *Step Into*—Single-step through the code, entering called procedures if encountered. Shortcut: press F8.

- *Step Over*—Single-step through the code, stepping over procedure calls. Shortcut: press Shift+F8.

- *Step Out*—Step out of the current procedure. Shortcut: press Ctrl+Shift+F8.

For an example, refer back to Figure 12.2. Visual Basic has stopped at a breakpoint but can single-step to the next line, as shown in Figure 12.3. As you can see, the arrow at left in the code window has moved to the next line; Visual Basic has executed the previous line of code. By single-stepping in this way, you can move through your code to debug it.

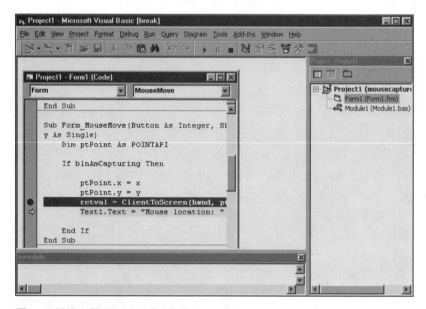

Figure 12.3   Single-stepping in Debug mode.

Examining The Value Of An Expression While Debugging

Debugging gives you a useful "behind-the-scenes" view of your code. You can take a look at the value of an expression—including an individual variable—with the Quick Watch window.

To examine the value in a variable or expression in the code window when execution has stopped at a breakpoint, select the variable or expression you want to examine with the mouse and choose the Debug|Quick Watch menu item. Doing so opens the Quick Watch window, shown in Figure 12.4. You can see the value of the variable named **x** in that window.

Besides quick watches, you can use the Immediate window, as we'll see in the next topic.

Figure 12.4 *Examining a variable with a Quick Watch window.*

Evaluating Expressions Using The Immediate Window

You can use the Immediate window to examine expressions or variables immediately, simply by typing them in. The Immediate window appears at lower left when Visual Basic is in its Debug state, as shown in Figure 12.5.

You can enter an expression to evaluate in the Immediate window by preceding it with a question mark and then pressing the Enter key. For example, here's how to check the value of a variable named **x**:

```
?x
```

Visual Basic displays the values of the expression you're examining in the Immediate window on the line after your query. For instance, in Figure 12.5, **x** holds a value of 299.

12: The Debugger

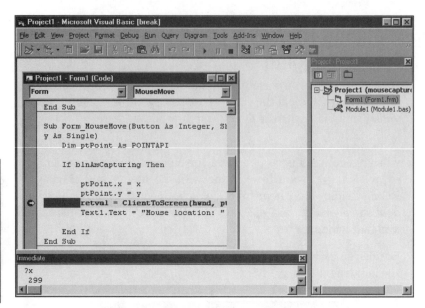

Figure 12.5   *The Immediate debugging window appears at lower left when Visual Basic is in its Debug state.*

You can also test the value of expressions; here's how to check the value of the expression **x + 1**:

```
?x + 1
```

Using The Watches Window In The Debugger

Here's a powerful aspect of the Visual Basic debugger: You can display the values of selected variables or expressions continuously as you execute your program by adding the Watches window to your debugging session.

To add the Watches window, select the variable or expression you want to watch with the mouse and choose the Debug|Add Watch menu item. Doing so opens the Add Watch dialog box; be sure the variable or expression you want to watch appears in the Expression box and click on OK. When you do, Visual Basic adds the Watches window to the debug session, as you can see at the bottom of Figure 12.6, where we're watching the value of the variable **x**.

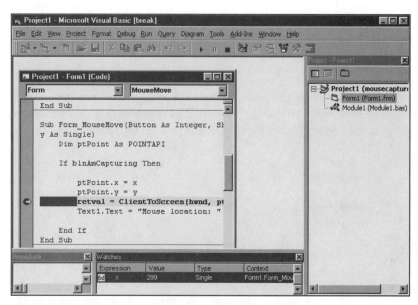

Figure 12.6 *A Watches window joins the debug session.*

Being able to continuously watch the values of your program's variables as the program executes can be a great asset in debugging, because you can see unexpected values as they appear.

Using The Debugger: An Example

This topic summarizes information from some of the previous topics and gives you an example of the power of the Visual Basic debugger—notably, the ability to single-step through your code as it executes.

The most common way to debug is to place a *breakpoint* at a particular line in your code. When execution reaches that line, it will halt; Visual Basic will then enter the Debug state, giving you access to your code and variables. You can examine the contents of those variables and work through your code line by line, watching program execution behind the scenes.

For example, you might write the following code, which is meant to increment the value in text box **Text1** each time you click on a button:

```
Private Sub Command1_Click()
    Dim intCounter As Integer
```

```
        intCounter = intCounter + 1
        Text1.Text = intCounter

End Sub
```

Instead, the value 1 appears in the text box each time you click on the button. It's time to debug! To start that process, place a breakpoint (see the "Setting A Breakpoint" topic) at this line in the code:

```
Private Sub Command1_Click()
        Dim intCounter As Integer

        intCounter = intCounter + 1
        Text1.Text = intCounter

End Sub
```

Now, when you run the program and click on the button, execution halts at the breakpoint, and the code window appears. See the "Examining The Value Of An Expression While Debugging" topic for information on how to examine the contents of individual variables or entire expressions on the screen.

To move through your program step by step, you can select from three options in the Debug menu (see the "Debugging By Single-Stepping" topic).

Examining the contents of the **intCounter** variable shows that it's being reset to zero each time the code runs. You should declare that variable as static, this way:

```
Private Sub Command1_Click()
        Static intCounter As Integer

        intCounter = intCounter + 1
        Text1.Text = intCounter

End Sub
```

That's the process in overview—we've debugged the code.

Clearing All Breakpoints

If you have a large number of breakpoints in a program, you might be relieved to learn that you can clear them all at once: Simply choose the Debug|Clear All Breakpoints menu item. The shortcut for this menu item is Ctrl+Shift+F9.

Skipping Over Code

While you're debugging, you can skip over lines of code that you've already proofed. To do that, just click on the line of code at which you want execution to begin (after having skipped the lines you don't want to execute) and choose the Debug|Set Next Statement menu item.

You can also skip over code while single-stepping, using these Debug menu options:

- *Step Over*—Single-step through the code, stepping over procedure calls. Shortcut: press Shift+F8.
- *Step Out*—Step out of the current procedure. Shortcut: press Ctrl+Shift+F8.

Executing Up To The Cursor

During a debugging session, it can be tedious to single-step through many lines of code. You have another option, however—click on a line of code to place the text-insertion cursor at that line, and then select the Debug|Run To Cursor menu item. When you do, execution continues to the line you've selected.

Handling Trappable Errors

When a trappable error occurs, you can direct the execution of your program to an *error handler*—a section of code written specifically to deal with errors.

File handling is an area of programming very susceptible to runtime errors; let's write an example that will open a file and display its contents in a text box, as well as handle file errors.

When the user clicks on a button (**Command1**), you can display an
Open dialog box using a common dialog control (**CommonDialog1**):

```
Private Sub Command1_Click()
    With CommonDialog1

        .ShowOpen
            .
            .
            .
    End With
End Sub
```

In that dialog box, the user enters the name of the file to open; you
then open the file, read the text in the file, display the text in a multiline
text box with scroll bars (**Text1**, with its **Multiline** property set to
True and its **Scrollbars** property set to **Both**), and close the file:

```
Private Sub Command1_Click()
    With CommonDialog1

        .ShowOpen
        Open .FileName For Input As #1
        Text1.Text = Input$(LOF(1), #1)

        Close #1

    End With
End Sub
```

To handle errors, add an **On Error GoTo** statement. For example,
the following code indicates that the error-handling code will begin
at the label **FileError**:

```
Private Sub Command1_Click()

    On Error GoTo FileError

    With CommonDialog1

        .ShowOpen
        Open .FileName For Input As #1
        Text1.Text = Input$(LOF(1), #1)

        Close #1

    End With
```

Next, add that label—**FileError**—and indicate with a message box that a file error occurred:

```
Private Sub Command1_Click()

    On Error GoTo FileError

    With CommonDialog1

        .ShowOpen
        Open .FileName For Input As #1
        Text1.Text = Input$(LOF(1), #1)

        Close #1

    End With

FileError:
    MsgBox "File Error"
End Sub
```

You must also prevent execution of the normal code from continuing into the error handler. To do so, add an **Exit Sub** statement to the code before that error handler:

```
Private Sub Command1_Click()

    On Error GoTo FileError

    With CommonDialog1

        .ShowOpen
        Open .FileName For Input As #1
        Text1.Text = Input$(LOF(1), #1)

        Close #1

    End With

    Exit Sub

FileError:
    MsgBox "File Error"
End Sub
```

That's it—your error handler is in place. Now, if an error occurs, a message box with the message *File Error* will appear.

Customizing Error-Handling Code

In the previous topic, we used very rudimentary code in our error handler, but error handlers can be much more complex. For example, you can get the actual error code of the trappable error using the Visual Basic **Err** object's **Number** property, and you can make that number the basis of a Visual Basic **Select Case** statement to take the appropriate action depending on which error occurred.

For example, the following code specifically handles two types of errors: the case in which the user clicks on Cancel in the common dialog box (you must set the common dialog control's **CancelError** property to **True** for the common dialog control to generate an error when the user clicks on Cancel), and the case in which Visual Basic can't find the file to open:

```
Private Sub Command1_Click()

    On Error GoTo FileError

    With CommonDialog1

        .ShowOpen
        Open .FileName For Input As #1
        Text1.Text = Input$(LOF(1), #1)

        Close #1

    End With

    Exit Sub

FileError:
    Select Case Err.Number
        Case cdlCancel
            MsgBox "Please select a file."
            Resume
        Case 53
            MsgBox "File not found"
        Case Default
            MsgBox "File Error"
    End Select

End Sub
```

Now you're able to indicate to the user what error occurred.

Jumping To A Specific Code Location When Errors Occur

How do you make execution jump to a specific line of code when an error occurs? You use the Visual Basic **On Error GoTo** statement. When you execute an **On Error GoTo** *Label* statement in your code, execution is transferred to the code starting at *Label* if a trappable error has occurred. The code following that label is your error handler.

Let's look at an example to make this clear. This code executes a statement indicating that error-handling code begins at the label **FileError**:

```
Private Sub Command1_Click()

    On Error GoTo FileError
    .
    .
    .
```

Now, if an error occurs, you'll transfer program execution to the code that follows the label **FileError**. Error-trapping is enabled for all this code:

```
Private Sub Command1_Click()

    On Error GoTo FileError

    With CommonDialog1

        .ShowOpen
        Open .FileName For Input As #1
        Text1.Text = Input$(LOF(1), #1)

        Close #1

    End With

    Exit Sub
    .
    .
    .
```

The actual error-handling code follows the label **FileError**, like this:

```
Private Sub Command1_Click()

    On Error GoTo FileError

    With CommonDialog1

        .ShowOpen
        Open .FileName For Input As #1
        Text1.Text = Input$(LOF(1), #1)

        Close #1

    End With

    Exit Sub

FileError:
    Select Case Err.Number
        Case cdlCancel
            MsgBox "Please select a file."
            Resume
        Case 53
            MsgBox "File not found"
        Case Default
            MsgBox "File Error"
    End Select

End Sub
```

Resuming Execution After Handling An Error

When you're writing code for an error handler, you can return control to the main body of the procedure by using the **Resume** statement. Program execution starts again with the line that caused the error—and this can be very valuable if you're able to fix the error in the error handler.

For example, suppose your code opens a file that the user has selected with a common dialog Open dialog box. If the user clicks on Cancel, instead, you can display a message box with the text *Please select a file* and use the **Resume** statement to redisplay the Open dialog box. You do that by trapping the error generated when the user clicks on Cancel in the Open dialog box (set the common dialog control's **CancelError** property to **True** to ensure that a trappable error is generated when the user clicks on Cancel):

```
Private Sub Command1_Click()

    On Error GoTo FileError

    With CommonDialog1

        .ShowOpen
        Open .FileName For Input As #1
        Text1.Text = Input$(LOF(1), #1)

        Close #1

    End With

    Exit Sub

FileError:

    Select Case Err.Number
        Case cdlCancel
            MsgBox "Please select a file."
            Resume
        Case 53
            MsgBox "File not found"
        Case Default
            MsgBox "File Error"
    End Select

End Sub
```

Resuming Execution At A Specific Line After Handling An Error

When you're writing code for an error handler, you can return control to a particular line in the main body of the procedure by using the **Resume *Label*** statement. To label a line, just place the label's text directly into the code, followed by a colon (:).

Let's look at an example. The following code uses the **Resume *Label*** statement to retry a file-open operation if the user clicks on Cancel in the Open dialog box, using the label **TryAgain** (to make the common dialog Open dialog box return a trappable error if the user clicks on the Cancel button, set the common dialog control's **CancelError** property to **True**):

```
Private Sub Command1_Click()

    On Error GoTo FileError

    With CommonDialog1
TryAgain:
        .ShowOpen
        Open .FileName For Input As #1
        Text1.Text = Input$(LOF(1), #1)
        Close #1

    End With

    Exit Sub

FileError:

    Select Case Err.Number
        Case cdlCancel
            MsgBox "Please select a file."
            Resume TryAgain
        Case 53
            MsgBox "File not found"
        Case Default
            MsgBox "File Error"
    End Select

End Sub
```

Resume *Label* is useful if you're able to fix a trappable error in an error handler and want to resume execution at some specific line in the code. (Note that if you want to resume execution with the next line of code, it's easier to use the **Resume Next** statement.)

Turning Off Error-Trapping

To turn off error-trapping, you can use the **On Error GoTo 0** statement.

For example, the following code turns on error-trapping to catch the case in which the user clicks on Cancel in a common dialog control's Font dialog box (to make the Cancel button generate a trappable error, set the common dialog control's **CancelError** property to **True**); the code turns off error-trapping if the user doesn't click on Cancel:

```
Private Sub Command1_Click()
    On Error GoTo Cancel
    CommonDialog1.Flags = cdlCFBoth Or cdlCFEffects
    CommonDialog1.ShowFont
    On Error GoTo 0

    Text1.FontName = CommonDialog1.FontName
    Text1.FontBold = CommonDialog1.FontBold
    Text1.FontItalic = CommonDialog1.FontItalic
    Text1.FontUnderline = CommonDialog1.FontUnderline
    Text1.FontSize = CommonDialog1.FontSize
    Text1.FontName = CommonDialog1.FontName
Cancel:
End Sub
```

Part III

Common Tasks

Chapter 13

Multiple Forms, MDI, And Dialog Boxes

In Brief

In this chapter, we're going to take a look at some powerful window-handling techniques in Visual Basic: handling multiple forms, the Multiple Document Interface (MDI), and creating dialog boxes.

All three of these topics are very popular. For example, it's a rare professional program that doesn't support multiple windows or dialog boxes. MDI programs are also very common; a good example of an MDI program is the Visual Basic IDE itself. Let's take a look at these three areas of Visual Basic programming in a little more detail now.

Multiple Forms

All but the most basic Windows applications support more than one window, even if it's only to use dialog boxes (which you handle with multiple-form techniques in Visual Basic). Because each form has its own module in Visual Basic, coordinating multiple forms means working with code across several code modules; we'll see the techniques for doing that here.

Managing multiple forms means being able to open or close other forms in code, as well as determining which form is currently active. You'll also work with collections like the Visual Basic **Forms** collection, which holds an application's forms in an easily accessible format.

After you work with multiple forms, the next step is to corral those forms into one window: an MDI window.

MDI Forms

Besides standard forms, Visual Basic also supports Multiple Document Interface (MDI) forms; an MDI form appears in Figure 13.1.

You can see that an MDI form looks much like a standard form, with one major difference: The client area of an MDI form acts like a kind of holding pen for other forms. That is, an MDI form can display MDI child forms within itself, which is how the multiple-document interface works. In Figure 13.1, a document is open in the MDI form. This document is itself an MDI child form—these forms appear in MDI child windows, but otherwise are very much like standard forms.

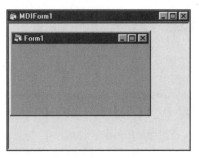

Figure 13.1 *An MDI form.*

Dialog Boxes

Every Windows user is familiar with dialog boxes—they're those special windows that applications display to get input from the user. In pre-Windows applications, users could type their input line by line into the application. However, Windows works differently—you use controls like text boxes and buttons to get input from the user, and very often it isn't appropriate to display those controls at all times.

For example, you'd hardly want the controls for changing printers always visible in a word-processor program (Windows is often crowded enough for most users, and it's important to simplify what's going on as much as possible). To unclutter the screen, you would put those controls into a dialog box that the program can display on the screen when needed.

Each dialog box should have (ideally) a single purpose. Examples of those purposes include printing a document, setting drawing colors, indicating an error condition, displaying print previews, getting text information from the user, setting fonts, opening files, and thousands of others. As long as Windows is around, there will be dialog boxes.

In this chapter, we'll attend to the special handling dialog boxes require, such as setting up a dialog box, making a dialog box *modal* (that is, requiring the user to dismiss the dialog box before continuing with the rest of the program), using the Visual Basic predefined dialog form, and more.

That's all the overview we need—it's time to turn to the Immediate Solutions part of this chapter.

Immediate Solutions

Adding A New Form To A Program

You begin working with multiple forms by adding those forms to your program. To add a new form, select the Project|Add Form menu item to open the Add Form dialog box shown in Figure 13.2.

You can select the type of form in the Add Form dialog box; when you click on Open, Visual Basic adds the form to your project. Figure 13.3 shows a new form added to a project.

For details on how to display your new form, see the next topic.

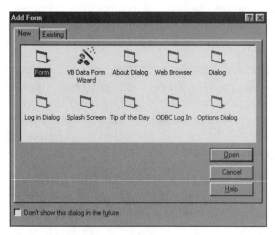

Figure 13.2   *The Add Form dialog box.*

Showing And Hiding Multiple Forms

To show a form on screen, use the **Show** method; here's an example that loads a new form (**Form2**) and then shows it:

```
Private Sub Command1_Click()
    Load Form2
    Form2.Show
End Sub
```

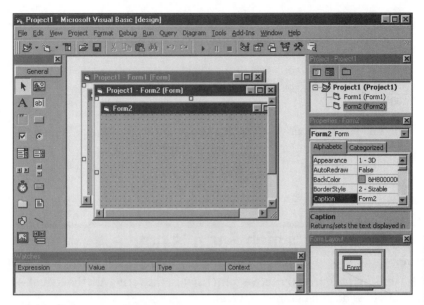

Figure 13.3   *A two-form project.*

After displaying a form, you can hide it with the **Hide** method and
unload it (although doing so isn't necessary) with the **Unload** statement. You usually unload forms if you have many of them and are
concerned about memory usage. Here's an example that hides **Form2**
and then unloads it:

```
Private Sub Command2_Click()
    Form2.Hide
    Unload Form2
End Sub
```

If you hide all windows in a Visual Basic program that has no **Main**
procedure in a module, the program will end.

Handling Multiple Forms

Let's say you need a second form (**Form2**) in your program, and that
form has a text box (**Text1**) in it. How can you reach that text box
from code in **Form1**, the program's main form?

In multiple-form programs, you have to specify the form you want to
work with if it isn't the current form. For example, to place the text

Hello from Visual Basic in **Form2**'s text box **Text1** from code in **Form1**, you can refer to that text box as **Form2.Text1** this way:

```
Private Sub Command1_Click()
    Form2.Text1.Text = "Hello from Visual Basic"
End Sub
```

In this way, you can work with multiple forms in a Visual Basic program. Just remember that you have to specify what form you want to work with if it isn't the current form—that's all there is to it.

Determining Which Form Is Active

Now, you have a multiform program and need to work with the controls on the currently active form (that is, the form with the focus)—but how do you determine which form is active?

You can use the Visual Basic Screen object's **ActiveForm** property to determine which form is active. For example, say you have a clock program with two forms (**Form1** and **Form2**), each of which has a label control (**Label1**) in which you can display the current time using a timer (**Timer1**). However, you'll update the time only in the active form—and the user can switch between the forms simply by clicking on them with the mouse.

To display the time, add the timer **Timer1** to **Form1** and set its **Interval** property to 1000 (as measured in milliseconds). Now you can use the **Label1** control in the currently active form in the timer's **Timer** event this way:

```
Private Sub Timer1_Timer()
    Screen.ActiveForm.Label1.Caption = Format(Now, _
        "hh:mm:ss")
End Sub
```

You also ensure that the second form—**Form2**—is shown when the program loads with **Form1**'s **Load** event:

```
Private Sub Form_Load()
    Form2.Show
End Sub
```

Now, when you click on one of the two forms, that form displays and updates the time; when you click on the other form, that form takes over.

Minimizing And Maximizing Forms In Code

To exert a little more control over the windows in your programs, you can set the **WindowState** property to maximize or minimize them. Here are the possible settings for that property and what they mean:

- *0*—Normal
- *1*—Minimized
- *2*—Maximized

The following example minimizes a form when the user clicks on a button:

```
Private Sub Command1_Click()
    WindowState = 1
End Sub
```

You can also set the **Enabled** property to enable or disable a window (when it's disabled, it will only beep if the user tries to give it the focus). You set the **Enabled** property to **True** to enable a window and to **False** to disable it.

Using The Visual Basic **Forms** Collection

You can loop over all the forms in a multiple-form application using the Visual Basic Global object's **Forms** collection.

Let's see an example that displays three forms, **Form1**, **Form2**, and **Form3**. The project displays **Form2** and **Form3** when **Form1** loads:

```
Private Sub Form_Load()
    Form2.Show
    Form3.Show
End Sub
```

Now, when the user clicks on a button in **Form1** named, say, **CloseAll**, you can hide all open forms using the **Forms** collection:

```
Private Sub CloseAll_Click()
    For Each Form In Forms
        Form.Hide
    Next Form
End Sub
```

Related solutions:	Found in:
Determining The Number Of Items In A Collection	Chapter 3
Using The **For Each** Statement	Chapter 5

Setting A Form's Startup Position

You can set the position of a form when it's first displayed by positioning it in the Visual Basic IDE's Form Layout window or by setting the **StartUpPosition** property at design time (this property isn't available at runtime). **StartUpPosition** has these possible values:

- *vbStartUpManual (0)*—No initial setting specified.
- *vbStartUpOwner (1)*—Center the form on the item to which the form belongs.
- *vbStartUpScreen (2)*—Center the form within the entire screen.
- *vbStartUpWindowsDefault (3)*—Position the form in the upper-left corner of the screen (the default).

Note, of course, that you can also position a form in the form's **Load** event handler by setting its **Left** and **Top** properties.

Creating Multiple Document Interface Programs

MDI frame windows can display multiple child windows within themselves; in fact, the Visual Basic IDE is an MDI frame window.

For example, if you already have a program based on a single form (**Form1**) and you want to make that form into an MDI child window within an MDI frame, follow these steps:

1. Add a new MDI form to the project by choosing the Project|Add MDI Form menu item.

2. Set the **MDIChild** property of the form you want to use as the MDI child form to **True**, as shown in Figure 13.4.

3. Run the program; the form you've made into an MDI child form appears in the MDI form.

That's all there is to it—now you're using MDI forms.

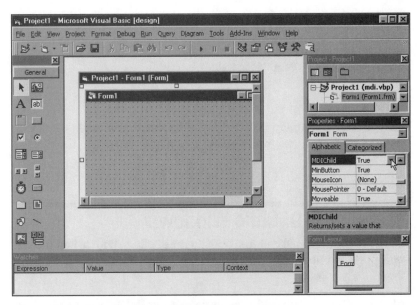

Figure 13.4   *Setting a form's **MDIChild** property to **True**.*

Using Different Types Of MDI Child Windows

In Visual Basic, you can use all kinds of MDI children in an MDI form, as long as each child form's **MDIChild** property is set to **True**. In other words, you can use different types of forms as MDI children in the same program. You can also use **Show** and **Hide** on those windows to manage them as you like.

Opening A New MDI Child Window

You can open multiple documents in an MDI frame window in one of two ways. First, you can create all the forms you want to use at design time and set each form's **Visible** property to **False** so it doesn't appear when the program starts. When you want to show or hide a form, use the **Show** or **Hide** method.

You can also create new forms as needed. For example, this code creates and displays a new MDI child form (assuming **Form1**'s **MDIChild** property is set to **True**) and sets its caption:

```
Private Sub NewWindow_Click()
    Dim NewForm As Form1
    Set NewForm = New Form1
    NewForm.Caption = "Document"
    NewForm.Show
End Sub
```

If you want to display text in a new child form, you might use a rich text box to cover the form's client area when you design it.

Arranging MDI Child Windows

You can arrange MDI children with their **Left**, **Top**, **Width**, and **Height** properties, but there's an easier way—you can use the MDI form method **Arrange**.

For example, if you add a menu item to an MDI form named, say, **ArrangeAll**, you can use the **Arrange** method to cascade all the windows in the form:

```
Private Sub ArrangeAll_Click()
    Me.Arrange vbCascade
End Sub
```

Using this method results in a standard cascade arrangement of the MDI child windows.

The possible values you can pass to **Arrange** to specify the way you want to arrange MDI children appear in Table 13.1.

Table 13.1   Ways of arranging MDI child windows.

Constant	Value	Does This
vbCascade	0	Cascades all nonminimized MDI child forms
vbTileHorizontal	1	Tiles all nonminimized MDI child forms horizontally
vbTileVertical	2	Tiles all nonminimized MDI child forms vertically
vbArrangeIcons	3	Arranges icons for minimized MDI child forms

Creating Arrays Of Forms

Wouldn't it be nice if you could use arrays of forms in Visual Basic and simply refer to each form with a single array index? Being able to do so would certainly help when working with multiple forms in MDI programs.

In fact, you *can* use arrays of forms in Visual Basic—you create an array of forms just as you would create an array of any other kind of object. This example creates an array of **Form1** objects, because that's the type of form you'll use as MDI children in an MDI program:

```
Dim Forms(1 To 20) As Form1
```

If you declare this **Forms** array as a form-level array in the MDI form, you can refer to that array in all procedures in the MDI form. For example, you might want to create and display a new MDI child form in a procedure named **mnuViewNewWindow_Click( )**:

```
Private Sub mnuViewNewWindow_Click()


End Sub
```

Next, you set up a static variable (**NumberForms**) to hold the total number of MDI child forms and increment that variable when you add a new form:

```
Private Sub mnuViewNewWindow_Click()
    Static NumberForms
    NumberForms = NumberForms + 1
    .
    .
    .
End Sub
```

Now, create a new form and add it to the form array:

```
Private Sub mnuViewNewWindow_Click()
    Static NumberForms
    NumberForms = NumberForms + 1
    Set Forms(NumberForms) = New Form1
    .
    .
    .
End Sub
```

Throughout the rest of the program, you can refer to the new form as a member of the form array. For example, this code sets the new form's caption and shows it, referring to it with an index value in the form array:

```
Private Sub mnuViewNewWindow_Click()
    Static NumberForms
    NumberForms = NumberForms + 1
    Set Forms(NumberForms) = New Form1
    Forms(NumberForms).Caption = "Document" & Str(NumberForms)
    Forms(NumberForms).Show
End Sub
```

Adding A Dialog Box To A Project

To add a dialog box to a project, select the Project|Add Form menu item. You could add a simple form and make it into a dialog box, but Visual Basic provides a predefined dialog box form, named **Dialog**, so select that option in the Add Form box and click on Open.

Doing so adds a new dialog box to the project, as shown in Figure 13.5.

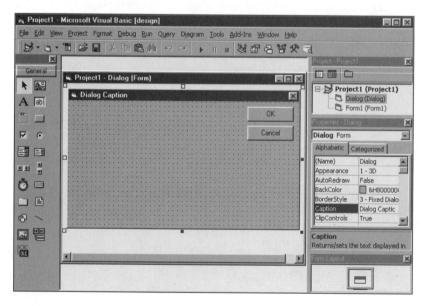

Figure 13.5   A new dialog box.

This dialog box comes with OK and Cancel buttons. Its **BorderStyle** property is set to 3, which gives it a fixed dialog-style border with only one control button: a close button.

In the next topic, we'll see how to use this dialog box in code.

Reading Values From A Dialog Box

In this topic, we'll work with the dialog box created in the last topic. Here, we'll see how to read data the user enters into the dialog box.

Add a text box (**Text1**) to the dialog box, as shown in Figure 13.5. Next, declare a **Public** string (**Feedback**) in the dialog box's (General) section; this string will hold the text that the user gives as feedback:

```
Public Feedback As String
```

When the dialog box opens, you can initialize **Feedback** to the empty string:

```
Private Sub Form_Load()
    Feedback = ""
End Sub
```

If the user clicks on Cancel, you'll leave the text in **Feedback** as the empty string and just hide the dialog box:

```
Private Sub CancelButton_Click()
    Hide
End Sub
```

On the other hand, if the user clicks on OK, you'll fill the **Feedback** string with the characters the user has typed into the text box and then hide the dialog box:

```
Private Sub OKButton_Click()
    Feedback = Text1.Text
    Hide
End Sub
```

That completes the dialog box.

In the program's main form, you can show the dialog box when required. You'll pass a value of 1 to the **Show** method, which displays the dialog box as *modal*, which means that the user must dismiss the dialog box before continuing with the rest of the program. (The default value passed to **Show** is 0, which displays windows in a nonmodal way.) The code to show the dialog box is as follows:

```
Private Sub Command1_Click()
    Dialog.Show 1
    .
    .
    .
End Sub
```

Next, you can display the feedback that the user has given (if any) by examining the dialog box's **Feedback** string this way:

```
Private Sub Command1_Click()
    Dialog.Show 1
    Text1.Text = Dialog.Feedback
End Sub
```

And that's it—now you're supporting dialog boxes, as shown in Figure 13.6.

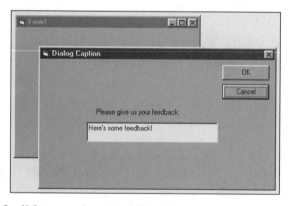

Figure 13.6   *Using a newly created dialog box.*

Making A Dialog Box Modal

When you simply use the **Show** method to display a dialog box, that dialog box works like any other form—the user can switch to other windows in the application before finishing with the dialog box.

Sometimes, you want to be sure the user finishes with a dialog box before moving on to other forms in the application; you do that by making the dialog box *modal*.

Doing this is easy; if you pass a value of 1 to the **Show** method, that method displays the dialog box as modal:

```
Private Sub Command1_Click()
    Dialog.Show 1
        .
        .
        .
End Sub
```

Always Provide A Cancel Button

Keep in mind this good rule for constructing dialog boxes: Always add a Cancel button, so that if users open a dialog box by mistake, they can close it without consequences.

Keeping A Dialog Box's Icon Out Of The Windows Taskbar

Windows treats a dialog box much like any other window, and that includes displaying an icon for the dialog box in the Windows Taskbar when the dialog box is on the screen. However, Visual Basic lets you keep the dialog box's icon out of the Taskbar, if you prefer.

To keep a dialog box's icon—or any other form's icon—out of the Windows Taskbar, simply set that form's **ShowInTaskbar** property to **False** at design time (this property is read-only at runtime). In fact, keeping dialog box icons out of the Taskbar is the most common use for this property.

Using The **MsgBox** Function

The **MsgBox** function acts as one of Visual Basic's built-in dialog box functions. You use the **MsgBox** function to display a message to the user and get a return value corresponding to one of the buttons in the message box. Here's the syntax:

```
MsgBox(prompt[, buttons] [, title] [, helpfile, context])
```

The **MsgBox** arguments are as follows:

* *prompt*—The string displayed as the message in the dialog box. (The maximum length of *prompt* is approximately 1,024 characters.)

  If *prompt* consists of multiple lines, you can separate the lines by placing between them a carriage return character (**Chr(13)**), a linefeed character (**Chr(10)**), or both (**Chr(13) & Chr(10)**).

* *buttons*—Tells Visual Basic what buttons and other items to put into the message box, as specified in Table 13.2. The default value for *buttons* is 0.

* *title*—The string displayed in the title bar of the dialog box. (If you don't specify *title*, Visual Basic places the application name in the title bar.)

* *helpfile*—A string that identifies the Help file to use to provide context-sensitive Help for the dialog box.

* *context*—The Help context number assigned to the appropriate Help topic.

The possible return values from **MsgBox** appear in Table 13.3.

Table 13.2   MsgBox constants.

Constant	Value	Description
vbOKOnly	0	Displays an OK button only.
vbOKCancel	1	Displays OK and Cancel buttons.
vbAbortRetryIgnore	2	Displays Abort, Retry, and Ignore buttons.
vbYesNoCancel	3	Displays Yes, No, and Cancel buttons.
vbYesNo	4	Displays Yes and No buttons.
vbRetryCancel	5	Displays Retry and Cancel buttons.
vbCritical	16	Displays the Critical Message icon.
vbQuestion	32	Displays the Warning Query icon.
vbExclamation	48	Displays the Warning Message icon.
vbInformation	64	Displays the Information Message icon.
vbDefaultButton1	0	Makes the first button the default.
vbDefaultButton2	256	Makes the second button the default.

(continued)

Table 13.2   MsgBox constants (continued).

Constant	Value	Description
vbDefaultButton3	512	Makes the third button the default.
vbDefaultButton4	768	Makes the fourth button the default.
vbApplicationModal	0	Indicates that the application is modal; the user must respond to the message box before continuing work in the current application.
vbSystemModal	4096	Indicates that the system is modal; all applications are suspended until the user responds to the message box.
vbMsgBoxHelpButton	16384	Adds a Help button to the message box.
VbMsgBoxSetForeground	65536	Specifies the message box window as the foreground window.
vbMsgBoxRight	524288	Right-aligns the text.
vbMsgBoxRtlReading	1048576	Specifies that text should appear right to left, to be read on Hebrew and Arabic systems.

Table 13.3   MsgBox return values.

Constant	Value	Description
vbOK	1	OK
vbCancel	2	Cancel
vbAbort	3	Abort
vbRetry	4	Retry
vbIgnore	5	Ignore
vbYes	6	Yes
vbNo	7	No

Using The **InputBox** Function

The **InputBox** function acts as one of Visual Basic's built-in dialog box functions; you can use the **InputBox** function to get a string of text from the user. Here's the syntax for this function:

```
InputBox(prompt[, title] [, default] [, xpos] [, ypos] [, _
    helpfile, context])
```

The **InputBox** arguments are as follows:

- *prompt*—A string displayed as the message in the dialog box.

- *title*—A string displayed in the title bar of the dialog box. (If you don't specify *title*, Visual Basic places the application name in the title bar.)

- *default*—A string displayed in the text box as the default response if no other input is provided.

- *xpos*—A number that specifies (in twips) the horizontal distance from the left edge of the dialog box to the left edge of the screen.

- *ypos*—A number that specifies (in twips) the vertical distance from the upper edge of the dialog box to the top of the screen.

- *helpfile*—A string that identifies the Help file to use to provide context-sensitive Help for the dialog box.

- *context*—The Help context number assigned to the appropriate Help topic.

The **InputBox** function returns the string the user entered.

Programming Core Controls

In Brief

In this chapter, we're going to take a look at the basic controls available in Visual Basic, including text boxes, command buttons, checkboxes, option buttons, list boxes and combo boxes. These controls are fundamental to Visual Basic, and we'll investigate their core programming issues in this chapter.

Text Boxes

Text boxes are probably Visual Basic's most elementary controls. As the name indicates, you enter text into text boxes and display text there under program control. Visual Basic provides many kinds of text boxes, including simple, multiline, scrollable, and locked. In fact, text boxes are so popular that Visual Basic has also introduced the rich text box, which is practically a word processor in a control; it allows you to read and save files, format text, and handle huge amounts of text. In this chapter, we'll get to the core of text-box programming.

Command Buttons

If text boxes are the most basic Visual Basic control, command buttons aren't far behind. You click on a command button to perform some specific, individual action, such as connecting to the Internet, entering a digit into a calculator, or sending an email message.

Command buttons are easy to use and program, because they really have only one primary use: You click on a button and the program executes the associated code. In this chapter, we'll see what command buttons—perhaps the simplest controls in Visual Basic—have to offer.

Checkboxes And Option Buttons

The next step up in control complexity brings us to checkboxes and option buttons. These controls behave like standard command buttons, but they also give you an indication of their state: selected or not. Whereas command buttons "de-press" when you click on them and then pop back immediately, checkboxes and option buttons stay selected until you click on them again.

Checkboxes indicate their state—selected or not—by either displaying or not displaying an X. If you see an X, the checkbox is selected; if you don't see an X, it isn't selected. The same is true for option buttons, with two differences:

- Option buttons display a dot to indicate they've been selected.
- Option buttons work in groups. You can select only one option button in a group at a time. In other words, when you click on one option button in a group, all the others are automatically deselected.

The upshot is that you use checkboxes to set nonexclusive options (such as toppings on a pizza) and option buttons in a group to set exclusive options (such as the day of the week).

List Boxes And Combo Boxes

Like the controls already described, list boxes and combo boxes are also very popular in Visual Basic programs. Both of these types of controls hold text items that the user can select. As their name suggests, *list boxes* hold items in a list; the user clicks on those items to make selections. You can also hide a list box's list in a drop-down list box until the user needs to see it. A combo box is a combination of a text box and a list box; the user can enter text in the text box in addition to selecting from the items in the list box. In this way, list boxes let the user select from a preset list of items, whereas combo boxes do the same but also let users enter their own items.

That's all the introduction we need for these controls—we're ready to delve into the Immediate Solutions part of this chapter.

Immediate Solutions

Working With Text In A Text Box

To work with the text in a text box, use the **Text** property, like this:

```
Private Sub Command1_Click()
    Text1.Text = "Greetings from Visual Basic"
End Sub
```

That's all there is to it. In this case, when the user clicks on the command button **Command1**, the text *Greetings from Visual Basic* appears in the text box.

Supporting Multiline, Word-Wrap Text Boxes

By setting a text box's **MultiLine** property to **True**, you convert the text box into a multiline text box, complete with word wrap. Figure 14.1 shows such a text box. Now, your program's users can type in more than one line of text.

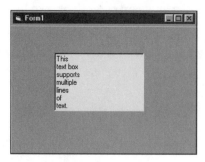

Figure 14.1   *A multiline text box.*

Aligning Text-Box Text

Text boxes have an **Alignment** property, with these three possible settings:

- *0*—Left-justified

- *1*—Right-justified
- *2*—Centered

If you set the **Alignment** property to **2** (Centered) at design time in all your text boxes and run your program, the text you enter appears as left-justified. The **Alignment** property doesn't seem to work—what's wrong?

You need to set the text boxes' **MultiLine** property to **True** before text alignment will work; it's simply a quirk of text boxes. When you set the **MultiLine** property to **True**, everything works as it should.

Supporting Scroll Bars In Text Boxes

Scroll bars allow users to enter much more text simply by scrolling appropriately. The text box **ScrollBars** property gives you four ways to add scroll bars to a text box. Here are the settings you use for **ScrollBars**, and the type of scroll bars each setting displays:

- *0*—None
- *1*—Horizontal
- *2*—Vertical
- *3*—Both

Note that in order for the scroll bars to actually appear, the text box's **MultiLine** property must be set to **True**.

Selecting Text In Text Boxes

To work with part of the text in a text box, use one of these three properties:

- *SelLength*—Returns or sets the number of characters selected.
- *SelStart*—Returns or sets the starting point of text selected; indicates the position of the insertion point if no text is selected.
- *SelText*—Returns or sets the string containing the currently selected text; consists of a zero-length string ("") if no characters are selected.

Note that text selected under program control this way does *not* appear highlighted in the text box.

Setting Text-Size Limits In Text Boxes

Although text boxes can hold up to 64K characters, that may be too much for you to handle conveniently—you may want to limit the maximum number of characters a text box can hold. You do that by setting the text box's **MaxLength** property to the maximum number of characters you want the user to be able to enter. (The default value for **MaxLength** is 0, which actually means 64K characters.)

On the other hand, if text boxes don't hold enough characters to suit your needs, you can use a rich text box. Rich text boxes can hold literally gigabytes of data.

Setting A Command Button's Caption

You use a button's **Caption** property to set its caption. This property is available at both design time and runtime.

After you add a button to a form, you set its caption by placing the appropriate text in the **Caption** property in the Properties window. You can also change the button's caption at runtime, of course, as follows:

```
Private Sub Command1_Click()
    Command1.Caption = "You clicked this button."
End Sub
```

Disabling Command Buttons

You can disable a button by setting its **Enabled** property to **False** when it's inappropriate to use that button. When a button is disabled, it is inaccessible to the user, and it can't accept the focus.

You can also disable a button at runtime, like this:

```
Private Sub Command1_Click()
    Command1.Enabled = False
End Sub
```

Rearranging Buttons On A Form At Runtime

If your program shows and hides buttons, you can rearrange the visible buttons to hide any gaps by using the buttons' **Move** method:

```
control.Move left, top, width, height
```

The **Move** method has these arguments:

- *left*—Value indicating the horizontal coordinate (x-axis) for the left edge of the object
- *top*—Value indicating the vertical coordinate (y-axis) for the top edge of the object
- *width*—Value indicating the new width of the object
- *height*—Value indicating the new height of the object

Here's an example:

```
Private Sub Command1_Click()
    Command1.Move 0, 0
End Sub
```

Showing And Hiding Buttons

To make a button disappear, simply set its **Visible** property to **False**. To make it reappear, set the **Visible** property to **True**. You can set this property at either design time or runtime. Here's how to make a button disappear when you click on it:

```
Private Sub Command1_Click()
    Command1.Visible = False
End Sub
```

Displaying A Picture In A Button

You can load an image into a button using the **Picture** property. To do so, just click on the button with the ellipsis (...) in the **Picture** property's entry in the Properties window and indicate an image file in the Load Picture dialog box that opens. You also have to set the button's **Style** property to **Graphical** (which has a numeric value of 1). Figure 14.2 shows an image loaded into a command button.

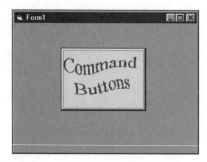

Figure 14.2   *An image loaded into a command button.*

When you set checkboxes and option buttons to **Graphical** style, they look just like graphical command buttons. The only difference is that when you click on a graphical checkbox or option button, it stays selected until you click on it again (and option buttons still function in groups, of course).

You can also set the **Picture** property at runtime—but don't try setting it directly to the name of a file. You can assign only Visual Basic **Picture** objects to the **Picture** property, such as those objects returned by the **LoadPicture** function:

```
Private Sub Command1_Click()
    Command1.Picture = LoadPicture("c:\image.bmp")
End Sub
```

Getting A Checkbox's State

You can determine whether a checkbox is selected by examining its **Value** property. Here are the possible **Value** settings for checkboxes:

- *0*—Unchecked
- *1*—Checked
- *2*—Grayed

This example changes a command button's caption if a checkbox (**Check1**) is checked, but not otherwise:

```
Private Sub Command1_Click()
    If Check1.Value = 1 Then
        Command1.Caption = "The checkbox is checked"
    End If
End Sub
```

Setting A Checkbox's State

You can set a checkbox's state by setting its **Value** property to one of the following:

- *0*—Unchecked
- *1*—Checked
- *2*—Grayed

This example checks a checkbox (**Check1**):

```
Private Sub Command1_Click()
    Check1.Value = 1
End Sub
```

Here's another example, which uses the Visual Basic **Choose** function to toggle a checkbox's state each time the user clicks on the command button **Command1**:

```
Private Sub Command1_Click()
    Check1.Value = Choose(Check1.Value + 1, 1, 0)
End Sub
```

Creating Option Button Groups

You can use the Frame control to group option buttons (you can also use the Picture Box control). Simply draw a frame for each group of option buttons you want on a form, and then add the option buttons to the frames. Each frame of option buttons acts as its own group; the user can select one option button in each group, as shown in Figure 14.3.

Figure 14.3 *Grouping option buttons using frames.*

TIP: *If appropriate, you might consider making the option buttons in each group into a control array; doing so can make handling multiple controls easier.*

Getting An Option Button's State

You can determine whether an option button is selected with the **Value** property. Unlike checkboxes, which have three **Value** property settings (corresponding to checked, not checked, and grayed), an option button's **Value** property has only two settings: **True** if the button is selected and **False** if it isn't selected.

Let's look at an example that shows how to see whether an option button is selected. In this case, the code displays a message in a message box that indicates whether the option button **Option1** is selected:

```
Private Sub Command1_Click()
    If Option1.Value Then
        MsgBox "The option button is selected."
    Else
        MsgBox "The option button is not selected."
    End If
End Sub
```

Setting An Option Button's State

You can set an option button's state using its **Value** property. The **Value** property can take two values: **True** or **False**. These lines set an option button (**Option1**) to its selected state by setting its **Value** property to **True**:

```
Private Sub Command1_Click()
    Option1.Value = True
End Sub
```

Placing Items In A List Box

You can add items to a list box using the **List** property and the **AddItem** method. Here's how you use the **List** property in code (keep in mind that you can get or set items in the list box with the **List** array):

```
ListBox.List(index) [= string]
```

How do you keep track of the total number of items in a list box? You use the **ListCount** property. That is, if you loop over the **List** array, you use **ListCount** as the maximum value to loop to.

You can also use the **AddItem** method this way:

```
Private Sub Form_Load()
    List1.AddItem ("These")
    List1.AddItem ("are")
    List1.AddItem ("items")
    List1.AddItem ("in")
    List1.AddItem ("a")
    List1.AddItem ("list")
    List1.AddItem ("box")
End Sub
```

Running this code results in the list box shown in Figure 14.4.

Note that when you place items in a list box, Visual Basic stores them by index; you can refer to them by their index with the **List** property.

Figure 14.4   *Placing items in a list box.*

Handling List Box **Click** And **DblClick** Events

You use two main events with list boxes: **Click** and **DblClick**. You work with the **Click** event much as you do a button's **Click** event, via a **Click** event handler. This example displays the item in a list box that a user has clicked on, using the **ListIndex** property (you can get the selected item's text using **List1.List(ListIndex)** or **List1.Text**):

```
Private Sub List1_Click()
    MsgBox "You clicked item " & Str(List1.ListIndex)
End Sub
```

The same is true for **DblClick**—simply add a **DblClick** handler with the code you want:

```
Private Sub List1_DblClick()
    MsgBox "You clicked item " & Str(List1.ListIndex)
End Sub
```

By the way, note that a **DblClick** event also triggers the **Click** event, because to double-click on an item, you must first click on it.

Sorting The Items In A List Box

You can alphabetize the items in a list box simply by setting its **Sorted** property to **True** (it's **False** by default) at design time or runtime.

Creating Multiselect List Boxes

A list box can also be a multiselect list box, meaning that the user can select a number of items in the list box at one time. You make a list box into a multiselect list box with the **MultiSelect** property. The user can then select multiple items by using the Shift and Ctrl keys. Here are the possible settings for **MultiSelect**:

- *0*—Multiple selection isn't allowed (this is the default).

- *1*—Simple multiple selection; you select or deselect an item in the list by clicking on it with the mouse or pressing the spacebar. (Arrow keys move the focus.)

- *2*—Extended multiple selection; you extend the selection from the previously selected item to the current item by pressing the Shift key and clicking on the item with the mouse or by pressing the Shift key and one of the arrow keys. Pressing the Ctrl key and clicking on an item with the mouse selects or deselects the item.

In a multiselect list box, you can determine which items the user has selected by using the **Selected** property:

```
For intLoopIndex = 0 To List1.ListCount - 1
    If List1.Selected(intLoopIndex) Then
    .
    .
    .
    End If
Next intLoopIndex
```

Getting The Item Count In A List Box

You use the **ListCount** property to determine how many items are in a list box. For example, let's search a list box to see whether it has an item whose caption is *Item 1*. First, you set up the loop over the indices of the items in the list box:

```
Private Sub Command1_Click()
    Dim intLoopIndex As Integer
    For intLoopIndex = 0 To List1.ListCount - 1
    .
    .
    .
    Next intLoopIndex
End Sub
```

Then, check each item for the caption *Item 1* and report if you find that item:

```
Private Sub Command1_Click()
    Dim intLoopIndex As Integer
    For intLoopIndex = 0 To List1.ListCount - 1
        If List1.List(intLoopIndex) = "Item 1" Then
            MsgBox "Found item 1!"
        End If
    Next intLoopIndex
End Sub
```

TIP: When setting up loops over the items in a list box, you should note that **ListCount** is the total number of items in a list, whereas index values start at 0, not 1. To accommodate the zero-based indices when you're looping over them, you should loop to **ListCount - 1** rather than **ListCount**.

Creating Combo Boxes

Visual Basic offers three types of combo boxes; you select which type you want with the combo box's **Style** property.

The default type of combo box is probably what you think of when you envision a combo box: It's made up of a text box and a drop-down list. However, you can also have a combo box in which the list doesn't drop down (the list is always open, and you must be sure to provide space for it when you add the combo box to your form) or a combo box in which the user can only select from the list.

Here are the settings for the combo box **Style** property:

- **VbComboDropDown**—0 (the default). This creates a drop-down combo list box, which includes a drop-down list and a text box. The user can select from the list or type in the text box.

- **VbComboSimple**—1. This creates a simple combo box, which includes a text box and a list that doesn't drop down. The user can select from the list or type in the text box. The size of a simple combo box includes both the edit and list portions. By default, a simple combo box is sized so that none of the list is displayed; increase the **Height** property to display more of the list.

- **VbComboDropDownList**—2. This creates a drop-down list box, which allows selection only from the drop-down list. This is a good style to keep in mind when you want to restrict the user's input (also consider a simple list box).

Placing Items In A Combo Box

A combo box is a combination of a text box and a list box. At design time, this means you can alter the text in the text box by changing the **Text** property. You change the items in the list box with the **List** property (this item opens a drop-down list when you click on it in the Properties window) at design time.

At runtime, you can add items to a combo box using the **AddItem** method, which adds items to the list box part. You can also add items to the list box using the **List** property, which holds an indexed array of items in the list box. If you want to put text in the text box, set the combo box's **Text** property.

Here's an example that adds four items to a combo box's list:

```
Private Sub Form_Load()
    Combo1.AddItem ("Item 0")
    Combo1.AddItem ("Item 1")
    Combo1.AddItem ("Item 2")
    Combo1.AddItem ("Item 3")
End Sub
```

You can also add items to the list with the **List** property. This code creates a fifth item and gives it a caption:

```
Private Sub Form_Load()
    Combo1.AddItem ("Item 0")
    Combo1.AddItem ("Item 1")
    Combo1.AddItem ("Item 2")
    Combo1.AddItem ("Item 3")
    Combo1.List(4) = "Item 4"
End Sub
```

That's all you need to do.

Handling Combo Box **Change** Events

When the user changes the text in a combo box, a **Change** event occurs, just as it does when the user types in a standard text box. You can read the new text in the text box with the **Text** property; for example, here's how to display the new text in the combo box every time the user changes that text by typing:

```
Private Sub Form_Load()
    Combo1.AddItem ("Item 0")
    Combo1.AddItem ("Item 1")
    Combo1.AddItem ("Item 2")
    Combo1.AddItem ("Item 3")
End Sub
```

14: Programming
Core Controls

```
Private Sub Combo1_Change()
    MsgBox "New text is: " & Combo1.Text
End Sub
```

Note that no **Change** event occurs when you use the mouse to select an item in a combo box's list, even if doing so changes the text in the combo's text box. Only the **Click** (or **DblClick**) event occurs when the user uses the mouse.

Handling Combo Box **Click** Events

Your program gets **Click** events when the user makes a selection in the list box using the mouse. You can determine which item the user clicked on by using the combo's **ListIndex** property, which holds the index of the clicked item. You can also get that item's text by using the **Text** property, because when you click on an item, it becomes the new selected item in the text box. Here's an example that uses the **ListIndex** property to report to the user which item in the combo box they've clicked on:

```
Private Sub Form_Load()
    Combo1.AddItem ("Item 0")
    Combo1.AddItem ("Item 1")
    Combo1.AddItem ("Item 2")
    Combo1.AddItem ("Item 3")
End Sub

Private Sub Combo1_Click()
    MsgBox "You clicked item " & Str(Combo1.ListIndex)
End Sub
```

Handling Combo Box **DblClick** Events

Simple combo boxes (that is, those with a **Style** property value of **VbComboSimple**, where **VbComboSimple** is a Visual Basic constant that equals 1), and *only* simple combo boxes, support the **DblClick** event. When you click once on an item in the list part of other types of combo boxes, the list closes. As a result, it's impossible to double-click on an item—except in a simple combo box, where the list stays open at all times.

A simple combo box can support the **DblClick** event this way:

```
Private Sub Form_Load()
    Combo1.AddItem ("Item 0")
    Combo1.AddItem ("Item 1")
    Combo1.AddItem ("Item 2")
    Combo1.AddItem ("Item 3")
End Sub

Private Sub Combo1_DblClick()
    MsgBox "You double clicked item " & Str(Combo1.ListIndex)
End Sub
```

Getting The Current Selection In A Combo Box

When you make a selection in a combo box, that new selection appears in the combo box's text box. So, it's easy to get the current selection—you just use the combo box's **Text** property.

For example, say you've added these items to a combo box:

```
Private Sub Form_Load()
    Combo1.AddItem ("Item 0")
    Combo1.AddItem ("Item 1")
    Combo1.AddItem ("Item 2")
    Combo1.AddItem ("Item 3")
End Sub
```

Then, when the user clicks on a command button, you can get the text of the current selection in the combo box this way, using the **Text** property:

```
Private Sub Command1_Click()
    MsgBox "New text is: " & Combo1.Text
End Sub
```

You can also get the currently selected item's index in the combo box's list using the **ListIndex** property. The **ListIndex** property's value will be **-1** in three cases:

- If no item is selected (for example, when the form first loads and the combo's text box is empty)

- If the user has altered the selection by typing in the text box (such that the selected item no longer matches the item in the combo box's list)

- If the user opens the combo box's list and then clicks outside that list without making a selection

Here's an example that displays the index of the currently selected item using **ListIndex**. First, you fill the combo box with items:

```
Private Sub Form_Load()
    Combo1.AddItem ("Item 0")
    Combo1.AddItem ("Item 1")
    Combo1.AddItem ("Item 2")
    Combo1.AddItem ("Item 3")
End Sub
```

Then, you can display the index of the current selection by using **ListIndex** when the user clicks on a command button:

```
Private Sub Command1_Click()
    MsgBox Str(Combo1.ListIndex)
End Sub
```

Getting The Number Of Items In A Combo Box

You can use a combo box's **ListCount** property to determine how many items are in the combo box's list. Let's see how to use **ListCount** in an example that searches the items in a combo box for one particular item with the caption *Item 1*; if we find the item, we'll display a message box.

Start by setting up a loop over the indices of all the items in the combo box (note that you subtract one from **ListCount** because indices are zero-based):

```
Private Sub Command1_Click()
    Dim intLoopIndex As Integer
    For intLoopIndex = 0 To Combo1.ListCount - 1
        .
        .
        .
    Next intLoopIndex
End Sub
```

Then, search the indexed **List** property for the item you want; if you find it, report that fact to the user:

```
Private Sub Command1_Click()
    Dim intLoopIndex As Integer
    For intLoopIndex = 0 To Combo1.ListCount - 1
        If Combo1.List(intLoopIndex) = "Item 1" Then
            MsgBox "Found item 1!"
        End If
    Next intLoopIndex
End Sub
```

Chapter 15

Programming More Advanced Controls

In Brief

In this chapter, we're going to take a look at some powerful Visual Basic core controls: timers, picture boxes, scroll bars, toolbars, and status bars. All these controls are very popular in Visual Basic, and we'll put their power to work for us in this chapter.

The Timer Control

Timer controls are perfect when you want to execute code at specific intervals. To use a timer, you add a timer control to your program and set its **Interval** property. From then on, while the timer is enabled, it creates timer events; these events are handled in an event-handling procedure, such as **Timer1_Timer**. You place the code you want executed each interval in that procedure.

The Picture Box Control

Just as the rich text control provides a sort of word-processor-in-a-control, the picture box provides a miniature graphics studio in Visual Basic. You can load images into a picture box, save images to disk, draw with some rudimentary graphics methods, print images, work pixel by pixel, set an image's scale, and more. Besides graphics handling, the picture box can also act as a container for other controls—and it's the only control that can appear by itself on an MDI form. We'll take a look at core programming for picture boxes in this chapter.

The Scroll-Bar Controls

Scroll bars are familiar to every Windows user. These rectangular controls display a small knob—called the *thumb*—that the user can move to scroll through data.

Vertical and horizontal scroll bars are intrinsic controls in Visual Basic, meaning that they appear in the toolbox. To use scroll bars, you add them to a project and set their **Min** and **Max** values to specify the range of values the user can set the controls to. Then, to interpret actions undertaken by the user, you read the **Value** property to get the control's setting in a **Change** event handler.

Change events occur after the user finishes changing the control's setting—you can also use the **Scroll** event to handle events as the user works with the control, as we'll see in this chapter.

The Toolbar Control

Toolbars generally appear at the top of a window, although they can appear other places, as well. These controls are filled with buttons and sometimes other controls, such as combo boxes.

As you no doubt know, toolbars provide the user with an easy way of executing commands in an application with a single button click. They're so easy to use and so handy that they've become very popular. You can also customize toolbars: Double-clicking on a toolbar at runtime opens the Customize Toolbar dialog box, which allows the user to hide, display, or rearrange toolbar buttons.

To place buttons on a toolbar, you add **Button** objects to its **Buttons** collection (usually by working with the toolbar's property pages). Each button can display text and/or an image; you set text with the **Caption** property and an image with the **Image** property for each **Button** object.

The Status-Bar Control

A status bar appears at the bottom of a window; it usually holds several panels in which you can display text. The status bar gives the user feedback on program operation, as well as showing information such as the time of day or key states (Caps Lock or Insert mode, for instance).

Status bars are built around the **Panels** collection, which holds the panels in the status bar. The collection can contain as many as 16 **Panel** objects. Each object can display an image and text. You can change the text, image, or width of any **Panel** object, using its **Text**, **Picture**, and **Width** properties.

That's all the introduction we need: It's time to turn to the Immediate Solutions part of this chapter.

Immediate Solutions

Placing A Timer Control On A Form

You add a timer control to your program just as you would any other intrinsic control—simply click on the timer control tool and draw the timer on your form.

The timer control is invisible when the program runs, so the size and location of the control don't really matter.

Now that you've added a timer, how do you get it running? See the next topic.

Setting Up A Timer Control

How do you start a timer control? You use these two properties:

- **Enabled**—Determines whether or not the timer creates timer events

- **Interval**—Specifies the number of milliseconds between timer events

When you place a timer in your program, you can set its **Enabled** property to **False** to prevent timer events from occurring. When you want to start the timer, you can set **Enabled** to **True**.

The **Interval** property sets the interval between timer events. Although measured in milliseconds (1/1000ths of a second), timer events can't actually occur faster than 18.2 times per second.

The interval can range from 0 milliseconds (in which case, nothing happens) to 64,767 milliseconds, which means that even the longest interval can't be much longer than one minute (about 64.8 seconds). However, you can design your code to wait for several intervals to pass before doing anything.

Note that if the system is busy, your application may not get timer events as often as the **Interval** property specifies. That is, the interval isn't guaranteed to elapse exactly on time. If you need greater assurance of accuracy, the timer event handler should check the system clock when needed.

Handling A Timer Control's Events

The main timer event is the **Timer** event. Double-clicking on a timer at design time creates a handler function for that event:

```
Sub Timer1_Timer()

End Sub
```

All you need to do is add to this procedure the code you want executed. For example, this code displays the current time in a label named **Label1** using the Visual Basic **Time$** function:

```
Sub Timer1_Timer()
    Label1.Caption = Time$
End Sub
```

This code will be called as often as the timer's **Interval** property specifies.

Using Timers To Write A Clock Application

To see how to create a clock application, create a new project now, and add to it a timer control (**Timer1**). Set the timer's **Interval** property to 1000 (that is, 1,000 milliseconds, or 1 second).

Next, add a label (**Label1**) that covers most of the form and give it a large font, such as 48-point Times New Roman. You'll display the time in that label each time the timer ticks, so add the **Timer1_Timer** event handler now:

```
Sub Timer1_Timer()

End Sub
```

All you have to do when a timer event occurs is update the clock. Use the Visual Basic **Time$** function to do that:

```
Sub Timer1_Timer()
    Label1.Caption = Time$
End Sub
```

That's all you need—now the clock is functional, as shown in Figure 15.1.

Figure 15.1   *A clock created with the timer control.*

Adding A Picture Box To A Form

Adding a picture box to a form is easy; just follow these steps:

1. Select the picture box tool in the toolbox and double-click on it to add a picture box to your form; or, click on it once and draw the picture box where you want it on the form.

2. If you want the picture box to resize itself to fit the picture you'll load into it, set its **AutoSize** property to **True**. If you don't want a border on the control, set its **BorderStyle** property to **None** (0).

3. If you want Visual Basic to refresh the picture box's contents when needed (for example, when another window obscuring the picture box is removed), set its **AutoRedraw** property to **True**.

4. Load the image you want to display into the picture box using its **Picture** property. Click on that property in the Properties window and click on the button with the ellipsis (...) to open the Load Picture dialog box. At runtime, you can load a picture using **LoadPicture( )** like this:

```
Private Sub Command1_Click()
    Picture1.Picture = _
        LoadPicture("c:\picturesandimages\image.bmp")
End Sub
```

Figure 15.2 shows an image loaded into the picture box following these steps—now the picture box is ready to go.

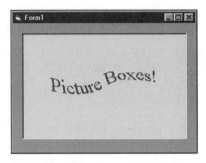

Figure 15.2   *A picture box on a form.*

Working With The Picture In A Picture Box

How do you place images in a picture box? You use the **Picture** property. A picture box is very versatile and can display images from bitmap (BMP), icon (ICO), metafile (WMF), JPEG (JPG), or GIF files—simply load the file's name into the **Picture** property.

At design time, click on that property in the Properties window and click on the button with the ellipsis (...) to open the Load Picture dialog box. Specify the file you want to load into the picture box and click on OK.

At runtime, you can use **LoadPicture** to load a picture as in this example, which loads an image when the user clicks on a command button:

```
Private Sub Command1_Click()
    Picture1.Picture = _
    LoadPicture("c:\picturesandimages\image.bmp")
End Sub
```

Another time to use the **Picture** property is if you want to access the picture in a picture box. For example, this code copies the picture from **Picture1** to **Picture2** when the user clicks on a command button:

```
Private Sub Command1_Click()
    Picture2.Picture = Picture1.Picture
End Sub
```

The **Picture** property is very useful in Visual Basic, because it provides such an easy way to handle images, as you can see in the previous two code snippets. Using the **Picture** property, you can store images and transfer them between controls.

Sizing Picture Boxes To Their Contents

When you load a picture into a picture control, the control doesn't adjust itself to fit the image—at least, not by default. A picture box will resize itself to fit its contents, however, if you set its **AutoSize** property to **True**.

If **AutoSize** is set to **True**, you don't have to worry about resizing the picture box, even if you load images into the picture box at runtime. This saves a lot of fiddling with the picture box's **Left**, **Top**, **Width**, and **Height** properties.

Placing Horizontal Or Vertical Scroll Bars On A Form

Although many novice programmers think that Visual Basic provides a single scroll bar tool that you use to add a scroll bar to a form and then set the scroll bar's orientation (vertical or horizontal), you're probably aware that the horizontal and vertical scroll bars are actually two different controls.

To add a horizontal scroll bar to a form, you use the horizontal scroll bar tool; to add a vertical scroll bar, you use the vertical scroll bar tool. A horizontal scroll bar (**HScroll1**) and a vertical scroll bar (**VScroll1**) appear in Figure 15.3.

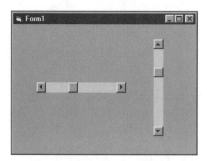

Figure 15.3   A horizontal and a vertical scroll bar.

Setting Scroll Bars' Minimum And Maximum Possible Values

When you add a scroll bar to a program, you should immediately set its range of possible values; the default range is 0 to 32767. A scroll bar's minimum value is stored in its **Min** property, and the maximum value is stored in the **Max** property. You can set the **Min** and **Max** properties for scroll bars at design time or at runtime; here's how to change those properties in a vertical scroll bar, **VScroll1**:

```
Private Sub Form_Load()
    VScroll1.Min = 1
    VScroll1.Max = 100
End Sub
```

Handling Scroll-Bar Clicks

When the user clicks on the scroll bar itself, rather than the thumb (that is, the scroll box) or an arrow button, the thumb should move toward the spot at which the user clicked by the amount set by the scroll bar's **LargeChange** property. For example, if the scroll bar's range is from 1 to 100, a reasonable **LargeChange** setting would be 10. You can set the **LargeChange** property at design time or at runtime.

This example sets the **LargeChange** property for two scroll bars, one horizontal and one vertical:

```
Private Sub Form_Load()
    VScroll1.Min = 1
    VScroll1.Max = 100
    VScroll1.LargeChange = 10

    HScroll1.Min = 1
    HScroll1.Max = 100
    HScroll1.LargeChange = 10
End Sub
```

Now, when the user clicks on the scroll bar between the thumb and the arrow buttons, the scroll bar's value will increase or decrease by 10.

> ***TIP:*** *On some occasions, you should change the **LargeChange** property while a program is running. For example, if you let the user scroll through a document with **LargeChange** while this property is set to 1, and the user loads a 30,000-line document, it might be wise to change the value of this property to avoid user frustration.*

Handling Scroll-Bar Arrow Clicks

As far as the user is concerned, there are three ways to change the setting of a scroll bar: by moving the thumb (that is, the scroll box), by clicking on the area of the scroll bar between the thumb and an arrow button, or by clicking on an arrow button. When the user clicks on an arrow button, the thumb moves by an amount stored in the **SmallChange** property.

When the user clicks on a scroll bar's arrow, the setting of the scroll bar is incremented or decremented (depending on which arrow the user clicked on) by the value in the **SmallChange** property. You can set a scroll bar's **SmallChange** property at design time or at runtime.

For example, this code sets the **SmallChange** property for two scroll bars, one horizontal and one vertical:

```
Private Sub Form_Load()
    VScroll1.Min = 1
    VScroll1.Max = 100
    VScroll1.SmallChange = 1

    HScroll1.Min = 1
    HScroll1.Max = 100
    HScroll1.SmallChange = 1
End Sub
```

Now, when the user clicks on an arrow button, the setting of the scroll bar will change by 1.

> ***TIP:*** *On some occasions, you should change the **SmallChange** property while a program is running. For example, if you let the user scroll through a document with **SmallChange** while this property is set to 1, and the user loads a 30,000-line document, it might be wise to change the value of this property to avoid user frustration.*

Getting And Setting A Scroll Bar's Current Value

You specify or get a scroll bar's current setting using the **Value** property. You can set this value either at design time or runtime, and you can read a scroll bar's setting while the program is running. The **Value** property holds values that can be in the range spanned by the values in the **Min** and **Max** properties.

Here's an example. The following code sets up two scroll bars (one horizontal and one vertical) and places the thumb of each scroll bar in the center of the range when the scroll bar first appears by setting the **Value** properties as follows:

```
Private Sub Form_Load()
    VScroll1.Min = 1
    VScroll1.Max = 100
    VScroll1.LargeChange = 10
    VScroll1.SmallChange = 1
    VScroll1.Value = 50

    HScroll1.Min = 1
    HScroll1.Max = 100
    HScroll1.LargeChange = 10
    HScroll1.SmallChange = 1
    HScroll1.Value = 50
End Sub
```

When the user makes a change in a scroll bar, you get the new setting from the **Value** property when the **Change** event is triggered.

Handling Scroll-Bar Events

How do you connect scroll bars to your program's code? When the user changes the setting in a scroll bar, a **Change** event occurs; you can react to those changes with an event handler attached to that event. For example, you can use scroll bars to move other controls around on the form (using those controls' **Move** methods), and when the user changes a scroll bar's setting, you'll be informed of the new value in the **Change** event handler.

Here's an example. The following code adds two scroll bars— **HScroll1** (horizontal) and **VScroll1** (vertical)—to a form and sets those controls' **Min**, **Max**, **SmallChange**, **LargeChange**, and **Value** properties when the form loads:

```
Private Sub Form_Load()
    VScroll1.Min = 1
    VScroll1.Max = 100
    VScroll1.LargeChange = 10
    VScroll1.SmallChange = 1
    VScroll1.Value = 50

    HScroll1.Min = 1
    HScroll1.Max = 100
    HScroll1.LargeChange = 10
    HScroll1.SmallChange = 1
    HScroll1.Value = 50
End Sub
```

Now, when the user changes the setting in a scroll bar, you can report the new setting in a text box (**Text1**) simply by using the new setting in the **Value** property, like this:

```
Private Sub HScroll1_Change()
    Text1.Text = "Horizontal scroll value: " & _
        Str(HScroll1.Value)
End Sub

Private Sub VScroll1_Change()
    Text1.Text = "Vertical scroll value: " & _
        Str(VScroll1.Value)
End Sub
```

That's all it takes—now you're handling scroll-bar events, as shown in Figure 15.4.

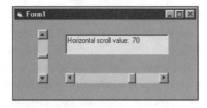

Figure 15.4   *Handling scroll-bar events.*

Handling Continuous Scroll-Bar Events

You can use the **Change** event to catch the user's scrolling actions, but another event is much better for many uses: the **Scroll** event.

When you use the **Change** event, nothing happens until the user finishes a scrolling action. After the action is completed, the **Change** event is triggered, and you find out what happened.

With the **Scroll** event, on the other hand, you get continuous updates as the action is happening. This means that you can update the screen immediately to show the user the results of scrolling actions. It's very useful to be able to update the screen as the user scrolls, especially when you're scrolling through a long document.

Let's look at an example that shows how to use the **Scroll** event. Basically, using this event is the same as using the **Change** event (unless you have an action that should be performed only after the user is done scrolling, in which case you should stick with the **Change** event). Begin by adding two scroll bars—**HScroll1** (horizontal) and **VScroll1** (vertical)—to a form. Set those controls' **Min**, **Max**, **SmallChange**, **LargeChange**, and **Value** properties when the form loads:

```
Private Sub Form_Load()
    VScroll1.Min = 1
    VScroll1.Max = 100
    VScroll1.LargeChange = 10
    VScroll1.SmallChange = 1
    VScroll1.Value = 50

    HScroll1.Min = 1
    HScroll1.Max = 100
    HScroll1.LargeChange = 10
    HScroll1.SmallChange = 1
    HScroll1.Value = 50
End Sub
```

Next, you simply add code to the two scroll bars' **Scroll** events to display the new setting in a text box (**Text1**):

```
Private Sub HScroll1_Scroll()
    Text1.Text = "Horizontal scroll value: " & _
        Str(HScroll1.Value)
End Sub
```

```
Private Sub VScroll_Scroll()
    Text1.Text = "Vertical scroll value: " & _
      Str(VScroll1.Value)
End Sub
```

With this code, the text box is continuously updated with the setting of the scroll bars as the user manipulates them. This is in contrast to using the **Change** event, which occurs only when the user has finished a scrolling action.

Placing A Toolbar On A Form

You create a toolbar by adding a toolbar control to a form. Here's how that works:

1. Select the Project|Components menu item.

2. Click on the Controls tab in the Components dialog box.

3. Select the Microsoft Windows Common Controls item, and then click on OK to close the Components dialog box.

Doing so adds the toolbar control tool to the Visual Basic toolbox. To place a toolbar on your form, simply double-click on the toolbar control tool.

Now you have a new toolbar; to work with this control, see the next couple of topics in this chapter.

Adding Buttons To A Toolbar

You add buttons to a toolbar control at design time by right-clicking on the control and clicking on the Properties item in the menu that appears. When the toolbar's Property Pages dialog box opens, click on the Buttons tab, as shown in Figure 15.5.

You insert new buttons by clicking on Insert Button and remove them by clicking on Remove Button. When you add a new button to a toolbar, you can associate a caption with it by filling in the Caption text box.

Each button is assigned a new **Index** value, which will be passed to the **Click** event handler. You can also give each button a **Key** value— a string that you can use to identify the button.

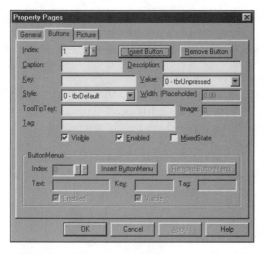

Figure 15.5   *Adding new buttons to a toolbar.*

When you're done, click on OK to close the Property Pages dialog box. Now that you've installed buttons on your toolbar, how do you handle button clicks? Take a look at the next topic.

Handling Toolbar Button Clicks

You've set up your toolbar with the buttons you want, but how can you make those buttons active? You do that with the toolbar control's **ButtonClick** event:

```
Private Sub Toolbar1_ButtonClick(ByVal Button As
MSComctlLib.Button)

End Sub
```

The button the user clicks on is passed to you in this event-handler procedure; you can determine which button was clicked on by checking either the button's **Index** or **Key** property. For example, this code uses a message box and the **Index** property to indicate which button was clicked on:

```
Private Sub Toolbar1_ButtonClick(ByVal Button As _
    MSComctlLib.Button)
    Text1.Text = "You clicked button " & Button.Index
End Sub
```

All buttons in a toolbar control have an **Index** value by default, so this code is ready to go. When the user clicks on a button, you can report which button the user clicked on, as shown in Figure 15.6.

Besides using the **Index** property, you can also give each button's **Key** property a text string (you do that at design time in the toolbar control's Property Pages dialog box). Then, you use a **Select Case** statement to determine which button was clicked on, like this:

```
Private Sub Toolbar1_ButtonClick(ByVal Button As _
    MSComctlLib.Button
        Select Case Button.Key
            Case "OpenFile"
                OpenFile
            Case "SaveFile"
                SaveFile
            Case "CloseFile"
                CloseFile
        End Select
End Sub
```

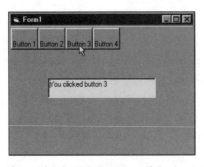

Figure 15.6   *Reporting which button the user clicked on.*

Placing A Status Bar On A Form

You create a status bar by adding a status bar control to a form. Here's how that works:

1. Select the Project|Components menu item.

2. Click on the Controls tab in the Components dialog box.

3. Select the Microsoft Windows Common Controls item, and then click on OK to close the Components dialog box.

Doing so adds the status bar control tool to the Visual Basic toolbox. To place a status bar on your form, simply double-click on the status bar control tool.

Now you have a new status bar—but how do you work with it? See the next few topics in this chapter.

Placing Panels In A Status Bar

After you've added a status bar to your program, you add panels to the status bar. The text in a status bar is displayed in those panels. A status bar control has a **Panels** collection; you add the panels you want to that collection. To do so at design time, follow these steps:

1. Right-click on the status bar and select the Properties item in the menu that opens.

2. Click on the Panels tab in the Property Pages dialog box, as shown in Figure 15.7.

3. Click on Insert Panel once for each panel you want in your status bar.

4. Close the Property Pages dialog box by clicking on OK.

It's also easy to add a new status bar panel at runtime—simply use the **Panels** collection's **Add** method. Here's an example that adds a panel to a status bar when the user clicks on a command button:

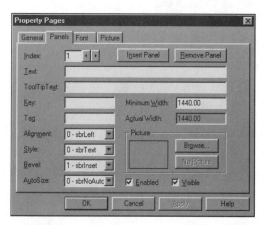

Figure 15.7 *Use the Panels tab of the Property Pages dialog box to add a panel to a status bar.*

```
Private Sub Command1_Click()
    Dim panel3 As Panel
    Set panel3 = StatusBar1.Panels.Add()
    Panel3.Text = "Status: OK"
End Sub
```

Now that you've added panels to the status bar, how do you display text in those panels? See the next topic.

Displaying Text In A Status Bar's Panels

The text in a status bar is displayed in the status bar's panels. Displaying text in a status bar's panels is easy—simply select the panel you want to work with as the index into the status bar's **Panels** collection, and then use that panel's **Text** property.

Let's look at an example. The following code displays the program status in the first panel of the status bar (note that the **Panels** collection is 1-based) when the user clicks on a command button (**Command1**):

```
Private Sub Command1_Click()
    StatusBar1.Panels(1).Text = "Status: OK"
End Sub
```

That's it—the result of this code appears in Figure 15.8. Now you've displayed text in a status bar.

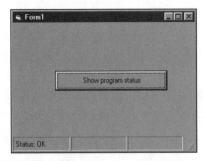

Figure 15.8 *Displaying text in a status bar control.*

Displaying Times, Dates, And More In Status Bars

Status bar controls are already set up to display common status items such as key states and dates. To display one of those items, simply right-click on the status bar, select the Properties item in the menu that appears, click on the Panels tab, and select the panel you want to work with. Then, set the **Style** property in the Style box to one of the following:

- *0 - sbrText*—This setting is the default; displays text and/or a bitmap. (Set text with the **Text** property.)

- *1 - sbrCaps*—Caps Lock key; displays the letters *CAPS* in bold when Caps Lock is enabled or dimmed when it's disabled.

- *2 - sbrNum*—Number Lock; displays the letters *NUM* in bold when the Num Lock key is enabled or dimmed when it's disabled.

- *3 - sbrIns*—Insert key; displays the letters *INS* in bold when the Insert key is enabled or dimmed when it's disabled.

- *4 - sbrScrl*—Scroll Lock key; displays the letters *SCRL* in bold when scroll lock is enabled or dimmed when it's disabled.

- *5 - sbrTime*—Time; displays the current time in the system format.

- *6 - sbrDate*—Date; displays the current date in the system format.

- *7 - sbrKana*—Kana; displays the letters *KANA* in bold when kana lock is enabled or dimmed when disabled. (This setting can be enabled only on Japanese operating systems.)

For example, Figure 15.9 displays the time in the third panel of the status bar.

Figure 15.9 *Displaying the time in a status-bar control.*

Coding ActiveX

In Brief

In this chapter, we're going to see how to create ActiveX controls. Visual Basic programmers are very familiar with ActiveX controls—you can add these controls to the Visual Basic toolbox using the Components dialog box. You add ActiveX controls to a Visual Basic program like you would add any other control. ActiveX controls can support properties, methods, and events.

Creating ActiveX Controls

You can create an ActiveX control in Visual Basic in three ways:

- By building it entirely from scratch (that is, you're responsible for its appearance)

- By building it on another control (such as a list box)

- By making it contain multiple existing controls (these ActiveX controls are said to contain *constituent* controls)

Visual Basic ActiveX controls are based on the Visual Basic **UserControl** object. When you create an ActiveX control, you create a control class file with the extension .ctl. Visual Basic uses that file to create the actual control, which has the extension .ocx. After you register the control with Windows, it will appear in the Visual Basic Components dialog box, ready for you to add to a program.

In this chapter, we'll see how to build ActiveX controls that have built-in properties, events, and methods. And that's really all we need for our overview of ActiveX controls—it's time to turn to the Immediate Solutions part of this chapter.

Immediate Solutions

Creating An ActiveX Control In Visual Basic

How do you create an ActiveX control? It isn't a difficult process: Simply select Visual Basic's File|New Project menu item to open the New Project dialog box, as shown in Figure 16.1.

Select the ActiveX Control icon in the New Project dialog box and click on OK. Doing so creates a new, empty ActiveX control, as shown in Figure 16.2.

You've created your first ActiveX control, **UserControl1**. You could even run the control by choosing the Run|Start menu item to display the control in Microsoft Internet Explorer (if you have it installed)—but there would be nothing to see, because the control is empty.

The default name of the ActiveX control project is Project1, but let's change it to FirstControl. To do that, select the Project|Project1 Properties menu item, type "FirstControl" in the Project Name box of the resulting Project Properties dialog box, and then click on OK. Save the project as firstcontrol.vbp. Instead of an FRM file, save the ActiveX control itself in a CTL file. Select the File|Save UserControl1 menu item and save the control as firstcontrol.ctl.

Now that we've seen how to create a new ActiveX control, it's time to make it do something. We'll see how that works starting in the next topic.

16: Coding ActiveX

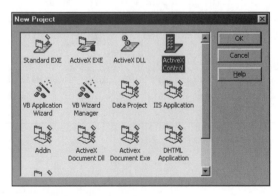

Figure 16.1   *The New Project dialog box.*

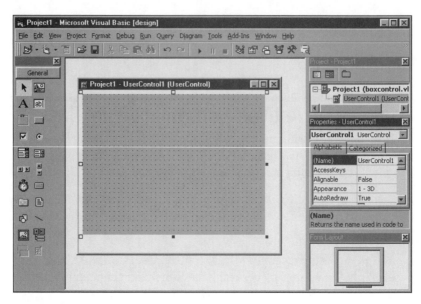

Figure 16.2   *A new ActiveX control.*

Designing An ActiveX Control's Appearance

You can design the appearance of your ActiveX control from scratch, creating an entirely new control (or, you can base your new control on existing controls, as you'll see later). In that case, you're responsible for creating the control's appearance. Later, you can add events to your control, as well as methods and properties.

To design the appearance of your new control, you can use the Visual Basic graphics methods that the **UserControl** object supports, such as **Circle**, **Line**, **PSet**, **Print**, **Cls**, and **Point**. You can also display an image in the **UserControl** object by setting its **Picture** property.

Let's look at an example that draws a box in an ActiveX control. Create a new ActiveX control now and double-click on it at design time to open the code window to the **UserControl_Initialize** function:

```
Private Sub UserControl_Initialize()

End Sub
```

This function is just like the form load procedure you're familiar with. Set the control's **AutoRedraw** property to **True**, so you can draw

graphics from **UserControl_Initialize**. Then, draw the lines to create the box in the control, using the **Line** method and **ScaleWidth**
and **ScaleHeight**, just as you would in a Visual Basic form:

```
Private Sub UserControl_Initialize()
    Line (ScaleWidth / 4, ScaleHeight / 4)-(3 * ScaleWidth _
        / 4, 3 * ScaleHeight / 4), , B
End Sub
```

Let's test this new ActiveX control in Microsoft Internet Explorer (as-
suming you have that browser installed). To do so, select the Run|Start
menu item. Doing so opens the Project Properties dialog box shown
in Figure 16.3.

Leave "UserControl1" in the Start component box and be sure the
Use Existing Browser checkbox is selected; then, click on OK. Doing
so registers your control with Windows, creates a temporary HTML
page with the control embedded in it, and starts Internet Explorer, as
you see in Figure 16.4.

Now you've designed an ActiveX control's appearance from scratch.
If you wanted to, you could add events, properties, and methods to
this control (we'll see how to do these things later in this chapter).

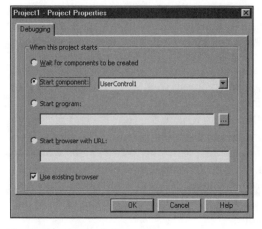

Figure 16.3   *The Project Properties dialog box.*

16: Coding ActiveX

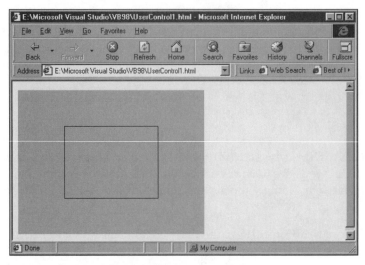

Figure 16.4   *An ActiveX control running in Internet Explorer.*

Designing An ActiveX Control Using An Existing Visual Basic Control

As we saw in the previous topic, you can design an ActiveX control from scratch, creating the control's appearance yourself. However, you can also base your ActiveX control on an existing Visual Basic control.

Let's look at an example that bases an ActiveX control on a Visual Basic command button. Create a new ActiveX control by selecting the ActiveX Control icon in the New Project dialog box. Now, draw a button (**Command1**) on the control (The button's size and position don't matter, because you'll set those values when the control runs.) Add this new button just as you would add a text box to a form—simply use the toolbox's button tool. You can even make the button cause the computer to beep by adding this code to the button's **Click** event handler:

```
Private Sub Command1_Click()
    Beep
End Sub
```

When Visual Basic first displays the control, you'll stretch the button to cover the control by placing this code in the ActiveX control **Initialize** event handler:

```
Private Sub UserControl_Initialize()
    Command1.Left = 0
    Command1.Top = 0
    Command1.Width = ScaleWidth
    Command1.Height = ScaleHeight
End Sub
```

That's it—select the Run|Start menu item. Then, click on OK if the Project Properties dialog box appears (it appears only when you run the control for the first time) to open the control in Internet Explorer, as shown in Figure 16.5.

As you can see in Figure 16.5, the ActiveX control displays a button, ready for use—when you click on it, the computer beeps. Now you've based an ActiveX control on an existing Visual Basic control.

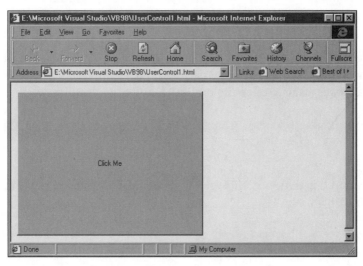

Figure 16.5   *Basing an ActiveX control on a button.*

Using Constituent Controls In An ActiveX Control

In the previous topics in this chapter, we've seen how to design an ActiveX control's appearance from scratch and how to base an ActiveX control on a Visual Basic control (or other ActiveX controls). ActiveX controls frequently contain more than one control; when they do, the controls are called *constituent controls*. How would you design such an ActiveX control in Visual Basic?

Let's take a look at this process now. You'll add two controls to an ActiveX control: a text box and a button. When the user clicks on the button, you'll display the message *Hello from Visual Basic* in the text box. In this way, you'll support two constituent controls—**Command1** and **Text1**—in an ActiveX control.

Create this new ActiveX control now, by choosing the File|New Project menu item, selecting the ActiveX Control item in the New Project dialog box, and clicking on OK.

You'll call this new control HelloControl; open the Project Properties dialog box and type "HelloControl" in the Project Name box. Windows will know your control under this name.

Now, use the toolbox to add two new controls to the ActiveX control: a command button (**Command1**) and a text box (**Text1**). Give the button the caption Click Me.

How do you display the text *Hello from Visual Basic* in the text box when the user clicks on the command button? You do that just as you would in any other Visual Basic program. Double-click on the button at design time to open the button's **Click** event handler:

```
Private Sub Command1_Click()

End Sub
```

When this button is clicked on, you display the message in the text box this way:

```
Private Sub Command1_Click()
    Text1.Text = "Hello from Visual Basic"
End Sub
```

And that's all there is to it: You've created an ActiveX control with two constituent controls. How can you test it? See the next topic.

Testing An ActiveX Control

You can test—and even debug—ActiveX controls in Microsoft Internet Explorer, as long as you have version 3 or later. Simply select Visual Basic's Run|Start menu item to see the ActiveX control you're designing at work.

Let's look at an example that runs the HelloControl ActiveX control you developed in the previous topic. To open this control in Internet Explorer, select the Project|Properties menu item to open the Project Properties dialog box. Click on the Debugging tab, as shown in Figure 16.6.

Although we've called our ActiveX control project HelloControl, this is the name that Windows knows the whole project by—we've left the actual control in the project named UserControl1 (although you can change that name in the Properties window). Why is the name of the project not the same as the name of the control? It's set up this way because a project can contain several ActiveX controls, as well as other items like forms. For that reason, leave the entry "UserControl1" in the Start Component box and be sure the Use Existing Browser checkbox is selected; then, click on OK. To run the control, select the Run|Start menu item. Doing so registers your control with Windows, creates a temporary HTML page with the control embedded in it, and starts Internet Explorer, as you see in Figure 16.7.

That's it—now you can use the ActiveX control.

Figure 16.6   *Setting Visual Basic debugging options.*

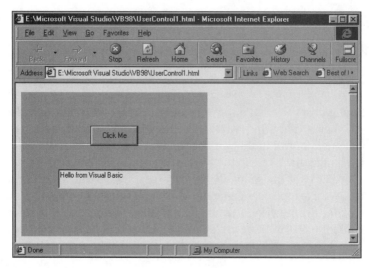

Figure 16.7   *Testing the control named UserControl1 in Internet Explorer.*

Testing An ActiveX Control With A Visual Basic Project Group

In the previous topic, we saw how to test an ActiveX control in a Web browser, but you can use ActiveX controls in Visual Basic programs, too. Can you test an ActiveX control in Visual Basic?

Yes you can—by creating a *project group*. How does that process work? As an example, let's see how to add the HelloControl ActiveX control (developed in the last two topics) to a program group. Just follow these steps:

1. Create a new Visual Basic standard EXE project named Project1.

2. Select the File|Add Project menu item.

3. Click on the Existing tab in the Add Project dialog box, select the name of the ActiveX HelloControl project (we used HelloControl.vbp earlier), and click on OK.

4. This adds the HelloControl ActiveX project to the current project and creates a program group. Choose the File|Save Project Group As menu item and accept all default file names, including the group file itself (group1.vbg). (You can give the file names any names you want, but because the defaults will suit this example just fine, let's accept them.)

5. Close the HelloControl project's window (that is, the design window in which you designed the HelloControl ActiveX control by adding text boxes, and so on). Doing so makes the HelloControl ActiveX control available to you in the new project; it will appear in the toolbox.

6. Add a new HelloControl control to **Form1** of Project1.

7. Select the Run|Start menu item to start Project1.

Following these steps creates the running program you see in Figure 16.8—now you're testing ActiveX controls in Visual Basic.

Figure 16.8   *Testing an ActiveX control in a program group.*

Registering Your ActiveX Control With Windows

To install an ActiveX control in a Windows program, you must register that control with Windows. You can do that either with the setup program or with the Windows regsvr32.exe utility.

Let's look at an example that registers an ActiveX control named activex.ocx with Windows. First, use the File|Make activex.ocx menu item to create activex.ocx. Next, you'll use regsvr32.exe (usually found in the c:\windows\system directory) to register that control with Windows. Here's how to register your ActiveX control:

```
c:\windows\system>regsvr32 c:\lvbbb\activex.ocx
```

After you register the ActiveX control, it will appear in the Visual Basic Components dialog box (accessible via the Project|Components menu item). You can now add it to the Visual Basic toolbox.

Placing Your Custom ActiveX Control In A Visual Basic Program

Now that you've registered your Visual Basic control with Windows (see the previous topic), how do you add it to a form in a Visual Basic project? You add your custom ActiveX controls to Visual Basic projects just as you add any other ActiveX controls, such as the ones that come with Visual Basic.

Let's see an example. After you register the HelloControl ActiveX control you've developed over the previous few topics in this chapter using the techniques in the previous topic, that control will appear in the Visual Basic Components dialog box. Start a new standard EXE project, and then open the Visual Basic Components dialog box by selecting the Project|Components menu item. Next, click on the Controls tab in the Components dialog box, as shown in Figure 16.9.

Click on the HelloControl entry (HelloControl was the name given to the project when you created this control) in the Components dialog box and close that dialog box to add the HelloControl control to the Visual Basic toolbox.

Next, draw a new HelloControl ActiveX control on the program's main form, creating the new control **UserControl1**; then, run the program, as shown in Figure 16.10.

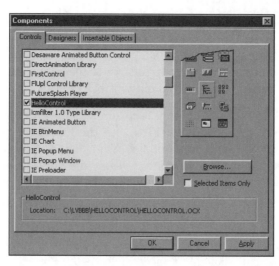

Figure 16.9   *The ActiveX control appears in the Components dialog box.*

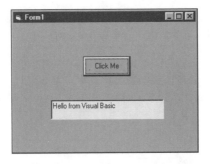

Figure 16.10   *Running the ActiveX control in a Visual Basic program.*

That's it—now you've created, registered, and added a functioning
ActiveX control to a Visual Basic program.

Giving An ActiveX Control A Property

In the previous topic, you added your custom HelloControl ActiveX
control (created in the last few topics in this chapter) to a Visual Basic program. The control has several properties already built into it,
as you can see in the Properties window in Figure 16.11.

These standard properties are called *ambient properties*; they're
stored in **AmbientProperties** objects, which you get from the
Ambient property. In addition, you can add your own properties to

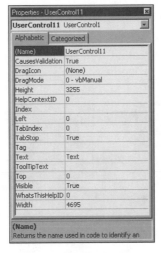

Figure 16.11   *The Visual Basic Properties window.*

an ActiveX control; these properties are stored in **Extender** objects, which you get from the **Extender** property.

Let's look at an example that adds a **Text** property to the HelloControl ActiveX control; this property will hold the text in the text box. After you add this property, programs that use HelloControl will be able to reach the **Text** property just as they reach any other control's properties, like this:

```
Private Sub Command1_Click()
    Text1.Text = UserControl1.Text
End Sub
```

Open the HelloControl project now and open the code window. Next, select the Tools|Add Procedure menu item to open the Add Procedure dialog box.

Be sure the Property option button in the Type box is selected, and give this new property the name **Text**, as shown in Figure 16.12.

Now, close the Add Procedure dialog box to create two new procedures for the **Text** property, **Get** and **Let**:

```
Public Property Get Text() As Variant

End Property

Public Property Let Text(ByVal vNewValue As Variant)

End Property
```

When another program wants to read the value in the **Text** property, the **Get** procedure is called. You return the text in the control's text box (**Text1**) in that procedure, like this:

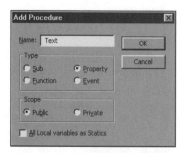

Figure 16.12   *Using the Add Procedure dialog box to give an ActiveX control a property.*

```
Public Property Get Text() As Variant
    Text = Text1.Text
End Property

Public Property Let Text(ByVal vNewValue As Variant)

End Property
```

On the other hand, when another program wants to set the value in the **Text** property, the **Let** procedure is called. You store that text in the text box this way:

```
Public Property Get Text() As Variant
    Text = Text1.Text
End Property

Public Property Let Text(ByVal vNewValue As Variant)
    Text1.Text = vNewValue
End Property
```

That's all it takes—now you're supporting a property in an ActiveX control. When other programs add this control, they can refer to this new **Text** property as they would any other property:

```
Private Sub Command1_Click()
    Text1.Text = UserControl11.Text
End Sub
```

In fact, you can put this **Command1_Click** code to work now in another program. Figure 16.13 shows the result of adding the previous code snippet to read the text in the HelloControl's **Text** property and to display that text in a text box. The ActiveX control is a success.

Figure 16.13   *Supporting a property in an ActiveX control.*

However, there's a problem—if the user places text in the HelloControl's **Text** property at design time, that text doesn't appear at runtime. To see how to make the HelloControl's **Text** property persistent between design time and runtime, see the next topic.

Making An ActiveX Control's Properties Persistent

You can store property settings in ActiveX controls by using the **PropertyBag** object. For example, if you want the property settings the user makes in your control at design time to apply when the program runs, you must make the properties persistent.

Let's look at an example that makes the **Text** property of the HelloControl ActiveX control developed in the previous few topics persistent. To do that, you first call the Visual Basic **PropertyChanged** procedure when the **Text** property is changed in its **Let** procedure. You pass the name of the property that's been changed to **PropertyChanged**, like this:

```
Public Property Let Text(ByVal vNewValue As Variant)
    Text1.Text = vNewValue
    PropertyChanged "Text"
End Property
```

When you call **PropertyChanged**, the control creates a **WriteProperties** event; you can write the new settings of properties to the **PropertyBag** object, which stores them on disk. Here's how you use **WriteProperty**:

```
UserControl.WriteProperty(propertyname, value [,default])
```

For example, to write the current settings of the HelloControl's property, you add this code to the **WriteProperties** event handler:

```
Private Sub UserControl_WriteProperties(PropBag As _
        PropertyBag)PropBag.WriteProperty "Text", Text1.Text
End Sub
```

When the control needs to read its stored properties, it creates a **ReadProperties** event. In that event's handler, you can use **ReadProperty**:

```
UserControl.ReadProperty(propertyname [,default])
```

Here's how to use **ReadProperty** to read stored properties:

```
Private Sub UserControl_ReadProperties(PropBag As _
     PropertyBag)
    Text1.Text = PropBag.ReadProperty("Text", "Text")
End Sub
```

Now the **Text** property is persistent.

Besides the **WriteProperties** and **ReadProperties** events, user controls also have **Initialize** events that occur when the control is opened at design time and **Terminate** events that occur when you switch to runtime from design time (that is, when the design-time instance of the control is terminated).

Here's the order of events that occur when you switch from design time to runtime:

• **WriteProperties**

• **Terminate**

• **ReadProperties**

And here's the order of events that occur when you switch from runtime to design time:

• **Initialize**

• **ReadProperties**

Giving An ActiveX Control A Method

How do you add a method to an ActiveX control? You do so in much the same way you add a property—with the Tools menu's Add Procedure dialog box.

Let's look at an example that adds a new **SetText** method to the HelloControl ActiveX control developed in the previous few topics in this chapter. When the control's **SetText** method is called, you'll display the message *Hello from Visual Basic* in the control's text box.

Open the HelloControl ActiveX project in Visual Basic and open the code window, as well. Next, select the Tools|Add Procedure menu item to open the Add Procedure dialog box. Give this new method the name **SetText**, as shown in Figure 16.14.

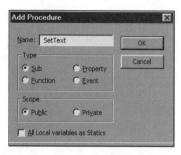

Figure 16.14   *Using the Add Procedure dialog box to give an ActiveX control a method.*

Select the Sub option button in the Type box to make the new method a Sub procedure, and be sure the Public option button in the Scope box is selected (this makes the method available to container programs outside the ActiveX control). Click on OK to close the Add Procedure dialog box.

Following these steps creates a new **SetText** procedure in the HelloControl ActiveX control:

```
Public Sub SetText()

End Sub
```

If you want arguments passed to this method, simply add them to the argument list between the parentheses, as you would for any subroutine.

In this case, you want to place the message *Hello from Visual Basic* in **Text1**, and you do that with this code:

```
Public Sub SetText()
    Text1.Text = "Hello from Visual Basic"
End Sub
```

That's all you need; now, create the HelloControl control and embed it in another program as **HelloControlControl1**. When you do, you can use the control's **SetText** method like this: **HelloControlControl1.SetText**.

For example, you can add a new button with the caption "Set text" to the project and add this code to the command button's **Click** event:

```
Private Sub Command2_Click()
    HelloControlControl1.SetText
End Sub
```

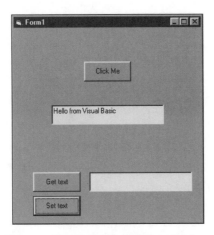

Figure 16.15 *Calling a custom ActiveX control method.*

The result appears in Figure 16.15—when the user clicks on Set Text, Visual Basic executes the HelloControl ActiveX control's **SetText** method. The ActiveX method example is a success.

Giving An ActiveX Control An Event

ActiveX controls can support events, of course, and the custom ActiveX controls you design with Visual Basic are no exception. You add events much as you add properties and methods—with the Tools|Add Procedure menu item. After you create a new event, it's up to you to raise that event with the **RaiseEvent** method.

Let's look at an example that adds an event named **HellocontrolClick** to the HelloControl ActiveX control developed in the previous few topics in this chapter. When the user clicks on the HelloControl control, the **HellocontrolClick** event will occur.

To add this event to the HelloControl ActiveX control, open the HelloControl ActiveX project in Visual Basic and open the code window, as well. Next, select the Tools|Add Procedure menu item to open the Add Procedure dialog box.

As shown in Figure 16.16, type "HellocontrolClick" in the Name box and select the Event option button in the Type box to indicate that you want to create a new event. Click on OK.

Doing so creates the new event by declaring it in the ActiveX control's (General) section:

16: Coding ActiveX

315

Figure 16.16   *Using the Add Procedure dialog box to give an ActiveX control an event.*

```
Public Event HellocontrolClick()
```

If you want to add arguments to this event's handler procedures, list them in the parentheses as you would for any procedure.

How do you make this new event active? It's up to you to raise this event when appropriate, using the **RaiseEvent** method. In this case, that's particularly easy—you'll use the user control's **Click** event. Add a **Click** event handler to the HelloControl ActiveX control now:

```
Private Sub UserControl_Click()

End Sub
```

This event handler will be called when the HelloControl control is clicked on. In this handler, you'll raise the **HellocontrolClick** event:

```
Private Sub UserControl_Click()
    RaiseEvent HellocontrolClick
End Sub
```

If your event supports arguments, you raise it and pass the arguments to it with the syntax

```
RaiseEvent eventname([argumentlist])
```

just as you would pass arguments to any procedure.

Now, when you embed the HelloControl control in a Visual Basic program, you'll find that it has a **HellocontrolClick** event to which you can add code. For example, here's how to use the **HellocontrolClick** event to display the text *You clicked the control* in a text box in a program that uses the new control:

```
Private Sub UserControl11_HellocontrolClick()
    Text2.Text = "You clicked the control"
End Sub
```

The result appears in Figure 16.17. As you can see, the program displays the message *You clicked the control* when the user clicks on the HelloControl ActiveX control.

In this way, you've added a new event to your ActiveX control.

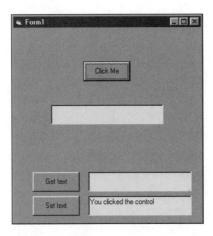

Figure 16.17 *The result of adding an event to an ActiveX control.*

Classes And Objects

In Brief

In this chapter, we'll see how to create and use classes and objects in Visual Basic. You're already very familiar with objects in Visual Basic—for example, you refer to controls in a Visual Basic program as *objects*. You access their properties, events, and methods using the dot (.) operator. For example, this code places the text *Hello from Visual Basic* in a text box (**Text1**) when the user clicks on a command button:

```
Private Sub Command1_Click()
    Text1.Text = "Hello from Visual Basic"
End Sub
```

Using classes, you can create your own objects; in fact, you can think of classes as templates for Visual Basic objects. As we'll see in this chapter, when you declare an object, you use that object's class as its *type*.

Although it's useful to create and use classes for their own sake, programmers usually create classes in Visual Basic to build code components (formerly called OLE automation servers). We'll also cover code components in some detail in this chapter.

Code Components

What is a code component? Code components are at the core of the Component Object Model (COM). You can think of a code component as a library of classes, ready to be used by other applications (called *client applications*).

For example, you might have a terrific record-sorting routine that you want to use in a dozen different programs. You can put the routine in a code component, register the code component with Windows, and then use the routine in that code component in other programs.

In other words, a code component is made up of one or more classes, and other applications can create objects from those classes and use the methods, properties, and events of those new objects.

Visual Basic supports a three-part ActiveX component set:

- ActiveX controls
- ActiveX documents
- Code components

You build code components as ActiveX EXEs or ActiveX DLLs, much as you create ActiveX controls or documents (the DLLs are in-process code components, and the EXEs are out-of-process code components).

When you create a code component, you add code in class module(s); when you register the code component with Windows, you make the class(es) available to client applications. Those applications in turn can add a *reference* to your code component and create a class object with the **New**, **CreateObject**, or other Visual Basic statement (we'll see how to create objects later in this chapter). When the client application includes an object corresponding to one of your classes, it can use that class's properties and methods.

Code components are all about reusing your code. You get an object corresponding to a class in a code component as in the following code snippet, which creates an object **objClock** of the class **ClockClass** from the hypothetical code component **ClockComponent**:

```
Dim objClock As Object
Set objClock = CreateObject("ClockComponent.ClockClass")
    .
    .
    .
```

Now, you can use that object's properties and methods to give you access to the code in the class:

```
Dim objClock As Object
Set objClock = CreateObject("ClockComponent.ClockClass")

objClock.Hours = 3                    'Use a property
intSeconds = objClock.GetSeconds      'Use a method
    .
    .
    .
```

If you've created your code component as an ActiveX EXE, that code component is an out-of-process server that runs separately from the client application. If you've created your code component as an ActiveX DLL, that code component is an in-process server that will run as part of the client application's process.

That's it for our overview—now we'll put classes, objects, and code components to work in the Immediate Solutions part of this chapter.

17: Classes And Objects

Immediate Solutions

Creating A Class

How do you create a class in Visual Basic? You use a class module. To add a class module to a project, select the Project|Add Class Module menu item to open the Add Class Module dialog box, as shown in Figure 17.1.

Simply select the Class Module icon in the Add Class Module dialog box and click on Open. Doing so adds a new, empty class module (that is, an empty code window) to your project. The name of this new class (as set in the Properties window) is **Class1**. To find out how to create an object of this new class, see the next topic.

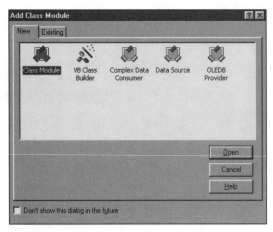

Figure 17.1   *Adding a class module to a project.*

Creating An Object From A Class

When you have a class to work with, you can create objects of that class in a variety of ways. For example, if you have a **Class1** class and you want to create an object of that class in a form in the same project, you can use the **Set** and **New** keywords, like this:

```
Private Sub Command1_Click()
    Dim obj As Object
    Set obj = New Class1
End Sub
```

When you want to create an object from a code component, however, you must first add a reference to that code component using the Visual Basic Project|References menu item (note that the code component must be registered with Windows).

In general, you can create objects in Visual Basic in three ways:

- Declare the variable using the **New** keyword (in statements such as **Dim**, **Public**, or **Private**). Visual Basic will automatically assign a new object reference the first time you use the variable (that is, when you refer to one of its methods or properties). This technique works only with code components that supply *type libraries* (as the code components created with Visual Basic do), which specify what's in the code component.

- Assign a reference to a new object in a **Set** statement by using the **New** keyword or the **CreateObject** function.

- Assign a reference to a new or existing object in a **Set** statement by using the **GetObject** function.

Let's look at some examples. Here we'll assume you've already added a reference to the code component containing the classes you'll work with.

If the code component you're using supplies a type library (as the ones built with Visual basic do) or if you're declaring an object of a class in the same project, you can use the **New** keyword to declare and create the object. For example, this code creates an object named **objAdder** of the **Adder** class:

```
Dim objAdder As New Adder
objAdder.Add
```

Visual Basic actually creates the object only when you refer to it for the first time.

Regardless of whether a code component supplies a type library, you can use the **CreateObject** function in a **Set** statement to create a new object and assign an object reference to an object variable. To use **CreateObject**, you pass it the name of a code component and class. For example, here's how to use **CreateObject** to create a new

Sheet object named **objExcel** from the Microsoft Excel code component library:

```
Dim objExcel As Object
Set objExcel = CreateObject("Excel.Sheet")
```

Note the way you specify the name of the class from which to create the object: **Excel.Sheet** (that is, *CodeComponent.Class*). Because the code components you create with **CreateObject** don't need a type library, you must refer to the class you want to use as *CodeComponent.Class* rather than just *Class*, as you can with **New**.

You can also use the **GetObject** function to assign a reference to a new class, although this function is generally used to assign a reference to an existing object. You use **GetObject** as follows:

```
Set objectvariable = GetObject([pathname] [, class])
```

Here's what the arguments of this function mean:

* *pathname*—The path to an existing file or an empty string; this argument can be omitted.

* *class*—The name of the class you want to create an object of. If *pathname* is omitted, then *class* is required.

Passing an empty string for the first argument makes **GetObject** work like **CreateObject**: It creates a new object of the class whose name is in the *class* argument. For example, this code creates an object of the class **ClockClass** in the code component **ClockComponent** using **GetObject** (once again, you refer to the class you're using as *CodeComponent.Class*):

```
Set objClockComponent = GetObject("", _
  "ClockComponent.ClockClass")
```

Using Classes In The Same Project

After you've created a new class named, say, **Class1**, you can create objects of that class in other modules in the same project using the **Set** and **New** keywords. For example, here's how to create an object named **obj** of class **Class1** when the user clicks on a command button:

```
Private Sub Command1_Click()
  Dim obj As Object
```

```
    Set obj - New Class1
End Sub
```

Now you can refer to the properties, events, and methods of the new
obj object as you would for any other Visual Basic object. For example, assuming that **obj** has a property named **Text**, you can display the value of that property in a text box (**Text1**):

```
Private Sub Command1_Click()
    Dim obj As Object
    Set obj - New Class1
    Text1.Text - "Text property - " & obj.Text
End Sub
```

Using Code Components In Client Applications

Code components provide libraries of classes across application
boundaries. In fact, you can treat OLE automation servers like Excel
as code components, adding them to your program and using them as
desired. To do that, you add a reference to the code component to
your program, create an object from that code component, and then
use the properties and methods of that object.

Let's look at an example that uses Microsoft Excel in a Visual Basic
program to multiply 1 * 2 * 3 and display the result in a text box. To
begin, add a reference to Excel by choosing the Project|References
menu item, selecting the Microsoft Excel Object Library item, and
clicking on OK.

Now, add a button (**Command1**) with the caption *Multiply 1 * 2 * 3
Using Microsoft Excel* to the program; also add a text box (**Text1**) in
which to display the results of the multiplication. When the user clicks
on the button, you create an object (**objExcel**) from the Excel library using the Visual Basic **CreateObject** function:

```
Private Sub Command1_Click()
    Dim objExcel As Object
    Set objExcel - CreateObject("Excel.Sheet")
    .
    .
    .
```

Note that Excel will stay hidden throughout the program's execution.

Now that you have your new object, you can use its properties as in the following code, which places 1, 2, and 3 in cells (1,1), (2,1), and (3,1), respectively:

```
Private Sub Command1_Click()
    Dim objExcel As Object
    Set objExcel = CreateObject("Excel.Sheet")

    objExcel.Cells(1, 1).Value = "1"
    objExcel.Cells(2, 1).Value = "2"
    objExcel.Cells(3, 1).Value = "3"
    .
    .
    .
```

To multiply these values, place an Excel formula in cell (4,1), the cell beneath these three:

```
Private Sub Command1_Click()
    Dim objExcel As Object
    Set objExcel = CreateObject("Excel.Sheet")

    objExcel.Cells(1, 1).Value = "1"
    objExcel.Cells(2, 1).Value = "2"
    objExcel.Cells(3, 1).Value = "3"

    objExcel.Cells(4, 1).Formula = "=R1C1 * R2C1 * R3C1"
    .
    .
    .
```

Finally, you display the resulting product in the text box **Text1** and quit Excel, like this:

```
Private Sub Command1_Click()
    Dim objExcel As Object
    Set objExcel = CreateObject("Excel.Sheet")

    objExcel.Cells(1, 1).Value = "1"
    objExcel.Cells(2, 1).Value = "2"
    objExcel.Cells(3, 1).Value = "3"

    objExcel.Cells(4, 1).Formula = "=R1C1 * R2C1 * R3C1"
    Text1.Text = "Microsoft Excel says: 1 * 2 * 3 = " & _
        objExcel.Cells(4, 1)
```

```
        objExcel.Application.Quit
End Sub
```

The result appears in Figure 17.2. Congratulations—you've created your first code component client application.

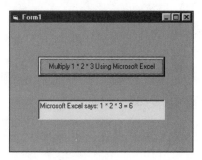

Figure 17.2 *Using Microsoft Excel as a code component.*

Writing A Code Component

You can create two types of code components: in-process components and out-of-process components.

- When you create a code component as an ActiveX DLL, it will run as an in-process component, in the same process as the client application.

- When you create a code component as an ActiveX EXE, it will run as an out-of-process component, in a different process than the client application.

As it turns out, there are also two ways to create each type of code component in Visual Basic. From the New Project window, you can create an ActiveX DLL or ActiveX EXE by selecting the appropriate icon and clicking on OK to create the files you'll need. Or, you can set the project type using the Project|Properties menu item in a standard project to convert it to an ActiveX DLL or ActiveX EXE project.

Let's use the first (shorter) way here. Select the ActiveX EXE icon in the New Project dialog box, as shown in Figure 17.3, to create a new project.

Next, set the project name in the Project Properties dialog box to the name of the new code component. For example, let's use the name **ClockComponent** and create a new component that will have built-in clock functions.

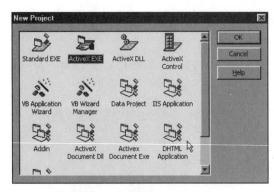

Figure 17.3   *Creating a new code component.*

Set the class module's **Name** property to the name you want to use for your new class (in this case, **ClockClass**) and that's it—you've created a new class. However, there isn't much going on in this class, so let's add a **strTime** property to the **ClockClass** class. To do that, add this code to the class module:

```
Option Explicit

Public strTime As String
    .
    .
    .
```

Declaring a variable as **Public** in a class module makes it available as a property to client applications, as we'll see when we discuss properties later in this chapter. To set the value of your new property to the time an object of this class is created, add code using the **Time$** function to the class's **Initialize** event, which occurs when Visual Basic first loads the code component:

```
Option Explicit

Public strTime As String

Private Sub Class_Initialize()
    strTime = Time$
End Sub
```

Now you've created a new code component and a new class that supports a property. To make this component available to client applications, simply create its EXE file using the File|Make ClockComponent.exe menu item, and then run that EXE file to register the code component with Windows. Now you can add a reference to **ClockComponent** in another program, create objects from the **ClockClass** in that component, and use the **strTime** property of that object this way:

```
Dim objClock As Object

Private Sub Form_Load()
    Set objClock = CreateObject("ClockComponent.ClockClass")
End Sub

Private Sub Command1_Click()
    Text1.Text = objClock.strTime
End Sub
```

Making A Code Component In-Process Or Out-Of-Process

There are two types of code components: in-process components and out-of-process components.

• When you create a code component as an ActiveX DLL, it will run as an in-process component, in the same process as the client application.

• When you create a code component as an ActiveX EXE, it will run as an out-of-process component, in a different process from the client application.

Both types offer advantages. For example, an in-process component runs more quickly, but an out-of-process component can self-register (just run the EXE file to register the component with Windows).

Giving A Class A Property

You can add properties to a class in a code component in two ways: by declaring them as **Public** variables or by using **Let** and **Get** functions. We'll take a look at the first technique here and the second technique in the next topic.

The first way to create properties in a class module is very easy: You simply declare the property you want as a **Public** variable in the class module's (General) declarations area. Making a variable public in a class module makes it a property of that module.

You can also declare variables in a class module as **Private** (meaning they aren't available outside the module) or as **Friend**. When you declare **Friend** variables, they're available to the other objects in your code component but not to client applications—in other words, **Friend** works as a sort of local **Public** declaration.

Let's look at an example. In the "Writing A Code Component" topic earlier in this chapter, we created a class named **ClockClass** and added a **strTime** property to that class by simply declaring the property as a public variable:

```
Option Explicit

Public strTime As String
   .
   .
   .
```

In addition, we initialized the value of that property with the **Initialize** event when Visual Basic first loads the class:

```
Option Explicit

Public strTime As String

Private Sub Class_Initialize()
    strTime = Time$
End Sub
```

To use this new property, you add a reference to **ClockComponent** in another program; then, you can create an object from **ClockClass** in that component and use the **strTime** property of that object this way:

```
Dim objClock As Object

Private Sub Form_Load()
    Set objClock = CreateObject("ClockComponent.ClockClass")
End Sub

Private Sub Command1_Click()
    Text1.Text = objClock.strTime
End Sub
```

That's one way to add a property to a class, but note that client applications have full access to this property—they can read it and set it any time and any way they wish. If you want to restrict possible property values (for example, by ensuring that a **Date** property holds only legal dates), use the property **Get** and **Let** methods we'll look at in the next topic.

Giving A Class A **Get/Let** Property

You can add properties to a class in a code component in two ways: by declaring them as **Public** variables or by using **Let** and **Get** functions. We covered the first technique in the previous topic; we'll discuss the second technique here.

Suppose programmers keep setting your class's **sngDayOfTheMonth** property to values greater than 31. How can you watch for those settings? If you want to be in control when client applications set or get your class's properties, use **Get** and **Let** methods to allow the client application to get or set the property.

To set up a property with **Get/Let** methods in a class module, open the class module's code window and select the Tools|Add Procedure menu item; doing so opens the Add Procedure dialog box shown in Figure 17.4. Select the Property option button in the Type box and the Public option button in the Scope box, and then click on OK to close the Add Procedure dialog box. Doing so adds the **Get/Let** procedures for this property—it's up to you to customize them.

Let's look at an example that adds a new **sngDayOfTheMonth** property to the **ClockClass** class developed in the previous few topics in this chapter. This new property can be set only to values less than or equal to 31.

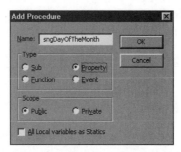

Figure 17.4   *Using the Add Procedure dialog box to give a class a Get/Let property.*

To add this new property to **ClockClass**, open that class module's code window and select the Tools\Add Procedure menu item. Set this property's name to **sngDayOfTheMonth** (as shown in Figure 17.4), select the Property and Public option buttons, and click on OK.

When you do so, Visual Basic adds two new procedures to the class module for this property:

```
Public Property Get sngDayOfTheMonth() As Variant

End Property

Public Property Let sngDayOfTheMonth(ByVal vNewValue As Variant)

End Property
```

When client applications want to get the value in the **sngDayOfTheMonth** property, the **sngDayOfTheMonth Get** procedure is called; when they want to set the value in the **sngDayOfTheMonth** property, the **sngDayOfTheMonth Let** procedure is called.

Visual Basic gives this new property the default type **Variant**; you can change this type to one appropriate for your property. In this case, let's make **sngDayOfTheMonth** a **Single** value:

```
Public Property Get sngDayOfTheMonth() As Single

End Property

Public Property Let sngDayOfTheMonth(ByVal vNewValue _
    As Single)

End Property
```

At this point, you're ready to add code to support the **sngDayOfTheMonth** property. For example, you can store the actual value in this property in an internal variable named **sngDay**:

```
Option Explicit

Public strTime As Single
Private sngDay As Single
    .
    .
    .
```

Now, when a client application asks for the value in the **sngDayOfTheMonth** property, you pass back the value in **sngDay**:

```
Public Property Get sngDayOfTheMonth() As Single
    sngDayOfTheMonth = sngDay
End Property
```

On the other hand, if a client application tries to set the value in **sngDayOfTheMonth**, you'll check first to be sure the value is less than or equal to 31 before storing it in **sngDay**:

```
Public Property Let sngDayOfTheMonth(ByVal vNewValue _
  As Single)
    If vNewValue <= 31 Then
        sngDay = vNewValue
    End If
End Property
```

To use this new property, add a reference to **ClockComponent** in another program. Then, you can create objects from the **ClockClass** in the component and use the **sngDayOfTheMonth** property of that object as follows:

```
Dim objClock As Object

Private Sub Form_Load()
    Set objClock = CreateObject("ClockComponent.ClockClass")
End Sub

Private Sub Command1_Click()
    objClock.sngDayOfTheMonth = 18
    Text1.Text = objClock.sngDayOfTheMonth
End Sub
```

In this way, you can control the values stored in the properties in code components.

Giving A Class A Method

You can add a method to a class in a code component as easily as you add a property. Methods can be either public subroutines or functions; you can add them to a class module with the Tools|Add Procedure menu item.

Besides declaring procedures **Public** in a class module, you can also declare them as **Private** (meaning they aren't available outside the module) or as **Friend**. **Friend** procedures are available to the other objects in your code component, but not to client applications—in other words, **Friend** works as a sort of local **Public** declaration.

Let's look at an example that adds a method to the **ClockClass** class developed in the previous few topics. This new method—**sngGetDay**—will return the value currently in the class's **sngDayOfTheMonth** property.

To add this method, open the **ClockClass**'s code window and select the Tools|Add Procedure menu item. In the resulting Add Procedure dialog box, add a new public function named **sngGetDay**. When you close the dialog box by clicking on OK, Visual Basic adds this code to the class module:

```
Public Function sngGetDay()

End Function
```

As it stands, this function returns a **Variant**. Let's make it return a **Single** value, the same type as the **sngDayOfTheMonth** property:

```
Public Function sngGetDay() As Single

End Function
```

Now you're ready to write the code for this method, which simply returns the value in the **sngDayOfTheMonth** property (that value is stored in the **sngDay** variable):

```
Public Function sngGetDay() As Single
    sngGetDay = sngDay
End Function
```

That's all it takes—now you've added a new method to the **ClockClass** class. To use this new method, add a reference to **ClockComponent** in another program; then, you can create objects from the **ClockClass** in the component and use the **sngGetDay** method of that object this way:

```
Dim objClock As Object

Private Sub Form_Load()
```

```
    Set objClock = CreateObject("ClockComponent.ClockClass")
End Sub

Private Sub Command1_Click()
    objClock.sngDayOfTheMonth = 12
    Text1.Text = objClock.sngGetDay
End Sub
```

Passing Arguments To A Class Method

You can pass arguments to class methods just as you can to other procedures—simply specify an argument list in the method's declaration.

Certain method arguments should be declared **ByVal** for out-of-process components and **ByRef** for in-process components. When you're declaring methods for objects provided by an out-of-process component, use **ByVal** to declare arguments that will contain object references. In addition, if you expect client applications to pass large strings or **Variant** arrays to a method, and the method doesn't modify the data, declare the parameter **ByVal** for an out-of-process component but **ByRef** for an in-process component.

Creating And Registering An In-Process Code Component

How do you create and register the real code component for use in actual client applications? You can create the actual code component in two ways: one way if you're creating an in-process code component (an ActiveX DLL) and another way if you're creating an out-of-process code component (an ActiveX EXE). We'll take a look at in-process code components here and out-of-process code components in the next topic.

To create the in-process server's DLL file, select the File|Make *ProjectName*.dll menu item. To register that DLL file with Windows, you use a Windows utility—such as regsvr32.exe—like this:

```
c:\>c:\windows\system\regsvr32 ProjectName.dll
```

Creating And Registering An Out-Of-Process Code Component

How do you create and register the real code component for use in actual client applications? You can create the actual code component in two ways: one way if you're creating an in-process code component (an ActiveX DLL) and another way if you're creating an out-of-process code component (an ActiveX EXE). We took a look at in-process code components in the previous topic, and we'll cover out-of-process code components here.

To create the out-of-process code component's EXE file, select the File|Make *ProjectName*.exe menu item. To register that out-of-process code component with Windows, simply run the EXE file. Your code component is now ready to use.

Using A Class's **Initialize** Event

The **Initialize** event occurs when a client application creates an instance of a class—you can use this event to initialize the object that's being created. No arguments are passed to this event's handler.

Let's look at an example. When we created the class **ClockClass** in the **ClockComponent** code component earlier in this chapter, we set up a property named **strTime** and initialized it to the current time in the **Initialize** event handler, like this:

```
Option Explicit

Public strTime As String

Private Sub Class_Initialize()
    strTime = Time$
End Sub
```

Using A Class's **Terminate** Event

An object's **Terminate** event occurs when the object goes out of scope or when you set it to the **Nothing** keyword. You can use this event to clean up after the object—for instance, by releasing allocated memory or resources.

Here's an example that you can add to the class **ClockClass** in the **ClockComponent** code component developed earlier in this chapter. In this case, you use the **Terminate** event to display a message box to the user, indicating that the **ClockClass** object the user created is being terminated:

```
Private Sub Class_Terminate()
    MsgBox "Terminating now!"
End Sub
```

Destroying An Object

An object can be destroyed in two ways. It's destroyed automatically when it goes out of scope. If you don't want to wait for that to happen, you can set its variable using the Visual Basic **Nothing** keyword—doing so destroys the object and releases its memory:

```
Set objBigObject = Nothing
```

Programming With
Database Controls

In Brief

This is the first of two chapters on databases—an immense topic in Visual Basic. To cover the subject adequately, I'd need whole volumes, but that kind of space isn't available here. However, we'll cover some of the most common database-handling techniques. Due to space constraints, we'll restrict ourselves to working with the database objects originally designed to work with Visual Basic: Data Access Objects (DAO). The DAO standard serves Visual Basic programmers well. However, if you need more database programming depth, turn to one of the large books written expressly on Visual Basic database programming.

You can work with Visual Basic databases in two ways; we'll discuss one in this chapter and the other in the next chapter.

Database Controls Vs. Database Objects

The first way to work with databases uses the special controls that support databases:

- The data control, which supports DAO

- The remote-data control, which supports Open Database Connectivity (ODBC)

- ADO data control, which supports Active Data Objects (ADO)

You use those controls to connect to and move through databases, but they don't actually display data—you *bind* them to other Visual Basic controls, and those bound controls handle the display.

You can also work with the three database object sets directly in code, without using controls like the data control; we'll try that technique in the next chapter when we examine the DAO objects in code.

Besides DAO, Visual Basic now supports Remote Data Objects (RDO) and ADO. At first, Visual Basic supported only DAO, which connected it to the Microsoft Jet database engine. Then, Microsoft created the ODBC standard and supported ODBC with RDO in Visual Basic. Finally, Microsoft created ADO, which forms a flexible standard that allows connections on the same computer, over networks, and the

Web; it's intended to supercede ODBC. ADO is also called OLE DB, and it's based on COM programming techniques.

Let's get started exploring the DAO database controls now as we turn to the Immediate Solutions part of this chapter.

18: Programming With Database Controls

Immediate Solutions

What's A Database?

The fundamental concept behind a database is a simple one. Say you're in charge of the inventory at a publishing house and you keep a list of book titles and the quantity of each title you have in the warehouse. This list could be made into a table, with one row for each book and two columns: "Title" for book titles and "Number" for the number of books in the warehouse, as you see in Table 18.1.

At this point, you've already created a database—or, more specifically, a database *table*. The transition from a table on paper to one in a computer is natural: With a computer, you can sort, index, update, and organize large tables of data easily (and without wasting paper). You can even connect tables, creating *relational* databases.

Each individual data entry in a table—such as a book's name—goes in a *field*. A collection of fields, such as the Title and Number fields in our table, makes up a *record*. Each record has its own row in a table, and each column in that row represents a different field.

A collection of records—that is, rows of records in which each column is a field—becomes a table. What, then, is a *database*? A database is simply a collection of one or more tables. In fact, you can go farther than that in Visual Basic—you can create collections of databases. In DAO, those collections are called the *workspace*. A database can also have *indices* that provide pointers to specific fields, either in the current database or another one.

Now that you've set up a database, how do you work with the data in it? One popular way is to use Structured Query Language (SQL). You use SQL to set up a *query*, which (when applied to a database) yields

Table 18.1   Data for the books database.

Title	Number
Riding the Rails	1000
Roving the Roads	2000
Sailing the Seas	3000
Mastering the Mountains	4000

a *recordset*. This recordset contains the records from the database that matched your query—for example, you might ask for all book titles of which you have fewer than 1000 copies in the warehouse. We'll see more about working with databases in code in the next chapter.

Related solution:	Found in:
Executing SQL In Code	Chapter 19

Using The Visual Data Manager To Create Databases

Visual Basic comes with a tool for working with databases: the Visual Data Manager. You open this tool from the Visual Basic Add-Ins menu, as shown in Figure 18.1.

You can use the Visual Data Manager to create and modify databases. You create a new database with the File|New menu item and open an existing database with the File|Open menu item.

Let's look at an example that creates a new database with the Visual Data Manager. Click on the Table Type Recordset button (at the far

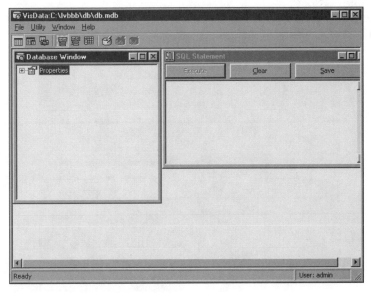

Figure 18.1   *The Visual Data Manager.*

left on the toolbar) and the Use Data Control On New Form button (fourth button from the left).

Next, select the FileINew menu item. The Visual Data Manager lets you design databases in several different formats; for this example, choose Microsoft Access Version 7 MDB (or later, if a later version is indicated). The Visual Data Manager will ask you for a name and path for this new database; enter the name "db.mdb" and click on OK.

Now that you've created a new database, you'll add a table to it in the next topic.

Creating A Table With The Visual Data Manager

To add a table named *books* to the db.mdb database created in the previous topic, right-click on the Properties item in the Visual Data Manager's Database Window to open the Table Structure dialog box.

Name the new table by typing "books" in the Table Name box, as shown in Figure 18.2. That's it—you've very quickly created a new table.

Now that you've created a new table, you'll add fields to it in the next topic.

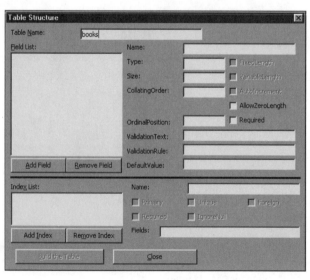

Figure 18.2   The Visual Data Manager's Table Structure dialog box.

Creating A Field With The Visual Data Manager

How do you add a field to a record in a database? To add fields to the books database table created in the previous topic, click on the Add Field button in the Visual Data Manager's Table Structure dialog box. Doing so opens the Add Field dialog box; note that some default values are filled in automatically when the dialog box opens.

Name this new field by typing "Title" in the Name box, as shown in Figure 18.3; then, click on OK. The Add Field dialog box will stay open, and Visual Basic will add the new field to the books table. Add another field by typing Number in the Name box; then, click on OK to add the field and click on Close to close the Add Field dialog box.

Now, in the Table Structure dialog box, click on the Build The Table button. Doing so incorporates the two new fields—Title and Number—into the table you created in the last topic, and it opens that table in the Visual Data Manager's Database Window, as you can see in Figure 18.4.

In the next topic, you'll enter data into the new table.

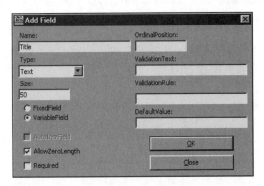

Figure 18.3   *The Visual Data Manager's Add Field dialog box.*

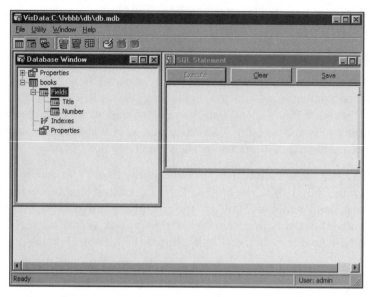

Figure 18.4   *The newly created database.*

Using The Visual Data Manager To Place Data In A Database

To enter data into a table in the Visual Data Manager, right-click on the table's entry in the Database Window and select the Open item from the resulting menu.

In this case, doing so opens the Table:books dialog box. You'll use this dialog box to enter data into your database's records—in this case, the data from Table 18.1—but you can also use it to edit that data.

Type "Riding the Rails" in the Title box and "1000" in the Number box for the first book in the Table:books dialog box, as shown in Figure 18.5. Then, click on Update to add that new record to the database; when the Visual Data Manager displays a message box asking if you want to save the new record to the database, click on Yes.

Now, click on the Add button (which appears after you click on Update) and add another new record with the Title "Roving the Roads" and the Number "2000"; then, click on Update and answer Yes when the Visual Data Manager asks you if you want to save the new record to the database.

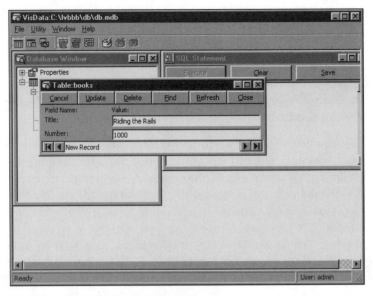

Figure 18.5 *Entering a record in a database.*

When you finish entering the records from Table 18.1, click on Close in the Table:books dialog box. Finally, close the database by choosing the Visual Data Manager's File|Close menu item.

You've created a new database; in the next several topics, you'll see how to work with it.

Placing A Data Control On A Form

The data control is the only intrinsic database control—it already appears in the toolbox. Double-click on that tool now to add a data control to your form.

Stretch the data control as desired. When you stretch the control beyond its original size, you'll see a space for text in the center of the control. Set the control's **Caption** property to the name of the database table you'll be working with: books.

That's all it takes to add a data control to your program.

Using The Visual Basic Data Control

The data control displays a set of arrow buttons that enable you to move from record to record in a database. You can display and manipulate data from the records in bound controls. Figure 18.6 shows a data control operating with bound controls; we've placed the books table in a database and opened it with a data control.

It turns out that you can perform most data-access operations using the data control, without writing any code. Data-bound controls automatically display data from one or more fields for the current record while the data control performs all operations on the current record. If you move the data control to a different record, all bound controls automatically pass any changes to the data control to be saved in the database. The data control then moves to the requested record and passes back data from the current record to the bound controls in which it's displayed.

When an application begins, Visual Basic uses data-control properties to open a selected database, create a DAO **Database** object, and create a **Recordset** object. The data control's **Database** and **Recordset** properties refer to those **Database** and **Recordset** objects, and you can manipulate the data using those properties. For example, if you need to execute an SQL statement, you place it in the data control's **RecordSource** property—the result appears in the **Recordset** property.

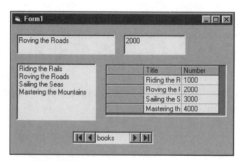

Figure 18.6   Using a data control.

Using The Visual Basic Data-Bound Controls

You can bind certain controls to the data control; those controls are called *bound controls*. To bind a control to a data control, use a property like **DataSource** to specify the database control, and then use a property like **DataField** or **BoundColumn** to specify which field to display in the bound control.

The following controls can function as bound controls: picture boxes, labels, text boxes, checkboxes, image controls, OLE controls, list boxes, masked-edit controls, rich-text boxes, and combo boxes.

In addition, several special controls are designed for use as bound controls: DBList, DBCombo, FlexGrid, and MSHFlexGrid.

After installing a data control, you can connect that control to other controls through the data-binding process. You bind controls to a data control using the data properties of the bound control. The standard bound controls and their data properties appear in Table 18.2. Using the information in that table, you can connect the listed Visual Basic controls to data controls.

For example, refer back to Figure 18.6. We've added to the form a number of controls bound to a data control (**Data1**): two text boxes, a DBList control, and a FlexGrid control (you can add the FlexGrid control or DBList control using the Project|Components menu item). The data control, in turn, is connected to the db.mdb database created earlier in the chapter. When you move through the database with

Table 18.2   The bound controls.

Control	Properties To Set
Checkbox	DataField = desired Boolean field, DataSource = data control's name
Combo box	DataField = desired field, DataSource = data control's name
DBCombo	BoundColumn = desired field, DataField = desired field, DataSource = data control's name, ListField = desired field, RowSource = data control's name
DBList	DataField = desired field, DataSource = data control's name, RowSource = data control's name
FlexGrid	DataSource = data control's name
Image	DataField = desired field, DataSource = data control's name
Label	DataField = desired field, DataSource = data control's name
List box	DataField = desired field, DataSource = data control's name
Masked edit	DataField = desired field, DataSource = data control's name
MSHFlexGrid	DataSource = data control's name
Picture box	DataField = desired field, DataSource = data control's name
Rich-text box	DataField = desired field, DataSource = data control's name
Text box	DataField = desired field, DataSource = data control's name

18: Programming With Database Controls

the data control, the data in each bound control is updated. The code for this program—db.frm—appears in Listing 18.1.

Listing 18.1   The db.frm code.

```
VERSION 6.00
Object = "{5E9E78A0-531B-11CF-91F6-C2863C385E30}#1.0#0"; _
   "MSFLXGRD.OCX"
Object = "{FAEEE763-117E-101B-8933-08002B2F4F5A}#1.1#0"; _
   "DBLIST32.OCX"
Begin VB.Form Form1
      Caption         =   "Form1"
      ClientHeight    =   3195
      ClientLeft      =   60
      ClientTop       =   345
      ClientWidth     =   5655
      LinkTopic       =   "Form1"
      ScaleHeight     =   3195
      ScaleWidth      =   5655
      StartUpPosition =   3  'Windows Default
      Begin MSDBCtls.DBList DBList1
         Bindings     =   "Form1.frx":0000
         Height       =   1425
         Left         =   120
         TabIndex     =   3
         Top          =   960
         Width        =   2055
         _ExtentX     =   3625
         _ExtentY     =   2514
         _Version     =   393216
         ListField    =   "Title"
      End
      Begin MSFlexGridLib.MSFlexGrid MSFlexGrid1
         Bindings     =   "Form1.frx":0014
         Height       =   1335
         Left         =   2400
         TabIndex     =   2
         Top          =   960
         Width        =   3135
         _ExtentX     =   5530
         _ExtentY     =   2355
         _Version     =   393216
      End
      Begin VB.TextBox Text2
         DataField    =   "Number"
         DataSource   =   "Data1"
         Height       =   495
         Left         =   2880
```

```
      TabIndex        =   1
      Top             =   240
      Width           =   1575
   End
   Begin VB.TextBox Text1
      DataField       =   "Title"
      DataSource      =   "Data1"
      Height          =   495
      Left            =   120
      TabIndex        =   0
      Top             =   240
      Width           =   2535
   End
   Begin VB.Data Data1
      Caption         =   "books"
      Connect         =   "Access"
      DatabaseName    =   "C:\lvbbb\db\db.mdb"
      DefaultCursorType=  0   'DefaultCursor
      DefaultType     =   2   'UseODBC
      Exclusive       =   0    'False
      Height          =   345
      Left            =   1560
      Options         =   0
      ReadOnly        =   0    'False
      RecordsetType   =   1   'Dynaset
      RecordSource    =   "books"
      Top             =   2640
      Width           =   2100
   End
End
Attribute VB_Name = "Form1"
Attribute VB_GlobalNameSpace = False
Attribute VB_Creatable = False
Attribute VB_PredeclaredId = True
Attribute VB_Exposed = False
```

Opening A Database In Code With The Data Control

To connect a data control to a database, you simply set the data control's **DatabaseName** property to the path and name of the database file you want to open. Let's look at an example that uses the db.mdb file created at the beginning of this chapter:

```
Private Sub Form_Load()
    Data1.DatabaseName = "c:\lvbbb\db\db.mdb"

    .
    .
    .

End Sub
```

In addition, you select the table you want to work with in that file using the data control's **RecordSource** property:

```
Private Sub Form_Load()
    Data1.DatabaseName = "c:\lvbbb\db\db.mdb"
    Data1.RecordSource = "books"
End Sub
```

Now you've connected your database to your data control.

Adding A Record In Code

You can add a new record to a database with the **AddNew** method of the **Recordset** property of a data control.

Let's look at an example. When the user clicks on the Add button, you can add a new record like this:

```
Private Sub cmdAdd_Click()
    Data1.Recordset.AddNew
End Sub
```

This code adds a new, blank record. You can enter the data you want in the record's fields using bound controls; to update the database, use the **Update** method.

Related solution:	Found in:
Recordsets: Adding A Record In Code	Chapter 19

Deleting A Record In Code

You can delete a database record with the **Delete** method of a data control's **Recordset** property.

For example, when the user clicks on the Delete button, you can delete a record like this:

```
Private Sub cmdDelete_Click()
    Data1.Recordset.Delete
End Sub
```

Related solution:	Found in:
Recordsets: Deleting A Record In Code	Chapter 19

Updating A Database In Code

After changing the fields in a record (by changing the data in the data-bound controls), you can update a database with the **UpdateRecord** method of the data control.

For example, when the user clicks on the Update button, you can update the database with the new record in the data control like this:

```
Private Sub cmdUpdate_Click()
    Data1.UpdateRecord
End Sub
```

Related solution:	Found in:
Recordsets: Updating A Database In Code	Chapter 19

Moving To The First Record In Code

You can move to a database's first record with the **MoveFirst** method of a data control's **Recordset** property. Let's look at an example. When the user clicks on the First button, you can move to the first record like this:

```
Private Sub cmdFirst_Click()
    Data1.Recordset.MoveFirst
End Sub
```

Related solution:	Found in:
Recordsets: Moving To The First Record In Code	Chapter 19

Moving To The Last Record In Code

You can move to a database's last record with the **MoveLast** method of a data control's **Recordset** property. Let's look at an example. When the user clicks on the Last button, you can move to the last record like this:

```
Private Sub cmdLast_Click()
    Data1.Recordset.MoveLast
End Sub
```

Related solution:	*Found in:*
Recordsets: Moving To The Last Record In Code	Chapter 19

Moving To The Previous Record In Code

You can move to the previous record of a database with the **MovePrevious** method of a data control's **Recordset** property.

For example, when the user clicks on the Previous button, you can move to the previous record like this:

```
Private Sub cmdPrevious_Click()
    Data1.Recordset.MovePrevious
End Sub
```

Related solution:	*Found in:*
Recordsets: Moving To The Previous Record In Code	Chapter 19

Avoiding Moving Before The Start Of The Database

When you use the **MovePrevious** method, be sure you don't try to move to a record before the first record of the database. You can check that you're not moving back too far by using the **BOF** (beginning of file) property of the data control's **Recordset** property:

```
Private Sub cmdPrevious_Click()
    If Not Data1.Recordset.BOF Then
```

```
        Data1.Recordset.MovePrevious
    End If
End Sub
```

Related solution:	Found in:
Recordsets: Avoiding Moving Past The First Record	Chapter 19

Moving To The Next Record In Code

You can move to the next record of a database with the **MoveNext** method of a data control's **Recordset** property.

For example, when the user clicks on the Next button, you can move to the next record like this:

```
Private Sub cmdNext_Click()
    Data1.Recordset.MoveNext
End Sub
```

Related solution:	Found in:
Recordsets: Moving To The Next Record In Code	Chapter 19

Avoiding Moving Past The End Of The Database

You can ensure that you're not moving past the last record of a database by using the **EOF** (end of file) property of a data control's **Recordset** object:

```
Private Sub cmdNext_Click()
    If Not Data1.Recordset.EOF Then
        Data1.Recordset.MoveNext
    End If
End Sub
```

You can also use the **RecordCount** property of a **Recordset** object to determine how many records you have to work with.

Related solution:	Found in:
Recordsets: Avoiding Moving Past The Last Record	Chapter 19

Putting It All Together: A Data-Editing Example

You can combine several of the database navigation and editing methods in an example, as shown in Figure 18.7, where the database control is connected to the db.mdb database developed earlier in this chapter.

The figure also shows the addition of two data-bound text boxes to display the fields in the database, as well as buttons with the captions Add Record, Update Record, Next Record, and Prev Record. To make those buttons work, use the corresponding methods, such as **AddNew** and **MoveNext**.

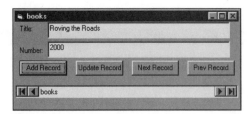

Figure 18.7   *Editing records in a database.*

The code for this example—dbedit.frm—appears in Listing 18.2.

Listing 18.2   *The dbedit.frm code.*

```
VERSION 6.00
Begin VB.Form Form1
    Caption        =    "books"
    ClientHeight   =    2145
    ClientLeft     =    1995
    ClientTop      =    1800
    ClientWidth    =    5760
    LinkTopic      =    "Form2"
    PaletteMode    =    1   'UseZOrder
    ScaleHeight    =    2145
    ScaleWidth     =    5760
    Begin VB.TextBox Text2
        DataField      =    "Number"
```

```
    DataSource      =   "Data1"
    Height          =   405
    Left            =   840
    TabIndex        =   7
    Top             =   480
    Width           =   4695
End
Begin VB.TextBox Text1
    DataField       =   "Title"
    DataSource      =   "Data1"
    Height          =   405
    Left            =   840
    TabIndex        =   6
    Top             =   0
    Width           =   4695
End
Begin VB.CommandButton cmdPrevious
    Caption         =   "Prev Record"
    Height          =   375
    Left            =   4440
    TabIndex        =   5
    Top             =   960
    Width           =   1215
End
Begin VB.CommandButton cmdNext
    Caption         =   "Next Record"
    Height          =   375
    Left            =   3000
    TabIndex        =   4
    Top             =   960
    Width           =   1215
End
Begin VB.CommandButton cmdUpdate
    Caption         =   "Update Record"
    Height          =   375
    Left            =   1560
    TabIndex        =   3
    Top             =   960
    Width           =   1215
End
Begin VB.CommandButton cmdAdd
    Caption         =   "Add Record"
    Height          =   375
    Left            =   120
    TabIndex        =   2
    Top             =   960
    Width           =   1215
End
```

```
Begin VB.Data Data1
   Caption          =   "books"
   Connect          =   "Access"
   DatabaseName     =   "C:\lvbbb\dbedit\db.mdb"
   DefaultCursorType=   0   'DefaultCursor
   DefaultType      =   2   'UseODBC
   Exclusive        =   0   'False
   Height           =   345
   Left             =   0
   Options          =   0
   ReadOnly         =   0   'False
   RecordsetType    =   1   'Dynaset
   RecordSource     =   "books"
   Top              =   1560
   Width            =   5760
End
Begin VB.Label lblLabels
   Caption          =   "Number:"
   Height           =   255
   Index            =   1
   Left             =   120
   TabIndex         =   1
   Top              =   600
   Width            =   735
End
Begin VB.Label lblLabels
   Caption          =   "Title:"
   Height           =   255
   Index            =   0
   Left             =   120
   TabIndex         =   0
   Top              =   60
   Width            =   615
End
End
Attribute VB_Name = "Form1"
Attribute VB_GlobalNameSpace = False
Attribute VB_Creatable = False
Attribute VB_PredeclaredId = True
Attribute VB_Exposed = False
Private Sub cmdAdd_Click()
  Data1.Recordset.AddNew
End Sub

Private Sub cmdNext_Click()
  Data1.Recordset.MoveNext
End Sub
```

```
Private Sub cmdPrevious_Click()
  Data1.Recordset.MovePrevious
End Sub

Private Sub cmdUpdate_Click()
  Data1.UpdateRecord
End Sub
```

Chapter 19

Programming With Database Objects

In Brief

In the last chapter, we examined the process of working with data controls in Visual Basic. In this chapter, we'll see that you can do the same kind of work—and more—without data controls, thanks to a set of Data Access Objects (DAO) Microsoft has added to Visual Basic:

- *DBEngine*—The Jet database engine
- *Workspace*—An area that can hold one or more databases
- *Database*—A collection of tables
- *TableDef*—The definition of a table
- *QueryDef*—The definition of a query
- *Recordset*—The set of records that makes up the result of a query
- *Field*—A column in a table
- *Index*—An ordered list of records
- *Relation*—Stored information about the specific relationship between tables

We'll work with these database objects in this chapter. Using database objects in code rather than data controls has several advantages: You save a great deal of memory and more programming power is available (of course, that power comes at a cost of greater complexity).

Using Recordsets

At the core of DAO database programming is the *recordset*. A recordset can hold the records from a table or the results of a database *query*, which creates a recordset of records that meet criteria you've specified. To work with data in DAO programming, you work with a recordset.

Although a recordset can hold many records, only one can be the *current record*. When you work with the data in a recordset, you usually work with the current record (you can specify the current record with a variety of methods, as we'll see in this chapter). To access the data in the current record's fields, you can use the recordset's **fields** collection.

Now, let's get started examining what the DAO code objects have to offer as we turn to the Immediate Solutions part of this chapter.

Immediate Solutions

Creating Databases In Code

It's time to create a new database—but how do you create a DAO database in code? You do so with the objects in the Microsoft DAO Object Library.

To add a reference to that library, choose the Project|References menu item, select the Microsoft DAO Object Library, and click on OK to close the References dialog box (several different versions of the DAO Object Library may be registered in your machine—it's usually best to select the most recent version). Now, you can use the data objects in that library to create a new database with the **CreateDatabase** method.

CreateDatabase is a method of the DAO **Workspace** object (the DAO **DBEngine** object's **Workspaces** collection contains a collection of **Workspace** objects). Here's how you use **CreateDatabase:**

```
Set database = workspace.CreateDatabase (name, locale _
   [, options])
```

The first two arguments to **CreateDatabase** are as follows:

- *name*—A string up to 255 characters long that's the name of the database file you're creating. It can be the full path and file name, such as C:\db.mdb. If you don't supply a file name extension, Visual Basic adds .mdb.

- *locale*—A string that specifies a collating order for creating the database, such as **dbLangGeneral** (which includes English), **dbLangGreek**, and so on.

Here are the possible settings for the *options* argument:

- *dbEncrypt*—Creates an encrypted database

- *dbVersion10*—Creates a database that uses the Jet engine version 1 file format

- *dbVersion11*—Creates a database that uses the Jet database engine version 1.1 file format

- *dbVersion20*—Creates a database that uses the Jet database engine version 2 file format

- ***dbVersion30***—The default; creates a database that uses the Jet database engine version 3 file format (compatible with version 3.5)

Here's an example. First, declare a database (**db**) as a form-wide variable:

```
Dim db As Database
```

Next, add a common dialog control (**CommonDialog1**) to the program and show it how to get the name of the database file the user wants to create:

```
Private Sub Command1_Click()
    CommonDialog1.ShowSave
    If CommonDialog1.FileName <> "" Then
        .
        .
        .
```

Then, create the new database, passing the **CreateDatabase** method the name of the database file and indicating that you want to use the default collating order by passing the constant **dbLangGeneral**:

```
Private Sub Command1_Click()
    CommonDialog1.ShowSave
    If CommonDialog1.FileName <> "" Then
        Set db = DBEngine.Workspaces(0).CreateDatabase_
        (CommonDialog1.FileName, dbLangGeneral)
    End If
End Sub
```

Now you've created a new, empty database. After you fill the database with data, save it to disk and close it with the **Close** method:

```
Private Sub Command2_Click()
    db.Close
End Sub
```

After creating a new database, the usual next step is to add a table or tables to it; we'll take a look at that process in this chapter.

Creating A Password For A Database

You can create a password for a new **Database** object by concatenating the password (starting with **;pwd=**) with a constant in the *locale* argument to **CreateDatabase**, like this:

```
dbLangGreek & ";pwd=NewPassword"
```

If you want to use the default *locale* but specify a password, simply enter a password string for the *locale* argument:

```
";pwd=NewPassword"
```

Creating A Database Table In Code

Can you create a table in a DAO database in code? Yes, you can: You define tables with a **TableDef** object. After you do so, you can append fields to the table, and then append the new table definition to a database's **TableDefs** collection.

Here's an example. First, create a new **TableDef** object (**td**), which you declare as a form-wide variable:

```
Dim td As TableDef
```

You create a new **TableDef** for a database object (**db**) using the name for the table the user has placed in **Text1**:

```
Sub CreateTable()
    Set td = db.CreateTableDef(Text1.Text)
    .
    .
    .
```

This code creates a new, empty **TableDef** object named **td**. An empty table isn't much use, though—we'll see about adding fields to this object in the next topic.

Adding Fields To A Table In Code

Now that you've added a table to a database object, how do you add fields to that table? You can use the **TableDef** object's **CreateField** method, passing it the name of the new field, and a constant indicating that field's type:

```
TableDef.CreateField(FieldName, FieldType)
```

The constants specifying the possible field types are as follows:

- **dbBigInt**
- **dbBinary**
- **dbBoolean**
- **dbByte**
- **dbChar**
- **dbCurrency**
- **dbDate**
- **dbDecimal**
- **dbDouble**
- **dbFloat**
- **dbGUID**
- **dbInteger**
- **dbLong**
- **dbLongBinary** (OLE object)
- **dbMemo**
- **dbNumeric**
- **dbSingle**
- **dbText**
- **dbTime**
- **dbTimeStamp**
- **dbVarBinary**

Here's an example to make this clearer. Let's say you have a **TableDef** object named **td**, created from a table name the user has placed in text box **Text1**:

```
Sub CreateTable()
```

```
Set td = db.CreateTableDef(Text1.Text)
     .
     .
     .
```

Let's add two fields to that **TableDef** object by declaring those fields in an array named **fields** of type **Field** (which is defined in the DAO library):

```
Dim fields(2) As Field
```

Assuming the user has specified names for those two new fields in two text boxes (**Text2** and **Text3**), you create the new fields this way:

```
Sub CreateTable()
    Set td = db.CreateTableDef(Text1.Text)

    Set fields(0) = td.CreateField(Text2.Text, dbText)
    Set fields(1) = td.CreateField(Text3.Text, dbText)
     .
     .
     .
```

Now that the new fields exist, you can append them to the actual **TableDef** object, **td**:

```
Sub CreateTable()
    Set td = db.CreateTableDef(Text1.Text)

    Set fields(0) = td.CreateField(Text2.Text, dbText)
    Set fields(1) = td.CreateField(Text3.Text, dbText)
    td.fields.Append fields(0)
    td.fields.Append fields(1)
End Sub
```

That's it—you've defined two new fields, named them, and appended them to a **TableDef** object. The next step is to append the table to a database object.

Appending A Table To A Database

To append a table to a database object, you use the **Append** method of the database object's **TableDefs** collection. This method adds the

table to the database. Here's how you use the **Append** method to
append a table to a database named **db**:

```
Sub CreateTable()
    Set td = db.CreateTableDef(Text1.Text)

    Set fields(0) = td.CreateField(Text2.Text, dbText)
    Set fields(1) = td.CreateField(Text3.Text, dbText)
    td.fields.Append fields(0)
    td.fields.Append fields(1)

    db.TableDefs.Append td
    .
    .
    .
```

You've set up your database and added a table. The next step is to get
a recordset so you can begin working with your data.

Creating A Recordset In Code

In Visual Basic DAO programming, you work with your data
in *recordsets*. After you've installed a table, you can use the
OpenRecordset method to open a recordset:

```
Set recordset = Database.OpenRecordset (source, type, _
    options, lockedits)
```

Here are the arguments for **OpenRecordset**:

- *source*—A string specifying the source of the records for the new
  Recordset object. The source can be a table name, a query name,
  or an SQL statement that returns records. (For table-type
  Recordset objects in Jet-type databases, the source must be a
  table name.)

- *type*—The type of **Recordset** object to open.

- *options*—A combination of constants specifying characteristics
  of the new **Recordset** object.

- *lockedits*—A constant that determines the locking for
  Recordset.

Here are the possible settings for the *type* argument:

- *dbOpenTable*—Opens a table-type **Recordset** object

- *dbOpenDynamic*—Opens a dynamic-type **Recordset** object, which is like an ODBC dynamic cursor

- *dbOpenDynaset*—Opens a dynaset-type **Recordset** object, which is like an ODBC keyset cursor

- *dbOpenSnapshot*—Opens a snapshot-type **Recordset** object, which is like an ODBC static cursor

- *dbOpenForwardOnly*—Opens a forward-only-type **Recordset** object (in which you must use **MoveNext** to move through the database)

Here are the possible settings for the *options* argument:

- *dbAppendOnly*—Allows users to append new records to the **Recordset**, but prevents them from editing or deleting existing records (Microsoft Jet dynaset-type **Recordset** only).

- *dbSQLPassThrough*—Passes an SQL statement to a Microsoft Jet-connected ODBC data source for processing (Jet snapshot-type **Recordset** only).

- *dbSeeChanges*—Generates a runtime error if one user is changing data that another user is editing (Jet dynaset-type **Recordset** only).

- *dbDenyWrite*—Prevents other users from modifying or adding records (Jet **Recordset** objects only).

- *dbDenyRead*—Prevents other users from reading data in a table (Jet table-type **Recordset** only).

- *dbForwardOnly*—Creates a forward-only **Recordset** (Jet snapshot-type **Recordset** only). This option is provided for backward compatibility; instead of using this option, you should use the **dbOpenForwardOnly** constant in the *type* argument.

- *dbReadOnly*—Prevents users from making changes to the **Recordset** (Microsoft Jet only). The **dbReadOnly** constant in the *lockedits* argument replaces this option, which is provided only for backward compatibility.

- *dbRunAsync*—Runs an asynchronous query (ODBCDirect workspaces only).

- *dbExecDirect*—Runs a query by skipping **SQLPrepare** and directly calling **SQLExecDirect** (ODBCDirect workspaces only).

- *dbInconsistent*—Allows inconsistent updates (Microsoft Jet dynaset-type and snapshot-type **Recordset** objects only).

- *dbConsistent*—Allows only consistent updates (Microsoft Jet dynaset-type and snapshot-type **Recordset** objects only).

Here are the possible settings for the *lockedits* argument:

- *dbReadOnly*—Prevents users from making changes to the **Recordset** object (default for ODBCDirect workspaces)

- *dbPessimistic*—Uses pessimistic (ultra-safe) locking to determine how changes are made to the **Recordset** object in a multiuser environment

- *dbOptimistic*—Uses optimistic (unchecked) locking to determine how changes are made to the **Recordset** object in a multiuser environment

- *dbOptimisticValue*—Uses optimistic (unchecked) record concurrency based on row values (ODBCDirect workspaces only)

- *dbOptimisticBatch*—Enables batch optimistic (unchecked) updating of records (ODBCDirect workspaces only)

Let's look at an example. After installing a table in a database, you open it for use with the **Database** object's **OpenRecordset** method, creating a new DAO recordset named **recordset**:

```
Sub CreateTable()
    Set td = db.CreateTableDef(Text1.Text)

    Set fields(0) = td.CreateField(Text2.Text, dbText)
    Set fields(1) = td.CreateField(Text3.Text, dbText)
    td.fields.Append fields(0)
    td.fields.Append fields(1)

    db.TableDefs.Append td

    Set recordset = db.OpenRecordset(Text1.Text, dbOpenTable)
End Sub
```

In this case, you're opening the new recordset as a standard DAO table by passing the constant **dbOpenTable**. You also declare **recordset** as a form-wide variable:

```
Dim recordset As Recordset
```

At this point, you've opened a table as a recordset, so you're ready to work with it and add data to it.

Opening An Existing Database

To open an existing DAO database, use the DAO **OpenDatabase** method, passing it the name of the database to open and these arguments:

```
Set database = workspace.OpenDatabase (dbname, [options [, _
   read-only [, connect]]])
```

Here are the arguments for **OpenDatabase**:

- *dbname*—The name of an existing database file or the data source name (DSN) of an ODBC data source

- *options*—**True** if you want to open the DAO database in exclusive mode; **False** (the default) to open the database in shared mode

- *read-only*—**True** if you want to open the database with read-only access; **False** (the default) to open the database with read/write access

- *connect*—A **Variant** (**String** subtype) that specifies various connection information, including passwords (optional)

Recordsets: Accessing Data In Fields

To access the data in the fields of the current record in a recordset, you use the recordset's **fields** array. For example, the following code places text from two text boxes into the first two fields of the current record:

```
Private Sub Command1_Click()
    recordset.fields(0) = Text1.Text
    recordset.fields(1) = Text2.Text
End Sub
```

Recordsets: Adding A Record In Code

To add a new record to a DAO recordset, use the **AddNew** method, which takes no parameters. After you've updated the fields of the current record, save that record to the database with the **Update** method.

Here's an example using **AddNew**, which adds a new record to a recordset when the user clicks on a command button:

```
Private Sub Command1_Click()
    recordset.AddNew
End Sub
```

Related solution:	*Found in:*
Adding A Record In Code	Chapter 18

Recordsets: Editing A Record In Code

The user might want to edit the existing records in a recordset. To do that, use the **Edit** method, like this:

```
Private Sub Command1_Click()
    recordset.Edit
End Sub
```

After the user edits the data in the record's fields, the user must update the database with the new data; the program does that with the **Update** method, as you'll see in the next topic.

Recordsets: Deleting A Record In Code

To delete the current record in a DAO recordset, use the **Delete** method; then, update the recordset. For example, here's how to use the **Delete** method to delete the current record when the user clicks on a button:

```
Private Sub Command1_Click()
    recordset.Delete
End Sub
```

Related solution:	*Found in:*
Deleting A Record In Code	Chapter 18

Recordsets: Updating A Database In Code

When the user changes the data in a record or adds a new record, you must update the database to record that change. You do so with the recordset **Update** method:

```
recordset.Update ([type [, force]])
```

Here are the method's arguments:

- *type*—A constant indicating the type of update, as specified in the **Settings** property. (ODBCDirect workspaces only)

- *force*—A **Boolean** value indicating whether to force the changes into the database, even if the data has been changed by another user (ODBCDirect workspaces only)

Let's look at an example. When the user clicks on a button, you can update the database with the new data for the current record. In this example, you get the new data for the current record from the text boxes **Text1** and **Text2** (where the user has entered that data) and load the data into the recordset's fields using the **fields** collection:

```
Private Sub Command1_Click()
    recordset.fields(0) = Text1.Text
    recordset.fields(1) = Text2.Text
    .
    .
    .
End Sub
```

After loading the data into the current record's fields, save that record to the database using the **Update** method:

```
Private Sub Command1_Click()
    recordset.fields(0) = Text1.Text
    recordset.fields(1) = Text2.Text
    recordset.Update
End Sub
```

Related solution:	Found in:
Updating A Database In Code	Chapter 18

Recordsets: Moving To The First Record In Code

To make the first record in a recordset the current record, use the **MoveFirst** method. For example, here's how to move to the first record when the user clicks on a button:

```
Private Sub Command1_Click()
    recordset.MoveFirst
End Sub
```

Related solution:	Found in:
Moving To The First Record In Code	Chapter 18

Recordsets: Moving To The Last Record In Code

To make the last record in a recordset the current record, use the **MoveLast** method. For example, here's how to move to the last record when the user clicks on a button:

```
Private Sub Command1_Click()
    recordset.Movelast
End Sub
```

Related solution:	Found in:
Moving To The Last Record In Code	Chapter 18

Recordsets: Moving To The Previous Record In Code

To move to the previous record in a recordset—making that record the current record—use the **MovePrevious** method.

For example, here's how to move to the previous record when the user clicks on a button:

```
Private Sub Command1_Click()
    recordset.MovePrevious
End Sub
```

Related solution:	Found in:
Moving To The Previous Record In Code	Chapter 18

Recordsets: Avoiding Moving Past The First Record

You can check whether you've gone past the beginning of the recordset with the **BOF** property; if this property is **True**, you should move forward one record, like this:

```
Private Sub Command1_Click()
    recordset.MovePrevious
    If recordset.BOF Then
        recordset.MoveNext
    End If
End Sub
```

Related solution:	Found in:
Avoiding Moving Before The Start Of The Databsase	Chapter 18

Recordsets: Moving To The Next Record In Code

To move to the next record in a recordset—making that record the current record—use the **MoveNext** method.

For example, here's how to move to the next record when the user clicks on a button:

```
Private Sub Command1_Click()
    recordset.MoveNext
End Sub
```

Related solution:	Found in:
Moving To The Next Record In Code	Chapter 18

Recordsets: Avoiding Moving Past The Last Record

You can check whether you've gone past the end of the recordset with the **EOF** property; if this property is **True**, you should move back one record, like this:

```
Private Sub Command1_Click()
    recordset.MoveNext
    If recordset.EOF Then
        recordset.MovePrevious
    End If
End Sub
```

Related solution:	Found in:
Avoiding Moving Past The End Of The Database	Chapter 18

Closing A Database In Code

To close a database in code, you simply use the **Close** method. Here's how it works:

```
Private Sub Command1_Click()
    db.Close
End Sub
```

Executing SQL In Code

When you execute an SQL statement, you create a new recordset of records that meet the criteria you've specified in that statement. You can execute an SQL statement when you create a DAO recordset using the **OpenRecordset** method by placing that SQL statement in the *source* argument:

```
Set recordset = Database.OpenRecordset (source, type, _
  options, lockedits)
```

Here are the arguments for **OpenRecordset**:

- **source**—A string specifying the source of the records for the new **Recordset** object. The source can be a table name, a query name, or an SQL statement that returns records. (For table-type **Recordset** objects in Jet-type databases, the source must be a table name.)
- **type**—The type of **Recordset** to open.
- **options**—A combination of constants specifying characteristics of the new **Recordset**.
- **lockedits**—A constant that determines the locking for **Recordset**.

Here are the possible settings for the *type* argument:

- *dbOpenTable*—Opens a table-type **Recordset** object
- *dbOpenDynamic*—Opens a dynamic-type **Recordset** object, which is like an ODBC dynamic cursor
- *dbOpenDynaset*—Opens a dynaset-type **Recordset** object, which is like an ODBC keyset cursor
- *dbOpenSnapshot*—Opens a snapshot-type **Recordset** object, which is like an ODBC static cursor
- *dbOpenForwardOnly*—Opens a forward-only-type **Recordset** object

Here are the possible settings for the *options* argument:

- *dbAppendOnly*—Allows users to append new records to the **Recordset**, but prevents them from editing or deleting existing records (Microsoft Jet dynaset-type **Recordset** only).
- *dbSQLPassThrough*—Passes an SQL statement to a Microsoft Jet-connected ODBC data source for processing (Microsoft Jet snapshot-type **Recordset** only).
- *dbSeeChanges*—Generates a runtime error if one user is changing data that another user is editing (Microsoft Jet dynaset-type **Recordset** only).
- *dbDenyWrite*—Prevents other users from modifying or adding records (Microsoft Jet **Recordset** objects only).
- *dbDenyRead*—Prevents other users from reading data in a table (Microsoft Jet table-type **Recordset** only).

- *dbForwardOnly*—Creates a forward-only **Recordset**
  (Microsoft Jet snapshot-type **Recordset** only). This option is
  provided for backward compatibility; instead, you should use the
  dbOpenForwardOnly constant in the *type* argument.

- *dbReadOnly*—Prevents users from making changes to the
  Recordset (Microsoft Jet only). The **dbReadOnly** constant in
  the *lockedits* argument replaces this option, which is provided
  only for backward compatibility.

- *dbRunAsync*—Runs an asynchronous query (ODBCDirect
  workspaces only).

- *dbExecDirect*—Runs a query by skipping **SQLPrepare** and
  directly calling **SQLExecDirect** (ODBCDirect workspaces only).

- *dbInconsistent*—Allows inconsistent updates (Microsoft Jet
  dynaset-type and snapshot-type **Recordset** objects only).

- *dbConsistent*—Allows only consistent updates (Microsoft Jet
  dynaset-type and snapshot-type **Recordset** objects only).

Here are the possible settings for the *lockedits* argument:

- *dbReadOnly*—Prevents users from making changes to the
  Recordset (default for ODBCDirect workspaces)

- *dbPessimistic*—Uses pessimistic (ultra-safe) locking to
  determine how changes are made to the **Recordset** in a
  multiuser environment

- *dbOptimistic*—Uses optimistic (unchecked) locking to
  determine how changes are made to the **Recordset** in a
  multiuser environment

- *dbOptimisticValue*—Uses optimistic (unchecked) record
  concurrency based on row values (ODBCDirect workspaces
  only)

- *dbOptimisticBatch*—Enables batch optimistic updating
  (ODBCDirect workspaces only)

Chapter 20

Creating Setup Programs And Help Files

In Brief

In this chapter, we're going to take a look at some deployment issues: creating setup programs and help files. After you've written your program and tested it, the next step is to get it out to the users—and we'll take a look at that process in this chapter.

Creating Setup Programs

You use setup programs to install your application on other computers. Visual Basic includes a great tool that will help you here: the Package and Deployment Wizard. Using this wizard, you can create setup files that you can distribute on CDs, multiple disks, or even across the Internet.

This wizard is extraordinarily helpful for one reason you might not think of immediately. Each Visual Basic application needs many files (usually DLL and OCX files) in order to work—but how can you determine exactly which files it needs? The Package and Deployment Wizard makes that determination for you and includes those files in the CAB data files you distribute along with the setup program.

Note that it's important to be sure you don't distribute licensed material or components without permission. Check first with the manufacturer of the DLL, OCX, or EXE files you want to distribute to determine whether the manufacturer's policy allows distribution.

Creating Help Files

Help files are an asset to any application, and just about all serious applications come with a help system of some sort. In this chapter, we'll see how to create Windows help files that you can display on the user's computer with standard Windows calls. You can build two kinds of help files: standard Windows help files and compiled HTML help files.

To create a standard Windows help file, you use the Microsoft Help Workshop, which creates a help *project*. You place the actual help text in a rich text (RTF) file and add that file to the help project. Why rich text? The Help Workshop uses RTF files so that you can embed hypertext jumps and commands directly into your help file, encoding those items with rich-text footnotes, hidden text, and so forth. When you finish your RTF files, use the Microsoft Help Workshop to compile them into a HLP file.

To create a compiled HTML help file, you use the HTML Help Workshop, which also creates help projects. Here, you can use the familiar format of HTML files to create help files with jumps, formatting, and figures. When you finish your HTML files, use the HTML Help Workshop to compile them into a HLP file. Note that to use your compiled HTML help file—which has the extension .chm—the user's computer must have the Microsoft hh.exe utility installed (for your own use, this utility comes with Visual Basic).

Now that you have a help file, how do you open it from Visual Basic? In this chapter, we'll see how to use the Windows API **WinHelp** function to open standard Windows help files and how to use the Windows API **ShellExecute** function to open compiled HTML help files.

That's all the introduction we need—it's time to turn to the Immediate Solutions part of this chapter.

Immediate Solutions

Creating An Application's Executable File

The first step in deploying your application is to create its EXE (or DLL or OCX) file. To do that, you simply select the File|Make *projectname*.exe (or DLL or OCX) menu item.

After Visual Basic creates your application's executable file, you're ready to create a setup program with which to deploy it; see the next topic.

Using The Package And Deployment Wizard

You create a setup program using the Visual Basic Package and Deployment Wizard; that wizard is an add-in that lets you deploy your application. If the Package and Deployment Wizard doesn't appear on the Visual Basic Add-Ins menu, use the Add-In Manager (which appears on the Add-Ins menu) to insert it.

It's important to be sure you don't distribute licensed material or components without permission. Check first with the manufacturer of the DLL, OCX, or EXE files you want to distribute, to determine whether the manufacturer's policy allows distribution.

Now, open the application you want to distribute in Visual Basic and open the Package and Deployment Wizard, as shown in Figure 20.1. As you can see, the wizard offers several options: You can create a new setup program, deploy a setup package to a distribution site, or manage the scripts you use with this wizard.

We'll create a setup program for a hypothetical application named *App* in the next few topics in this chapter, progressing step by step through the Package and Deployment Wizard. Click on the top button (Package) in the Package and Deployment Wizard to create a setup program for the App application.

Figure 20.1   *The Package and Deployment Wizard.*

Wizard Step 1: The Package Type

In the first step of the Package and Deployment Wizard, you select the package type you want to create. In this case, be sure the Standard Setup Package item is selected in the Package Type box, as shown in Figure 20.2.

Selecting this item tells Visual Basic to create a deployment package that can be installed using a setup.exe file. Now, click on Next to move to Step 2 of the Package and Deployment Wizard.

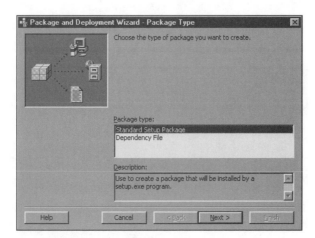

Figure 20.2   *Setting the package type.*

Wizard Step 2: The Build Folder

In Step 2 of the Package and Deployment Wizard, you select the folder in which Visual Basic will create your deployment package.

By default, this folder is named Package; the Package and Deployment Wizard will add it to your Visual Basic project's folder. For example, in the App project (which is in the c:\lvbbb\app folder), the deployment package will be created in the c:\lvbbb\app\Package folder. If you want to build the deployment package in another folder, select that folder now.

When you're ready, click on Next to move to the next step in the wizard.

Wizard Step 3: The Included Files

In Step 3 of the Package and Deployment Wizard, you can select the files you want included for distribution. These include your application's executable file and all necessary support files—the wizard determines which support files your application needs and adds them automatically, as shown in Figure 20.3.

The Package and Deployment Wizard presents a list of files it will include—you can deselect files you don't want to include. You can also include additional files in your deployment package (such as help or application-specific data files) by clicking on Add and specifying those files.

When you're ready, click on Next to move to the next step in the wizard.

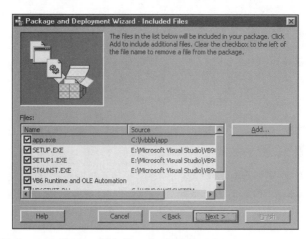

Figure 20.3 *Specifying which files are included.*

Wizard Step 4: The CAB Options

In Step 4 of the Package and Deployment Wizard, you specify how you want to distribute your application—as one single cabinet (CAB) file or over multiple disks.

If you select deployment with multiple CAB files, you can specify the capacity of each disk, from 360K to 2.88MB. The Package and Deployment Wizard will create a CAB file for each disk and let you know how many disks you need.

In this case, let's select the single-CAB option for the App application you're working with (see Figure 20.4).

When you're ready, click on Next to move to the next step in the wizard.

20: Creating Setup Programs And Help Files

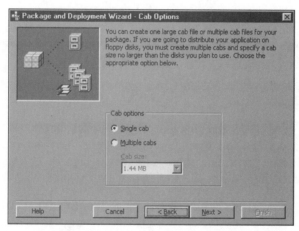

Figure 20.4 *Selecting the distribution type in the Package and Deployment Wizard.*

Wizard Step 5: The Installation Title

In Step 5 of the Package and Deployment Wizard, you enter the installation title for your application. This title will appear on the setup program's "wash" screen (which covers the whole screen) when the user installs the application.

Let's use the title "Project1", as shown in Figure 20.5, while creating the deployment package for the App application; you may also want to include your company's name in the title, if applicable.

When you're ready, click on Next to move to the next step in the wizard.

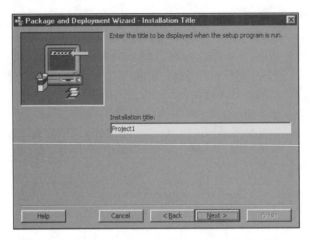

Figure 20.5   *Selecting a deployment package's installation title.*

Wizard Step 6: The Start Menu Items

In Step 6 of the Package and Deployment Wizard, you indicate what new program group(s) you want to add to Windows.

In this case, you're building a deployment package for the App application; so, you'll add only one program group—Project1, the internal name for the App application—as shown in Figure 20.6 (this is the default name the Package and Deployment Wizard has selected for you).

When you're ready, click on Next to move to the next step in the wizard.

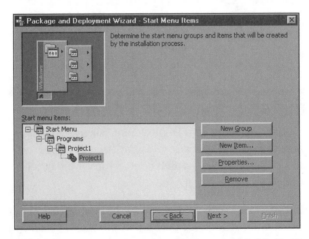

Figure 20.6   *Selecting program groups and icons to install in the Package and Deployment Wizard.*

Wizard Step 7: The Install Locations

In Step 7 of the Package and Deployment Wizard, you indicate where you want the parts of your application installed on the target computer, as shown in Figure 20.7.

By default, your application is placed into the directory the user specifies, which is represented in the Package and Deployment Wizard with the macro **$(AppPath)**.

When you're ready, click on Next to move to the next step in the wizard.

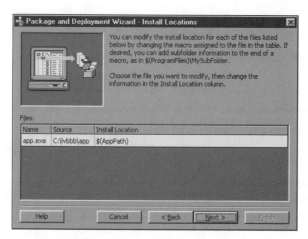

Figure 20.7   Setting installation locations.

Wizard Step 8: The Shared Files

In Step 8 of the Package and Deployment Wizard, you can indicate which files you want to register as shared files, as shown in Figure 20.8. These files may be used by several applications in the target computer, and will be uninstalled only if all applications that use them are uninstalled.

If in doubt, it's better to register files as shared—especially common DLLs and OCXs. (Don't forget to test your application's setup program.)

When you're ready, click on Next to move to the next step in the wizard.

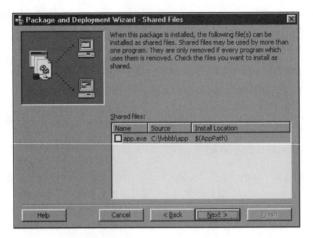

Figure 20.8   *Specifying shared files.*

Wizard Step 9: Finished!

Step 9 in the Package and Deployment Wizard is the last step in creating your application's deployment package. Simply click on Finish to create the CAB file(s), the setup.exe program itself, and the setup.lst file, which holds a list of the files to install and where they go (setup.exe reads setup.lst to know what to install where).

When you click on Finish, the Package and Deployment Wizard also displays a packaging report, indicating that the app.cab file has been created. Click on Close to close the packaging report dialog box; click on Close again to close the Package and Deployment Wizard.

And that's all it takes—now the user can run the setup.exe program to install your application, as shown in Figure 20.9.

When the setup program runs, it handles all the details of checking for adequate disk space, asks the user where to install the application, and installs the necessary files for you, using the CAB file and the setup.lst file—it's that simple.

You've completed the process. Using the Package and Deployment Wizard, you can now create setup programs to distribute your applications.

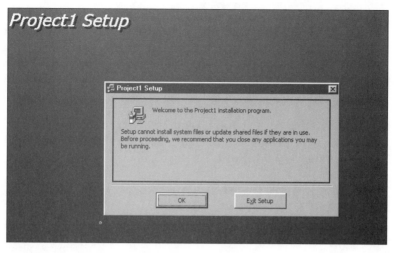

Figure 20.9   *Installing an application.*

Creating Windows Help Files

You can create standard Windows help files using the Microsoft Help Workshop, which appears in Figure 20.10. To see how the Help Workshop works, let's create a basic help file for an application named *helper* over the next few topics in this chapter.

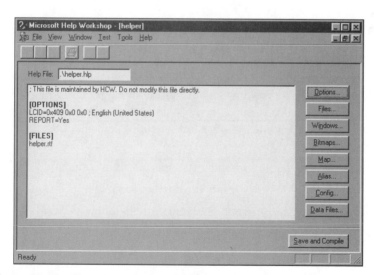

Figure 20.10   *The Microsoft Help Workshop.*

To create the help file (helper.hlp) for the helper application, you'll create a help project (helper.hpj) in the Help Workshop. This project keeps track of the files in your help system; in this example, you'll just have one such file—helper.rtf—which will hold the data for the help file. In that RTF file, you'll set up the help topics to display to the user and the jumps in the help file that will connect those topics.

After adding helper.rtf in the helper.prj file, you can compile that RTF file to create helper.hlp. To open the helper.hlp help file, use the Windows API function **WinHelp**:

```
Private Declare Function WinHelp Lib "user32" Alias _
    "WinHelpA" (ByVal hwnd As Long, ByVal lpHelpFile As _
    String, ByVal wCommand As Long, ByVal dwData _
    As Long) As Long
```

To create a new help project, first choose Help Workshop's File|New menu item. Select the Help Project item in the New dialog box that opens and click on OK. Using the File|Save As menu item, save the new help project as helper.hpj. The new help project appears in the Help Workshop (refer back to Figure 20.10).

Now that you've created a new help project, you'll add the actual help text to that project. You do that by creating an RTF file, as you'll see in the next topic in this chapter.

Creating A Windows Help File's RTF File

You use help-file RTF commands to create *help jumps* (which work like hyperlinks). As you'll see in the following topics, you use rich-text format codes to support these and other help features. For example, here are some rich-text format codes and what they do, as far as the Help Workshop is concerned:

- *\footnote*(*footnote*)—Indicates special topic commands
- *\page* (*page break*)—Ends the current topic
- *\strike* (*strikethrough*)—Indicates a help jump
- *\ul* (*underline*)—Indicates a link to a pop-up topic
- *\uldb* (*double underline*)—Indicates a help jump
- *\v* (*hidden text*)—Indicates the topic ID to jump to

We'll see how to use these format codes in the following topics. In fact, you'll build your help file's RTF file (helper.rtf) in Microsoft Word; you won't have to deal directly with these codes.

Using Microsoft Word, create the file helper.rtf (save the file in RTF format). Next, add it to your help project in the Help Workshop by clicking on the Files button in the Help Workshop, clicking on the Add button in the Topic Files dialog box that appears, selecting helper.rtf, and clicking on OK.

In the following topics in this chapter, we'll see how to create the text in the helper.rtf file to build the help file.

Entering Text In A Windows Help File

How do you format the text in a standard Windows help file? You simply type the text directly into the RTF file. In addition, the text in a help file is divided into pages; only one page is displayed at a time. To divide your text into pages in Microsoft Word, enter a page break by choosing the Insert|Break menu item or pressing Ctrl+Enter. The first page in the RTF file is the first page displayed when your help file is opened.

Let's make the first page of the helper.hlp file a welcome page by entering this text directly into helper.rtf and following it with a page break:

```
Contents

Welcome to helper example application. This help file gives you
help on the menu items in helper.
```

Now, this text will greet the user when the helper.hlp file first opens.

Actually, this text isn't enough by itself—you should allow the user some way to jump to the help pages they want to look at. You'll do that in the next topic.

Creating A Windows Help "Hyperlink"

To let the user move around in a help file, you use *help jumps*, which act much like hyperlinks. Help jumps appear underlined in help files—when the user clicks on a jump, the help system jumps to the target of that jump and opens the associated help page.

To see how jumps work, let's add two jumps to the opening help page developed in the last topic. Here, as shown in Figure 20.11, you'll let the user jump to two new help pages: one about the application's File menu items and another about the application's Help menu.

To add those jumps to the helper.rtf file, enter this text (to make the *File Menu Items* and *Help Menu Items* into help jumps, you give them a double underline, using the Microsoft Word Format|Font menu item):

```
Contents

Welcome to helper example application. This help file gives you
help on the menu items in helper.

To get help for the menu you are interested in, click a topic:

File Menu Items

Help Menu Items
```

Now that you've created two help jumps, you'll connect a label—called a *jump tag*—to each jump to indicate where you want to go when the user clicks on the jump. In this case, add the jump tags

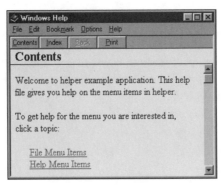

Figure 20.11   *Adding two help jumps to a help file.*

FILE_MENU_ITEMS and HELP_MENU_ITEMS to your jumps this way, marking them as *hidden text* with the Word Format|Font menu item (hidden text appears in a Word document with a dotted underline):

```
Contents

Welcome to helper example application. This help file gives you
help on the menu items in helper.

To get help for the menu you are interested in, click a topic:

File Menu ItemsFILE_MENU_ITEMS

Help Menu ItemsHELP_MENU_ITEMS
```

For an example of how the dotted underline appears in Word, refer to Figure 20.12 in the next topic.

Because you've made the new jump tags hidden text, they won't appear in the help file; however, when the user clicks on a help jump, the help system will look for the page that has the same tag as the jump the user clicked on. How do you give a help page a tag? We'll look at that topic next.

Creating A Windows Help "Hyperlink" Target

To connect a help jump with a page in a help file, place Word's blinking insertion cursor at the very beginning of the target page in the help file's RTF file; then, select Word's Insert|Footnote menu item.

In the Footnote And Endnote dialog box that appears, select Custom Mark in the Numbering box, type the special footnote character "#" in the Custom Mark box, and click on OK. Doing so inserts a new footnote in the document and opens a window showing the document's footnotes at the bottom of the window. To connect a help jump to the current page, simply enter the jump's tag as the footnote text.

Let's look at an example. In the previous topic, you created two help jumps; in this topic, you'll create the target that the help system will jump to when the user clicks on the File Menu Items jump—the tag for this jump is FILE_MENU_ITEMS.

To create the page to jump to when the user clicks on the File Menu Items jump, insert a page break to start a new page, and then add the title *File Menu Items* to that page. On this new page, you can list the menu items in the application's File menu, each with a jump to a new page, like this:

```
Contents

Welcome to helper example application. This help file gives you
help on the menu items in helper.

To get help for the menu you are interested in, click a topic:

File Menu ItemsFILE_MENU_ITEMS
━━━━━━━━━━━━━━━━━━━━.............
Help Menu ItemsHELP_MENU_ITEMS
━━━━━━━━━━━━━━━━━━━..............
---------------------------Page Break---------------------------
File Menu Items

Select the menu item you want to get help on:

    NewNEW
    ━━...
    OpenOPEN
    ━━....
    CloseCLOSE
    ━━.....
```

Next, to connect the FILE_MENU_ITEMS jump tag with the new page, place the insertion cursor at the beginning of that page. Select the Insert|Footnote menu item and give the footnote the custom mark "#" and the text "FILE_MENU_ITEMS", as shown in the footnotes pane in Figure 20.12.

Now you've connected the File Menu Items jump to the next help page you just created. When the user clicks on the File Menu Items jump, the help file will jump to this new page, as shown in Figure 20.13.

Using footnotes, you can do more than just create help jumps—you can title a help page. We'll see how to do that in the next topic.

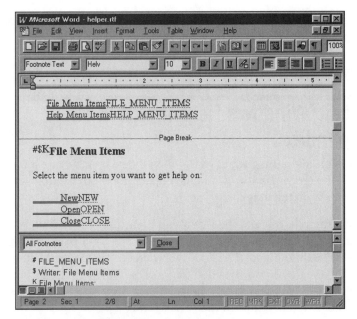

Figure 20.12   *Setting up a help jump target.*

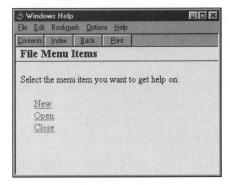

Figure 20.13   *Jumping to a help target page.*

Titling A Windows Help Page

To add a title to a help page, add a footnote to the page, giving it the custom mark "$" and the text you want to use as the page's title.

Let's see an example. In this case, you'll add the title *File Menu Items* to the appropriate page in the helper.rtf file you've been developing for the previous few topics. To do that, position the insertion cursor at the beginning of the File Menu Items page, add a footnote with the custom mark "$", and give that footnote the text "File Menu Items" (refer back to Figure 20.12).

Placing Windows Help Topics In The Help Index

You can add a help topic to the help index by inserting a footnote with the custom mark "K" and giving that footnote the text you want to appear in the index.

For example, you add the File Menu Items item to the help index by adding a footnote—"K"—to the appropriate help page in helper.rtf (refer back to Figure 20.12). Now, when the user uses the help file's index, the items you've added (such as as File Menu Items and Help Menu Items) appear in that index. When the user clicks on an item, the help system jumps to the corresponding page.

Compiling Windows Help Files With The Help Workshop

You've created your RTF file with the help text and jumps you want to use, and you've also created your help project in the Help Workshop. How do you create the actual HLP file? You use the Help Workshop's File|Compile menu item.

Choosing that menu item opens the Compile A Help File dialog box. Click on Compile to create the help file; in the case of the example developed over the previous few topics, this file is helper.hlp.

Now, you've created a new help file. But how do you launch it from Visual Basic? We'll take a look at that subject in the next topic.

Displaying A Windows Help File From Visual Basic

To display a help file from a Visual Basic program, you can use the Windows API function **WinHelp**:

```
Declare Function WinHelp Lib "user32" Alias "WinHelpA" (ByVal_
   hwnd As Long, ByVal lpHelpFile As String, ByVal _
   wCommand As Long, ByVal dwData As Long) As Long
```

Here's what the arguments to this function mean:

- **hwnd**—Handle of the window opening the help file
- **lpHelpFile**—Name of the help file to open
- **wCommand**—Open command; see the following list
- **dwData**—Additional data as required for the help-file-opening operation

You can use these possible values for the **wCommand** argument:

- **HELP_CONTEXT = &H1**
- **HELP_QUIT = &H2**
- **HELP_INDEX = &H3**
- **HELP_CONTENTS = &H3&**
- **HELP_HELPONHELP = &H4**
- **HELP_SETINDEX = &H5**
- **HELP_SETCONTENTS = &H5&**
- **HELP_CONTEXTPOPUP = &H8&**
- **HELP_FORCEFILE = &H9&**
- **HELP_KEY = &H101**
- **HELP_COMMAND = &H102&**
- **HELP_PARTIALKEY = &H105&**
- **HELP_MULTIKEY = &H201&**
- **HELP_SETWINPOS = &H203&**

Let's look at an example that opens the helper.hlp help file in an application named *helper* when the user selects the application's Help|Help menu item.

To start, you declare **WinHelp** and the constants it can use:

```
Const HELP_CONTEXT = &H1
Const HELP_QUIT = &H2
Const HELP_INDEX = &H3
Const HELP_CONTENTS = &H3&
Const HELP_HELPONHELP = &H4
Const HELP_SETINDEX = &H5
Const HELP_SETCONTENTS = &H5&
```

```
Const HELP_CONTEXTPOPUP = &H8&
Const HELP_FORCEFILE = &H9&
Const HELP_KEY = &H101
Const HELP_COMMAND = &H102&
Const HELP_PARTIALKEY = &H105&
Const HELP_MULTIKEY = &H201&
Const HELP_SETWINPOS = &H203&


Private Declare Function WinHelp Lib "user32" Alias _
    "WinHelpA" (ByValhwnd As Long, ByVal lpHelpFile As _
    String, ByVal wCommand As Long, ByVal dwData As Long) As Long
```

Then, when the user selects the appropriate menu item, you display
the helper.hlp file with **WinHelp** this way:

```
Private Sub mnuHelp_Click()
    retVal = WinHelp(Form1.hwnd, "c:\helper\helper.hlp",_
    HELP_INDEX, CLng(0))
End Sub
```

And that's it—now the user can open the helper.hlp file from a Visual
Basic application.

Creating Compiled HTML Help Files

There's an easier way to create help files than writing standard Windows help files—you can create compiled HTML help files. Note, however, that using compiled HTML help files depends on having the
Microsoft hh.exe utility installed; some of your users may not have
this utility.

To create a compiled HTML help file, use the HTML Help Workshop,
which appears in Figure 20.14.

Here's how the process works. You create the help files you want in
HTML format, including hyperlinks and graphics. Then, you add these
HTML files to a help project in the HTML Help Workshop. Finally,
you use the HTML Help Workshop to create the compiled HTML file.

We'll see how to follow these steps in the following topics in this
chapter.

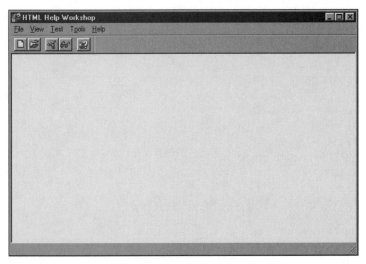

Figure 20.14 *The HTML Help Workshop.*

Creating HTML Files For Use With The HTML Help Workshop

To generate a compiled HTML help file, you first create a help system using HTML files. You can test that help system with a Web browser, if you wish. When the help system is ready to go, you add it to a help project in the HTML Help Workshop.

For example, suppose you have two HTML files: help1.htm and help2.htm. The help1.htm file is as follows, including an image and a hyperlink to help2.htm:

```
<HTML>

<H2>Help Topic 1</H2>
<BR>
Here's the help text...
<BR>
<BR>
<A HREF = "help2.htm">Help Topic 2</A>
<BR>
<HR>
<IMG WIDTH=244 HEIGHT=112 SRC="help.jpg">

<HR>

</HTML>
```

And here's help2.htm, which includes an image and a link to help1.htm:

```
<HTML>

<H2>Help Topic 2</H2>
<BR>
Here's the help text...
<BR>
<BR>
<A HREF = "help1.htm">Help Topic 1</A>
<BR>
<HR>
<IMG WIDTH=244 HEIGHT=112 SRC="help.jpg">

<HR>

</HTML>
```

Now, you're ready to add these two HTML files to an HTML Help Workshop project; see the next topic.

Creating A Help Project With The HTML Help Workshop

To create a help project in the HTML Help Workshop, choose the File|New menu item, select Project in the New dialog box that appears, and click on OK. Doing so opens the New Project Wizard.

Click on Next in the New Project Wizard. Then, fill in the name and path of the new help project you want to create; give it the extension .hhp, as you see in Figure 20.15. Then, click on Next.

The next step in the New Project Wizard allows you to add files to create a help table of contents, a help index, and the HTML files that display the actual help. In this example, you'll add to the help project the help1.htm and help2.htm files developed in the previous topic. To do so, select the option button marked HTML (HTM) files and click on Next to move to the next step.

Next, specify the HTML files you want to add to the project. Use the Add button to add the two HTML files help1.htm and help2.htm.

In the next (and final) step, click on Finish to create your new help project. The project then opens in the HTML Workshop, as shown in Figure 20.16.

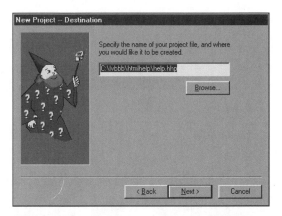

Figure 20.15   *Setting a new project's name in the HTML Help Workshop.*

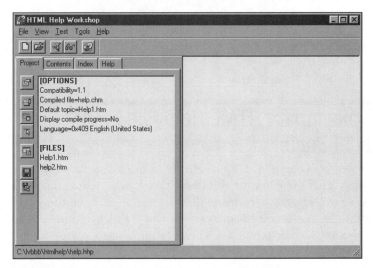

Figure 20.16   *The new project in the HTML Help Workshop.*

That's all it takes—now you've created a new help project in the HTML Help Workshop. To create the compiled HTML help file itself, see the next topic.

Compiling An HTML Help File

To create a compiled HTML help file after you've set up a help project in the HTML Help Workshop, simply choose the File|Compile menu item. Doing so opens the Create A Compiled File dialog box; click on Compile to create your help project's compiled HTML (CHM) file.

Now you can open the compiled help file, as shown in Figure 20.17.

Congratulations—you've created a compiled HTML Help file.

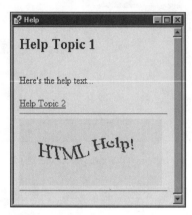

Figure 20.17   *Opening a new HTML help file.*

Displaying An HTML Help File From Visual Basic

To display a compiled HTML help file from a Visual Basic application, you can use the Windows **ShellExecute** function. Note that the computer on which you're using the function must have the Microsoft utility hh.exe—which displays compiled HTML help files—installed. The **ShellExecute** function's declaration is as follows:

```
Private Declare Function ShellExecute Lib "shell32.dll" _
    Alias "ShellExecuteA" (ByVal hwnd As Long, ByVal _
    lpOperation As String, ByVal lpFile As String, ByVal _
    lpParameters As String, ByVal lpDirectory As String, _
    ByVal nShowCmd As Long) As Long
```

Here are the arguments for the **ShellExecute** function:

- *hwnd*—The handle of the window using this function
- *lpOperation*—The operation you want performed (in this case, "open")
- *lpFile*—The name and path of the file to open
- *lpParameters*—Parameters to pass to the opened file
- *lpDirectory*—The new default directory (which you set if the opened file needs to read other files)

- *nShowCmd*—How to show the newly opened file, selected from one of the options set out next

The possible settings for the *nShowCmd* argument are as follows:

- *SW_HIDE*—Hides the window
- *SW_SHOWNORMAL*—Shows the window normally
- *SW_NORMAL*—Opens the window normally
- *SW_SHOWMINIMIZED*—Shows the window minimized
- *SW_SHOWMAXIMIZED*—Shows the window maximized
- *SW_MAXIMIZE*—Maximizes the window
- *SW_SHOW*—Shows the window
- *SW_MINIMIZE*—Minimizes the window
- *SW_RESTORE*—Restores the window
- *SW_SHOWDEFAULT*—Shows the window using default settings

For example, here's how you can display a compiled HTML file named help.chm when the user selects a Help menu item:

```
Const SW_HIDE = 0
Const SW_SHOWNORMAL = 1
Const SW_NORMAL = 1
Const SW_SHOWMINIMIZED = 2
Const SW_SHOWMAXIMIZED = 3
Const SW_MAXIMIZE = 3
Const SW_SHOWNOACTIVATE = 4
Const SW_SHOW = 5
Const SW_MINIMIZE = 6
Const SW_SHOWMINNOACTIVE = 7
Const SW_SHOWNA = 8
Const SW_RESTORE = 9
Const SW_SHOWDEFAULT = 10
Const SW_MAX = 10
Private Declare Function ShellExecute Lib "shell32.dll" _
Alias "ShellExecuteA" (ByVal hwnd As Long, ByVal _
  lpOperation As String, ByVal lpFile As String, ByVal _
  lpParameters As String, ByVal lpDirectory As String, _
  ByVal nShowCmd As Long) As Long

Private Sub mnuHelp_Click()
    Call ShellExecute(hwnd, "open", "c:\htmlhelp\help.chm", "", _
    "", SW_NORMAL)
End Sub
```

Index

& (ampersand)
   breaking long strings, 22
   concatenating strings, 79-80
' (apostrophe), comments, 19-20
* (asterisk), multiplication, 68
\ (backslash), integer division, 69
^ (caret), exponentiation, 69-70
$ (dollar sign), titling Windows Help
   pages, 395-396
. (dot operator)
   accessing members in user-
      defined data types, 56-57
   accessing properties, events,
      and methods, 320
= (equal sign)
   assignment operator and variable
      values, 64, 67
   comparison operator, 70-71
/ (forward slash), division, 69
> (greater-than sign), comparison
   operator, 70-71
< (less-than sign), comparison
   operator, 70-71
- (minus sign), subtraction, 68
+ (plus sign)
   addition, 67-68
   concatenating strings, 79-80
_ (underscore), continuation
   character, 19

A

Access characters, menu items, 199,
   207-208
Access procedures, protecting
   sensitive data, 22

ActiveForm property, multiple
   forms, 244
ActiveX controls, 297-317
   See also Code components,
      Controls.
   Add Procedure dialog box, 313-317
   adding to projects, 190-191, 308-309
   AmbientProperties object, 309
   AutoRedraw property, 300-301
   Click event, 316
   Components dialog box, 308
   constituent controls, 303-304
   creating, 298-299, 300
   designing, 300-303
   Extender property, 310
   Get procedure, 310-311
   HellocontrolClick event, 315-317
   Initialize event handler, 302-303
   Let procedure, 310-311
   Line method, 301
   naming, 305
   New Project dialog box, 299
   persistent properties, 312-313
   Project Properties dialog box,
      301, 305
   properties, 309-312
   PropertyBag object, 312
   PropertyChanged procedure, 312
   RaiseEvent method, 315, 316
   ReadProperty event, 312-313
   registering, 307
   SetText method, 313-315
   testing, 304-307
   Text property, 310-312
   UserControl object, 298, 300
   UserControl_Initialize function,
      300-301
   WriteProperty event, 312

P

Package and Deployment Wizard, 382-389
  CAB Options dialog box, 385
  Finish button, 388
  Included Files dialog box, 384
  Install Locations dialog box, 387
  Installation Title dialog box, 385, 386
  overview, 380, 382
  Package folder, 384
  Package Type dialog box, 383
  Shared Files dialog box, 387, 388
  Start Menu Items dialog box, 386
Panels collection, status bars, 279, 293-294
ParamArray keyword, passing indefinite number of arguments, 113
Parameter list, procedures, 108
Pascal calling convention, Windows API, 156-157
Passing arguments. *See* Arguments.
Passwords, DAO, 365
Pentium Pro processor optimization, project options, 16-17
Persistent properties, ActiveX controls, 312-313
Picture box control, 282-284
  adding images to, 283
  adding to forms, 282, 283
  AutoRedraw property, 282
  AutoSize property, 282, 284
  LoadPicture function, 282, 283
  overview, 278
  Picture property, 282, 283
Picture property
  displaying pictures on buttons, 263-264
  picture box control, 282, 283
PlaySound function, Windows API procedures, 153-157
Pop-up menus, 212-215
  creating, 212-214
  displaying, 214-215
  MouseDown event handler, 214
  PopupMenu method, 214-215
Precedence, of operators, 75-77

Prefixes
  control, 34-37
  data type, 29
  data variable, 38-39
  Hungarian notation and passing arguments to functions, 155-156
  menu and constant, 38-39
  variable, 34-39
  variable scope, 39
Preserve keyword, **ReDim** statement, 50
Print # statement, writing sequential-access files, 138-139
Private keyword
  code components, 330, 334
  declaring Windows API functions, 154
Procedures, 99-114
  access, 22
  Add Procedure dialog box, 183-184, 313-315
  calling in other modules, 107
  defined, 100
  "divide and conquer" dictum, 100
  event. *See* Event procedures.
  functions, 100-101, 104-107
  global variables and, 22
  GoSub statement, 114
  optional arguments, 111-113
  parameter list, 108
  passing arguments by reference, 109, 156-157
  passing arguments by value, 108, 157
  passing indefinite number of arguments, 113
  preserving values between calls to, 109-110
  returning values from functions, 110
  singularity of purpose, 21
  specifying argument types in calls to, 108
  startup (**Main** subroutine), 187
  subroutines, 100-103, 106
  types of, 100-101
  Windows API, 153-158
Program flow, 83-97
  Choose function, 89-90
  conditional statements, 84-85, 87-89

Q

R

RaiseEvent method, ActiveX
controls, 315, 316
Random-access files, 143-147
accessing any record, 147
overview, 134-135
reading records, 145-147
writing records, 143-144
Range, variable, 29-30
Reading binary files, **Get** statement,
148-149
Reading random-access
records, 145-147
Get statement, 145-146, 147
Put statement, 147
record types, 145
Reading sequential-access
files, 139-142
Input$ statement, 142
Input # statement, 140
Line Input # statement, 141-142
Reading values from dialog boxes,
251-252
ReadProperty event, ActiveX
controls, 312-313
Record types
reading random-access records, 145
writing random-access records, 143
Records, database controls and, 342
Recordset object, data control, 348
Recordset property
AddNew method, 352
Delete method, 352-353
EOF property, 355
MoveFirst method, 353
MoveLast method, 354
MoveNext method, 355
MovePrevious method, 354-355
Recordsets (DAO), 368-378
AddNew method, 371-372
BOF property, 375
Close method, 376
creating, 368-370
database controls, 343
Delete method, 372
Edit method, 372
EOF property, 376

fields array, 371
MoveFirst method, 374
MoveLast method, 374
MoveNext method, 375
MovePrevious method, 374-375
OpenDatabase method, 371
OpenRecordset method, 376-378
overview, 362
SQL statements, 376-378
Update method, 371, 373
RecordSource property, opening
databases with data control, 352
ReDim statement, arrays, 50-51
Redrawing contents of forms, 124-125
Reference
code component, 321, 323
DAO libraries, 363
passing arguments by, 109, 156-157
Registering ActiveX controls, 307
ReleaseCapture function
mouse capture, 164-165, 167
setting title bar text, 168-169
Removing
items from collections, 60
modules from projects, 13-14
project files, 14
Resize event, 118-119
Resume statement, debugger, 232-233
Resume *Label* statement,
debugger, 233-234
Return values
declaring Windows API
functions, 154
MsgBox function
(dialog boxes), 255
Reusing code, code components, 321
Right function, creating substrings, 81
RTF (Rich Text Format) files, Help
Workshop, 380-381, 390-391
RTrim function, creating substrings, 80
Runtime properties, described, 180

S

Saving
files, 136
projects, 12